D1598517

Cate Haste

KEEP THE HOME FIRES BURNING

Propaganda in the First World War

Allen Lane

ALLEN LANE
Penguin Books Ltd,
17 Grosvenor Gardens, London SW1W OBD

First published in 1977

Copyright © Cate Haste, 1977

ISBN 0 7139 08173

Set in Ehrhardt monotype

Printed in Great Britain by
Ebenezer Baylis and Son Ltd,
The Trinity Press, Worcester, and London

To Eric and Margaret and Melvyn

The nature of propaganda lies essentially in its simplicity and repetition. Only the man who is able to reduce the problems to the simplest terms and has the courage to repeat them indefinitely in this simplified form, despite the objection of the intellectuals, will in the long run achieve fundamental success in influencing public opinion.

Goebbels, *Diary*, 29 January 1942

Contents

	List of Illustrations	ix
	Acknowledgements	x
1	The Nature of Propaganda in the First World War	1
2	Road to War	5
3	The Machinery of Propaganda	21
4	Getting the Troops	49
5	The Evil Hun	79
6	Aliens and Spies	108
7	Propaganda for Peace	140
8	Peace	179
	Postscript	199
	Notes	203
	Bibliography	215
	Index	223

List of Illustrations

1. Buy War Bonds by Frank Brangwyn (Imperial War Museum)
2. Crush the Germans (Imperial War Museum)
3. Who's Absent? Is It *You*? (Imperial War Museum)
4. In Belgium – Help by Louis Raemaekers (Imperial War Museum)
5. 1914 – La Revanche (Imperial War Museum)
6. *Pas de Parade!* (Imperial War Museum)
7. *A la broche . . . l'alboche . . .* (Imperial War Museum)
8. *Das Kriegsanleihe!* (Imperial War Museum)
9. They Mutilate (Imperial War Museum)
10. Surrender! British Cavalry Beat and Cow the Hun (*War Illustrated*, 1917)
11. Britons Join Your Country's Army (Imperial War Museum)
12. *He* did *his* duty. Will *You* do *Yours*? (Imperial War Museum)
13. There is Still a Place in the Line for You (Imperial War Museum)
14. Come Along, Boys! (Imperial War Museum)
15. Have you any women-folk worth defending? (Imperial War Museum)
16. Remember Scarborough! (Imperial War Museum)
17. Go! It's Your Duty Lad (Imperial War Museum)
18. Britain Needs You at Once (Imperial War Museum)
19. These Women are Doing their Bit (Imperial War Museum)
20. On Her their Lives Depend (Imperial War Museum)
21. In the Trail of the Hun (*War Illustrated*, 1915)
22. A Great Naval Triumph (*Punch*, 7 April 1915)
23. The Elixir of Hate (*Punch*, 5 May 1915)
24. *Guglielmo il Sanguinario, Danza Macabra* (Imperial War Museum)
25. Poster by David Lindsay (Imperial War Museum)
26. Red Cross or Iron Cross? (Imperial War Museum)
27. Cold-Blooded Murder! (Imperial War Museum)

28. Coward Work of Germany's Military Murderers (*War Illustrated*, 1915)

29. Twelve Months of 'Kultur' (The *Passing Show*, 21 August 1915)

30. Patriotism is not Enough (The *Women's Dreadnought*, 1915)

31. The Fortunes of War (The *Daily Herald*, 18 August 1914)

32. No Scarcity of Food (The *Daily Herald*, 13 August 1914)

33. Militarism – 'Its Place in the Sun' (The *Daily Herald*, 20 August 1914)

34. Clyde-side (The *Herald*, 6 March 1915)

35. Three 'X'tra Points (The *Bystander*, 11 December 1918)

36. Once a German – Always a German! (Imperial War Museum)

37. The German Angel of Peace (*Punch*, 16 October 1918)

Acknowledgements

I would like to thank the people who have helped me in the preparation of this book, particularly Peter Copping, whose encouragement, advice and criticism were invaluable, and my husband for his constant support. Also Phillip Whitehead and Ian Hamilton for their helpful comments. I am grateful to Mike Moody and the Art Department of the Imperial War Museum who assisted in preparing the illustrations; and also the Controller of H.M. Stationery Office for the Public Records. A number of people gave me interviews about their war experience which were of great value in understanding the war – Lord Fenner Brockway, Bob Stewart, Edwin Routledge, George Miller and Wille and Henry Fell.

I am grateful to the following for permission to quote extracts: for the Wilfred Owen poem from Cecil Day Lewis, *Collected Poems of Wilfred Owen*, the Estate of Wilfred Owen and Chatto & Windus; for the Sassoon extracts, George Sassoon; for the Kipling poem, The National Trust and the Macmillan Co. of London and Basingstoke; for the Charles Sawley poem from *Marlborough and Other Poems*, The Cambridge University Press; for extracts from his unpublished manuscript, S. T. Kemp.

Chapter One

The Nature of Propaganda
in the First World War

Propaganda seeks to present part of the facts, to distort their relations, and to force conclusions which could not be drawn from a complete and candid survey of all the facts.

President Calvin Coolidge speaking to the
Association of Newspaper Editors, Washington.

So great are the psychological resistances to war in modern nations, that every war must appear to be a war of defence against a menacing, murderous aggressor. There must be no ambiguity about whom the public is to hate. The war must not be due to a world system of conducting international affairs, nor to the stupidity or malevolence of all governing classes, but to the rapacity of the enemy. Guilt and guilelessness must be assessed geographically and all the guilt must be on the other side of the frontier. If the propagandist is to mobilize the hate of the people, he must see to it that everything is circulated which establishes the sole responsibility of the enemy.

H. D. Lasswell, *Propaganda Techniques in World War I.*

The First World War was the first total war. As it progressed, war ceased to be the prerogative solely of military leaders, and came to involve the civilians of all belligerent countries on a scale never known before. For the first time the barometer of public morale needed as much careful attention as the efficiency of the troops in the front line and this revolutionized attitudes to propaganda. It thrust the role of propaganda as a weapon into new focus and gave it an importance it has retained ever since.

The aim of propagandists is the direction and control of public opinion towards certain ends. The word propaganda was originally coined to describe an activity of the Roman Catholic Church. In 1622 Pope Gregory XV established a Congregation '*de propaganda fide*', the purpose of which was to train priests to spread the faith throughout Asia and Africa. Since then, propaganda has been associated as much with politics as religion. It has been used to encourage recruitment and justify war, and has been an adjunct to political campaigning, especially electioneering, ever since the opinion of the broad mass of people had any influence on political events.

What distinguishes the propaganda of the First World War is that for the first time it was rationalized and modernized. During this war, propaganda – to the home front, which is the subject of this book – was carried out by the government, the press and by private patriotic organizations. The government role in propaganda at the start was confined to the routine activities of encouraging recruitment – a War Office responsibility – and justifying the war, an activity carried out by government leaders through public speeches and pamphlets. At the beginning, the government did not need to establish organized propaganda, since the population supported its policies. It was only later on, in response to increasing criticism of the conduct of the war, and when civilian morale was weakened by war weariness, that the government set up machinery actively to manipulate public opinion towards continued support of the war. By the end the government was engaged in organized propaganda to the home front, as well as to neutrals, allies and the enemy. Propaganda had been put on a professional basis.

Propaganda was also modernized. New developments in communications media enabled propagandists to influence the mass of the population in a more efficient way than had previously been possible. The development since the 1890s of the popular mass daily newspaper opened up the market of the newspaper reading public, while at the same time influencing the style of newspapers towards a more simplified and more sensational presentation of news which was particularly suited to wartime propaganda. By the end of the war, the new medium of film, which was attracting audiences of millions, was being used to convey information of a propagandist nature.

The role of the press in propaganda was crucial. The raw material of propaganda is information. Newspapers were the public's main source of information about the war. Propaganda is most effective if public access to truth is severely restricted, as it was in this war. The restrictions were partly imposed by government pressure. In the early stages the government controlled the amount of information available to the press, since newspaper correspondents were not allowed to the front and military leaders did not think the public had a right to know about military activities.

Information was not only restricted, it was also structured. Much of what reached the public was distorted and exaggerated for propagandist ends, through the activities of newspaper proprietors and editors. They often subordinated their responsibility of providing accurate information to other obligations which were to do with carrying out their patriotic duty: the duty to persuade men to fight, to keep up morale, to inspire patriotism and continually to denigrate the enemy. Information was structured to fit the prevailing demand: to justify the war and assist recruitment.

Censorship compounded this. By excluding publication of details of the war on the grounds that, for instance, they would affect civilian or military morale, or could provide useful information to the enemy, censorship contributed to a distorted picture of the war.

The essence of propaganda is simplification. Through the methods adopted by the media and the organizations engaged in propaganda, a fabric of images about war was gradually built up, by eternal repetition over a long period, to provide indisputable justification for the fighting. Propagandists create images with simple human content which are believable because they chime with what people have already been taught to believe. As Goebbels put it in a later war, the task is 'to provide the naïvely credulous with the arguments for what they think and wish, but which they are unable to formulate and verify themselves'.[1]

In wartime, this means firstly building up an image of 'the enemy' which accords with preconceived ideas of the behaviour which can be expected of 'enemies'. It entails constantly denigrating the enemy in such a way as to inspire hatred of him, and excluding information which is sympathetic to his cause. In the First World War, by elaborating on atrocity stories, an image was created of 'The Evil Hun'. Atrocity stories have appeared in all wars, before and since. The intention is to create an image which acts as a repository for all the hatred and fear inspired by war. It also means building up the image of national and allied leaders as the embodiment of courage, heroism, and resolution, while the enemy leaders become the embodiment of evil and the scapegoats for the war. And propaganda builds an image of war itself which is acceptably glorious and heroic, and exciting enough to arouse the desire to take part, while excluding details which would shock soldiers and civilians enough to undermine their unqualified support.

The war is justified in the name of simple and universal ideals which everyone has learnt and with which nobody can be expected to disagree.

Ideals like Freedom, Justice, Democracy and Christianity, which are the embodiment of prevailing national virtues.

However, the danger in a long war is that the images become gradually less believable under the strain of wartime reorganization, and a rift develops between the professional fighting men who have experienced war at first hand, and the civilian home front, whose perception of war has been shaped by the black and white simplifications and absolute ideals defined by propagandists. This occurred in 1917 and manifested itself in general war-weariness and a growing tendency to question the government's war aims. It opened the way for the propaganda of dissenters – people who dissented from the agreed war aims, either from anti-war or revolutionary principle, or people whose faith in the war had been eroded – to have some impact on public opinion.

It became increasingly necessary to professionalize propaganda and make it an official branch of state control, instead of, as had hitherto been the case, leaving it in the hands of the patriotic press and voluntary organizations. Official government propaganda was established to counter the propaganda of 'subversive' groups, to refurbish the images tarnished by war, and to reinvigorate popular support for the war.

Chapter Two

Road to War

A whole generation had been born and brought up in the threat of this German war. A threat that goes on for too long ceases to have the effect of a threat, and this overhanging possibility had become a fixed and scarcely disturbing feature of the British situation . . . quite subconsciously it affected his attitude to a hundred things . . . It bored him; there it was, a danger, and there was no denying it, and yet he believed firmly that it was a mine that would never be fired, an avalanche that would never fall.

H. G. Wells, *Mr Britling Sees It Through*, p. 123.

When war did threaten in July 1914, opinion in Britain was divided. *The Times* led the call for British intervention, arguing on 1 August 1914: 'It is not enough to put civilization upon our standards; we must fight for it, or our standards and our civilization with them, will ultimately disappear. The peace of the world has no greater enemy than the doctrine on which the Austro–Hungarian action, and the German support of that action, are based.' The Liberal *Nation* on the same day found it 'safe to say that there had been no crisis in history in which the political opinion of the British people has been so definitely opposed to war as at this moment'. The *Daily News*, also Liberal, argued for neutrality that day in an article, 'Why We Must Not Fight', in which A. G. Gardiner, the editor, claimed:

For years under the industrious propaganda of Lord Northcliffe, Mr Strachey, Mr Maxse and the militarists, this country has been preached into an anti-German frame of mind that takes no account of the facts. Where in the wide world do our interests clash with Germany? Nowhere. With Russia we have potential conflicts over the whole of South Eastern Europe and Southern Asia.

Within four days of those statements, the Liberal government had declared war on Germany, backed up by almost unanimous support of the nation.

Wartime propaganda against Germany was to make an indelible mark on public opinion and public reaction to events for four and a half years of war. But the seeds of anti-German propaganda had been sown earlier by pressure groups and powerful individuals who continually fed an undercurrent of anti-Germanism. These groups and individuals, political figures and men who controlled the press, helped to guide public reaction to events through the presentation of, and interpretation they put on, political issues. Their activities helped to determine that war was seen as the inevitable solution to escalating international rivalries, and helped to build up an image of Germany as the main threat to Britain's imperial, commercial and diplomatic position in the world. They also established the themes which were to be amplified in wartime propaganda against the enemy.

From 1900, anxieties, especially Conservative anxieties, about Britain's position in the world, focused on Britain's defence position, in particular, her preparedness for war. This was not new. During the last decades of the nineteenth century, there had been regular scares on the subject. War was viewed not only as a necessary but an inevitable method of solving international rivalries. Despite the technological advances which indicated that modern warfare would be more terrible than ever before, war was a popular theme, the subject of popular serials, novels and music hall songs of the period. War was still wrapped in the cloak of honour and heroism. Imperialists like W. E. Henley believed in the 'iron beneficence' of war. His views were published in the *Observer* in 1892:

> Give us, O Lord
> For England's sake,
> War righteous and true,
> Our hearts to shake.[1]

War had a sensational value which was not missed by the burgeoning popular press. Norman Angell wrote in 1908, 'A sedentary urbanized people find the spectacle of war more attractive than the spectacle of football. Indeed our press treats it as a glorified football match.'[2] For the younger generation who were to be the soldiers in the First World War, the world, in the words of Rupert Brooke, was 'a world grown old and cold and weary', and there was a spirit abroad searching for what was described in a propagandist pamphlet advocating National Service, as 'some new note, some clarion call, as it were, which shall inspire us to march forward under new auspices to a new destiny'.[3]

Literature on the theme of war had enjoyed immense popularity since the publication in 1871 of Lt Col. Sir Tomkyns Chesney's serial, 'The

1

Frank Brangwyn

'There is something infinitely greater and more enduring . . . a new patriotism, richer, nobler and more exalted than the old . . . '

Lloyd George

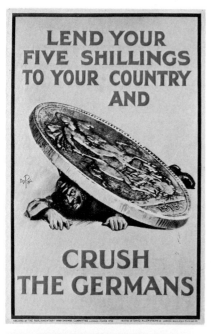

2

3

4. The first requirements were men and money to fight the war. Voluntary charities were set up to help Belgian refugees.

Louis Raemaekers

5

6

7

8. German propaganda—The Mailed Fist. 'That is the way to Peace—the Enemy wants it so! Therefore subscribe to WAR LOAN!' To the British, this was the symbol of Germany's aggressive ambitions. Clearly the Germans thought the same of British ambitions.

9. American image of German 'frightfulness'. Recruitment propaganda depicted the war as a crusade to save the future of civilization from the evils of barbarism.

Battle of Dorking' in *Blackwoods Magazine*. It was a propagandist tract which fictionalized the successful German invasion of Britain in order to expose what in Chesney's view was the British government's failure to take care of the navy. Published during a crucial period in the Franco–Prussian war, when the Germans had just reached Paris, it exploited fears about the vulnerability of Britain's defences with such success that Gladstone, the Prime Minister, was forced by the clamour to speak in parliament against the dangers of 'alarmist literature'. It spawned a new genre of war fantasies and spy stories which aimed primarily to highlight the defects of British defence policy through fictionalizing future wars. They included *The Great Naval War of 1887* by William Laird Clowes, Le Queux's *England's Peril*, Tracy's *The Final War* and Max Pemberton's *Pro Patria*, in which France was the enemy, and, after 1903, Childers' *The Riddle of the Sands* and Saki's *When William Came*, in which the enemy was Germany.

Alfred Harmsworth, later Lord Northcliffe, the rising star of Fleet Street, used the technique during his campaign as Conservative candidate for Portsmouth in the 1895 election. He commissioned a young Canadian journalist, Beckles Willson, to work in collaboration with William Laird Clowes, a leading naval expert and advocate of a big navy, on a series, *The Siege of Portsmouth*, to be published in his newly acquired paper, the *Portsmouth Daily Mail*. The serial described the successful invasion of that naval centre by Britain's traditional enemies, France and Russia. Harmsworth saw this not only as an election stunt, but as an opportunity to sell his newspaper. He advertised the serial on roadside hoardings and in the town with sensational pictures of the Town Hall crumbling to dust before advancing hordes of foreign troops. Willson was ordered to write a patriotic song to appeal to the dockyard workers, while Kennedy Jones, Harmsworth's business manager, ensured its repetition by employing twenty young men at 6d each to sit in the gallery at its performance and call for encores. The propagandist message of the fable was clear. This shocking state of affairs had only been possible because 'men had not sufficiently remembered that "England's Navy Is Her All"', and because, in one word, they were NOT READY'. It was the Conservative case against the Liberals at the election.

From 1900, propaganda increasingly centred on the 'Menace of Germany'. The man who perceived the danger more clearly than even his Conservative colleagues was Alfred Harmsworth. And he had in his power the makings of an influential propaganda machine. He was sitting on the largest newspaper empire in Fleet Street, which was based on the success of popular mass journalism, embodied in the *Daily Mail*. The *Daily Mail*, launched in 1896, rapidly acquired the largest circulation of any newspaper ever before. Its style was to appeal to the 'common man' – the suburban clerk who, Harmsworth found, liked his politics writ short and simply and interspersed with everyday events, serials, sensationalism, and competitions. The keynote of the paper's style was simplification. Political complexities were edited 'into a version fit for headlines'. It was an ideal medium for propaganda.

Harmsworth's views were reflected faithfully in his newspapers. From its inception, the *Daily Mail* bubbled away at establishing the image of Germany as Britain's inevitable enemy. In 1896, the *Daily Mail* warned: 'The keynote of modern Germany is militarism'. Already it was chiselling the stereotype of the sinister German and 'the inherent brutality of the German character which the saving grace of art and music has never destroyed'. In 1897, George Warrington Steevens, the *Mail*'s descriptive writer, was commissioned to write sixteen eye-witness accounts with the provocative title 'Under the Iron Heel'. In the first he warned, 'Germany will keep her hands free to deal with us. Let us make no mistake about it. For the next ten years fix your eyes very hard on Germany.'[4] By 1900, Harmsworth was writing to R. D. Blumenfield, editor of the Conservative *Daily Express*, 'My own view is that the Germans are being led definitely and irrevocably to make war on the rest of Europe, and we will have to take a part in it.'[5]

The campaign to shore up Britain's defences concentrated on criticism of the organization of both the army and the navy. The navy, on which Britain traditionally depended for the defence of her interests, aroused the greatest passion. But at the beginning of the century, attention focused for a while on what was considered to be the parlous state of the army. The existence of enormous Continental conscript armies roused the call for the reorganization of the British military system to include some form of compulsory military service, called 'National Service' – itself a propagandist concept which was retained until the 1960s.

The call was led by a pressure group, the National Service League, and backed by the Northcliffe press and a number of Tory journals. In 1905, Lord Roberts – 'Bobs', the popular veteran soldier of the Boer War and numerous other imperial adventures – became its president. The League was started in 1901 in the groundswell of a publication by George Shee entitled 'The Briton's First Duty – The Case for Conscription'. Shee

Punch, 7 December 1904

Figure 1 *A Tall Order*

German Eagle (to *Dove of Peace*): '*Teach me how to coo!*'

As early as 1904, the image of Germany was of a warmongering nation which would threaten peace

argued from the sub-Darwinian principles, by then firmly rooted in the consciousness of most European nations, and from principles of militant imperialism, that

just as necessity made man a warrior in order to defend the community in the early 'struggle for existence', so necessity calls for the armed services of every citizen in order to preserve the enormous accumulation of the fruits of industry from the aggression of jealous competitors in the new 'struggle for existence' – the struggle for the markets.[6]

He claimed that invasion – by the conscript armies of Russia or France – was imminent. Moreover, he argued, military training was good for the nation – indeed, the advantages were so great 'from the physical, moral, intellectual and educational point of view that, to paraphrase a celebrated saying, if the necessity for it did not exist, it would be the highest wisdom to invent it'.

Very few agreed. Freedom from conscription was held at the time to be one of the ancient liberties of the British race. Most Liberals, all Labour Party members and some Conservatives believed it was the height of folly and would bind the nation in the chains of militarism. The National Service League started a campaign to convince the population of conscription's virtues by pressurizing Members of Parliament and publicizing their views at public meetings and in pamphlets, leaflets and their monthly *National Service Journal* (later renamed *A Nation in Arms*). Although they had little success in their main objective, the adoption of conscription, they did help to propagate the view that war with Germany was becoming increasingly inevitable, and to contribute to the image of Germany as an aggressive, ambitious and brutal nation.

Harmsworth, now Lord Northcliffe, started a campaign for conscription in the *Daily Mail* in 1907. It was the tail end of another *Daily Mail* venture – the publication the previous year of William Le Queux's alarmist tale, *The Invasion of 1910*. This serial was a graphic account of a German invasion worked out in minute detail with the assistance of Lord Roberts and the *Daily Mail*'s naval expert, H. W. Wilson. It served a number of purposes. Not only did it add texture to Lord Roberts' arguments, it highlighted the more despicable methods of warfare which Germany could be expected to employ, and which, once war broke out, the propagandists had no difficulty in proving they were using. In particular it aired the legend of the ubiquitous German spy. Le Queux argued that invasion was made possible through the existence in Britain of a German civilian army, men who, having served in the German army, 'had come over to England and obtained employment as waiters, clerks, bakers, hairdressers and private servants, and being bound by their oath to their Fatherland, had served their country as spies'. This legend continued into the war and became a fruitful theme for the propaganda campaign which identified all enemy aliens as spies and traitors, making them the scapegoat for popular revenge against Germany. Northcliffe was motivated as much by patriotism as by a desire to increase the circulation of his newspaper. He complained that the route worked out by his experts was unsatisfactory, that is, bad for circulation. The Germans, he directed, had to pass through every sizeable town, 'not to keep to remote one-eyed villages where there was no possibility of large *Daily Mail* sales'.[8]

The serial was a resounding success. The book sold over a million copies and was translated into twenty-seven languages, one of them German. To advertise the serial, sandwichmen dressed as German soldiers paraded through the streets of London – 'a long file of veterans in spiked helmets and Prussian-blue uniforms', described by an eye-witness as 'a shattering portent'.[9] The display prompted two questions in parliament from people who were concerned about the spread of alarmism and anti-Germanism. The method was popular, however. In 1909 Guy du Maurier's play, *An Englishman's Home*, which dealt with invasion by 'the Emperor of the North', had such instant effect that recruiting stands were set up in Wyndham's Theatre to cope with the rush of recruits for the newly formed Territorial Force.

Lord Haldane's Liberal army reforms, which did not include conscription, received nothing but derision from Lord Roberts and his League, and from his Tory press supporters: notably the *Morning Post*, the *Daily Express* and Leo Maxse's platform of reaction, the *National Review*. Lord Roberts was constantly prodding them to keep up pro-conscription propaganda, urging Blumenfield of the *Daily Express* in 1911 not 'to drop . . . the question of our unpreparedness',[10] and in 1912, 'The time has come when the people must be made to understand the weakness of our Army, and the Territorials to feel that they are no use until the Force is raised under a system of Compulsory Military Training.'[11] In 1912 Lord Roberts made a speech in Manchester which unleashed floods of abuse from the Liberals who were consistently appalled at the scaremongering tactics of those bent on inflaming relations between England and Germany. In it Lord Roberts claimed that National Service was 'the only salvation of this nation and this Empire. The Territorial Force is now an acknowledged failure – a failure in discipline, a failure in numbers, a failure in equipment, a failure in energy.' This was bad enough. He then went on to raise further fears about Germany, arguing that the Germans knew 'that just as in 1866 and just as in 1870 – war will take place the instant the German forces by land and sea are, by their superiority at every point, as certain of victory as anything in human calculation can be made certain. Germany strikes when Germany's hour has struck' (Manchester, 22 October 1912).

The Liberal reaction was horror and indignation. To pacifist Liberals, Russia still represented as great a threat to Britain and the principles which Britain stood for as Germany. The *Manchester Guardian* expressed disgust at 'the insinuation that the German government's views of foreign policy are more cynical than those of other governments', while the *Daily News* used the opportunity to slam the National Service League as 'an attempt to set up, not defence, but an invasion of German territory . . . What the League wants is war.'

Though the number of Lord Roberts' Conservative supporters in parliament increased steadily up to the war, attempts to introduce even short-term National Service failed repeatedly. Conscription was not introduced until 1916. When the war went beyond Christmas, and victory seemed nowhere in sight, Lord Roberts' pre-war campaign was revived in the patriotic press. Lord Roberts, said the pundits, had been right, and Lord Haldane had been wrong, indeed Lord Haldane was accused of having deliberately failed to shore up Britain's defences because of his declared sympathy with Germany. The pre-war campaign laid the groundwork for the campaign for conscription in 1915. It also provided the patriots, when the time came to look for scapegoats for the war, with a target in the shape of Lord Haldane, on whose head fell the blame for the absence of a quick victory and, indeed, for the war itself.

On the navy question, passions were more easily roused. The German Navy Laws of 1898 and 1900, which initiated German naval expansion, had been noted in Britain, particularly by those who feared that the German programme would 'altogether upset the present balance of naval power'. This observation hastened plans for increased naval efficiency and, by 1904, the Admiralty was beginning to concentrate the Fleet in northern waters. According to the two-power standard, Britain insisted on retaining superiority over her two nearest rivals, plus 10 per cent. But the most important development, which took place under Admiral Sir John Fisher, who was made First Sea Lord in 1904, was the building of the *Dreadnought*. This gave Britain a qualitative as well as a quantitative lead over her rivals. It also rendered smaller British battleships obsolete, which meant that British superiority in numbers didn't count for so much.

In the 1906 election the Liberals were returned to power on the pledge to reduce armaments expenditure. But, during 1906–7, while the British government reduced naval expenditure, the Germans increased theirs. In January 1908, a new German Supplementary Naval Law precipitated further expansion and the development of the German Dreadnought programme. It marked a new acceleration of the arms race throughout Europe.

For those, mainly Conservatives, who feared that Britain was steadily losing her naval lead, it signalled a new period of activity. Conservatives, and especially Lord Northcliffe, who led the alarmist school in the press, used the facts of the navy race to highlight the menace of Germany. To the question, 'Why was Germany expanding her navy?', the simple answer had already been supplied by the *Daily Mail* in 1907: 'All the fine words in the world cannot disguise the fact that the naval competition between England and Germany is intense, and that Germany is now building a great fleet with the express object of meeting the British Navy at sea.'[12] And this, Northcliffe believed, was part of Germany's preparation for war with Britain and eventual German hegemony over Europe.

There was some truth in this claim, though it represented a simplification of political complexities. Admiral von Tirpitz, the man who expanded the German navy, had argued in 1897 in a 'Very Secret' memorandum for a large navy as a 'political power factor'. He wrote: 'For Germany the most dangerous naval enemy at the present time is England. It is also the enemy against whom we most urgently require a certain measure of naval force as a political power factor.' The main aim of Germany at the time was imperial and commercial expansion. This inevitably led to friction with established imperial powers, especially Britain. The navy was to be Germany's claim to world power. It was the prerequisite to a future German Empire. It was also a political instrument and a lever to be used against Britain. Germany, Tirpitz believed, could not 'expect fair play from Britain', the main block to German expansion, unless Germany's naval power could match Britain's. Only through the balance of naval power could Germany assert her rights to expansion. In 1900 Tirpitz declared that the German navy must be equal to her most difficult task: 'a naval battle with Britain in the North Sea'. Our fleet, agreed the German Chancellor, von Bülow, 'must be built with an eye on English naval policy'.[13]

From *Gott Strafe England*

Figure 2 *John Bull Embarrassed*

'*How much longer can I keep this up . . .?*'

German view of British ambitions – world domination

The arguments for a grand fleet were backed up by nationalists of the Pan German League and the Navy League and all who followed von Bülow's graphic dictum that the question for Germany was whether she was to become 'the hammer or the anvil' of world politics. The argument went that 'unless Germany owns a strong fleet she will be without colonies by the end of the twentieth century', and 'without colonial possessions she will suffocate in her small territory or else be crushed by the great world powers'.[14]

For the Kaiser, a large navy had the power 'to revive the patriotism of the classes and to fill them again with loyalty to, and love for the Emperor and the Reich',[15] in other words, to consolidate the right-wing forces against the rising influence of social democracy. In 1900, he announced 'I shall unswervingly complete the task of reorganizing My Navy so that . . . it shall be in a position, internationally, to win for the German Reich that place which we have yet to achieve.'[16]

The Kaiser's declarations of German ambition did nothing but anger those leaders of public opinion in Britain who were convinced of the threat from Germany. His claim, in 1904, to be 'Admiral of the Atlantic' was matched only by his claim for Germany's 'place in the sun'. It was perfectly clear to those who wanted to see it that both these ambitions could only be achieved at the expense of Britain. The Morocco Crisis in 1905, when Germany posed a direct challenge to the rights of Britain's ally, France, in Morocco, was seen as a portent of future German colonial tactics, and interpreted as blatant sabre-rattling.

Northcliffe, basing his view on information from his correspondents in Europe, saw clearly the threat to Britain, and determined to warn the nation of its peril. His most powerful ally was his new editor of the *Observer*, J. L. Garvin. Garvin had his feet placed firmly at the centre of Unionist politics. He was a thrusting and ambitious editor who was determined to use his newspaper influence to mould and formulate Unionist policies.

Garvin was the leading exponent of Chamberlain's Tariff Reform campaign, which had split the Unionist Party since 1900, and was a passionate advocate of anti-Germanism. Writing under the pseudonym of 'Calchas' in the *Daily Telegraph*, he had already roused the Kaiser's anger for his hostile articles on Germany, which were described by the Kaiser as 'a continual and systematic poisoning of the wells', involving 'the most unheard of and shameless lies against Germany and calumnies against myself'.[17]

For Garvin, the fortunes of the Unionist Party were as important as his patriotism, and the fortunes of the Unionist Party in 1908 were at a low ebb. The political advantage to the Conservatives of highlighting fears about the navy was that it could unite a divided party; it was also a way of attacking the Liberals while also appealing to wider patriotic support.

When he became editor of the *Observer* in 1908, Garvin had pledged to Northcliffe that he would increase its circulation and make it that part of his empire which wielded real political power. The debate on the

1908 Navy Estimates provided Garvin with the opportunity to make a sensational press issue of the subject. He had one enormous asset. His relationship with Admiral 'Jacky' Fisher was such that the Admiral actually provided him regularly with highly secret Admiralty documents. It worked for Fisher's benefit as well as Garvin's. Fisher was opposed at the time not only by the Liberals who were pledged to cut expenditure, but also by a group of Admiralty lords, led by Beresford, who opposed the Dreadnought programme. Garvin, having received complete advance details of the Navy Estimates from Fisher before they had been finally discussed in the Cabinet, printed a long article on 2 February 1908 under the headlines: THE NAVY AND THE NATION. ADMIRALTY AND THE GERMAN MENACE. A STRONG REPLY which firstly warned the Germans of the dangers of a naval race, and secondly backed up Fisher's case completely, arguing for economy in so far as it represented efficiency and the continuation of Dreadnoughts. There was an outcry in the Cabinet and at the Admiralty, but Garvin's article succeeded in bringing before the nation the central issue of the internal threat to the navy and the external threat from Germany.

It provoked the expected attack from the Liberal benches. In March 1908 Liberal industrialist Sir John Brunner accused Northcliffe's newspapers and the *Observer* of inflaming Anglo–German relations in order to make a base profit. He claimed:

A very large proportion of our newspapers have for years been nagging away at Germany. We have far too many newspapers, and the result of their competition, keen beyond precedent, is to be seen every day in the desperately unworthy expedients which they adopt . . . They live by sensations and scares, the more sensational the more profitable they are, and while they rake in the profits it is the people who have to pay the damage . . . I object to government by sensation mongers.[18]

Northcliffe had already been accused of being 'a footpad in politics' and 'an enemy of the human race'.

Garvin, choosing his moments judiciously, and guided by Fisher, pegged away for the rest of the year at the issue of naval competition which he saw as the core of imperial defence. The *Daily Mail* consistently backed up the *Observer*, a technique which served to advertise its sister paper. As Brunner had suspected, the circulation of the *Observer* did go up. In 1909, Garvin informed Northcliffe: 'The detailed figures clearly show that our naval campaign has accounted in successive movements for three-fifths of the increased circulation since January 1908.'[19]

The sustained agitation showed results in March 1909 over the question of Dreadnoughts.

The alarming rate of German building prompted the Admiralty, in the 1909 Estimates, to demand six new Dreadnoughts to retain British superiority. The Cabinet was divided. McKenna, First Lord of the Admiralty and a Liberal imperialist, was opposed by radicals led by Churchill and Lloyd George, who wanted a reduction of armaments expenditure and an increased programme of social reform.

The outcry started during the parliamentary debate, when McKenna admitted that the government had underestimated the speed of German naval expansion. The indignation expressed by the Opposition, who saw this as a stick to beat the Liberals, was echoed by the Tory and North-cliffe press, who exploited the opportunity to raise again the spectre of the German menace. The cry went up for eight Dreadnoughts.

Garvin pressed the issue on 21 March. Fearing that 'public agitation is no longer avoidable', he called on his readers to 'insist on the Eight, the whole Eight and nothing but the Eight, with more to follow, and break any man or faction who stands in the way'. The *Daily Mail* leader of 17 March 1909 had already declared, 'For England, there is nothing between sea supremacy and ruin . . . Our sea supremacy is in peril.' Agitation flared inside and outside Parliament. The slogan 'We Want Eight and We Won't Wait' became the rallying call for patriotism.

In parliament, meetings for the 'Eight' were held by the Parliamentary Naval Committee, chaired by Sir Edward Tennant, and the Navy League. Outside parliament, groups concerned with navy affairs – the Navy League, the London Chamber of Commerce Navy Committee, and the Naval and Military Committee of the City of London, chaired by Lord Roberts, held meetings during the week to put pressure for the 'Eight'. The Navy League, on 22 March, announced a campaign to hold meetings throughout the country to emphasize the importance of a large shipbuilding programme. The Imperial Maritime League launched a nationwide campaign to 'call on the government to take all possible measures to ensure the country's safety'.

The pacifist Liberal view was put by Sir John Brunner of the Liberal Reduction in Armaments Committee, who argued that, 'having regard to our established and continued friendly relations with foreign powers, and to the present burden of the cost of armaments, any increase of the Naval Estimates is inexpedient'.[20] The *Daily News* was more forceful. On 20

March it attributed the agitation to *The Times*, the *Daily Mail* and the *Observer*, and warned that 'never in its history has a nation whose sea power is the envy of the world abandoned itself to a more contemptible fit of hysteria . . . Such rivalries conducted in this spirit for another three years can only foster the expectation of an "inevitable war" . . .' The leader of 22 March, headed 'Panic', called this a 'horrible and dangerous phenomenon', instigated by the Northcliffe press, was thankful that the nation was not yet entirely 'tainted with the infection of their indecent panic' and complained of 'the scurrilous abuse poured upon a great nation with whom we are nominally, at all events, on terms of peace and friendship'.[21]

The *Daily Mail* meanwhile, reported that meetings up and down the country favoured the 'Eight', and devoted an enormous amount of space to the opinions of the press, and of leading men on the subject. The agitation bore fruit at the by-election in Croydon. The Unionist candidate, Herman Hodge, won in a campaign which was marked, as the *Daily News* reported, by 'rampant jingoism' on the navy issue, stirred up by the presence of the Imperial Maritime League among others, who held regular patriotic meetings and distributed pamphlets. At the victory celebration, Balfour, leader of the Opposition, claimed 'gradually the tide has been turning in our favour'. He accused the government of 'neglecting the interests of the Empire', welcomed 'a tide of Imperial sentiment [which] has spread with telegraphic rapidity to the farthest ends of the earth'; and concluded, 'I take it as an augury that London will be again what it has been in the past – the great heart of a great Empire (loud cheers).'[22]

The divided Cabinet settled on the 'Eight'. The agitation had been successful. As Churchill commented: 'Genuine alarm was excited throughout the country by what was for the first time widely recognized as a German menace.'[23]

The navy issue re-emerged during the 1910 election. In December 1909, Northcliffe added a little fuel to the flames by commissioning Robert Blatchford, editor of the *Clarion*, who was described by Churchill as 'a ridiculous jingo', and whose socialism, like a section of the socialist movement, was rabidly nationalist, to write a series of articles for the *Daily Mail*. 'I write these articles,' he began, 'because I believe that Germany is deliberately preparing to destroy the British Empire, and because I know that we are not able or ready to defend ourselves against such a sudden and formidable attack.' The *Daily News* called the articles 'ravings'. The *Manchester Guardian* called them a deliberate Tory trick to force the General Election away from the Liberals by 'deliberately raking the fires of hell for votes'.

Garvin, at the *Observer*, did just that. The Unionist Party was still divided over Protection, though united in opposition to Lloyd George's controversial budget of 1909. Garvin, wrote his biographer, A. M. Gollin, revived the question of naval rivalry 'in a last minute attempt to bolster up the election fortunes of the Unionists'.[24] It began 'as a purely electioneering device'. Garvin wrote to Sanders, Balfour's private secretary, on the question of election tactics: 'Now, what's our "cannon ball"? . . . Ought it not to be defence? . . . It would inspire the enthusiasm in the Party and would take the country. It would be intelligible to the dullest elector. It would be navally sound; and yet first class politics . . . Above all, it would put the other side in a fix. They could not talk of this subject except with two voices . . .'[25] Balfour replied with a directive to Garvin to continue raising this issue in the *Observer*. On 4 January 1910, Balfour made the navy the central plank in the Conservative election platform, to the disgust of the Liberals. Garvin's old friend, Admiral Fisher, was ecstatic in his praise of Garvin:

. . . You have lifted that boneless mob of guys [the Unionists] out of the pit of apathetic helplessness and said 'Lift up your hearts' & they did! If the proportion remains as at the moment of writing, you will have done a great work for the Navy for as McKenna says 'It has effectually crippled Lloyd George & Co. as regards the Navy.' (I need hardly say how sacredly private that last remark is) . . .[26]

The Conservatives made a remarkable come-back with 273 seats to the Liberals' 275, and the balance of power was held by the Irish Nationalists with eighty-two seats, while the Labour Party had forty.

The effect of the newspaper campaign had, by 1910, crystallized the object of fear in the public mind, and established the precise nature of the threat to the British Empire which had for so long haunted Northcliffe. As Lord Esher commented: 'The tension between England and Germany is a newspaper tension, but it is severe for all that.'[27]

The press campaign against Germany continued from 1910 till the outbreak of war. It was intensified by the Agadir crisis of 1911, when Germany sent the gunboat *Panther* to Morocco to stake her claim again. Churchill's comment on that occasion was: 'All the alarm bells throughout Europe began immediately to quiver.'[28] It caused acute anxiety about Germany's intentions even amongst the former leaders of the pacifists, Lloyd George and Churchill.

Sections of the press continued to portray Germany as the nation which wanted war and hegemony over Europe, though it was civil conflict which engaged the public's attention more than foreign affairs from 1911 onwards. However, an undercurrent that war was inevitable increasingly informed the published views of foreign affairs commentators in the Tory and Northcliffe press, who argued that the clash of interests between Germany and other European nations, including Britain, was irreconcilable, and who watched the escalating arms race, especially Germany's increased naval and military power, with undisguised alarm.

Nevertheless in the few days before Britain declared war on Germany, opinion in the country was divided. When war threatened in the last weeks of July, it was *The Times* which led the call for British intervention. The leader of 31 July 1914 argued,

We must make instant preparations to back our friends, if they are made the subject of unjust attack . . . The days of 'splendid isolation', if they ever existed, are over . . . We shall still work on for peace; work on for it to the very end; but the hour has come when we, too, may have to make instant preparations for war. We 'may almost hear the beating of his wings'. He may yet 'spare us and pass on'. But if he indeed visits those with whom we stand, we must pay our share of the fell tribute with stout hearts.

The majority of Liberal opinion was utterly opposed to *The Times*, to Grey's tactics, and to Britain's involvement in the war. They clamoured for neutrality, echoed by the Neutrality League and the Neutrality Committee, both set up specifically to disseminate arguments against Britain's participation in this Continental quarrel. The Labour Party held demonstrations in Trafalgar Square, addressed by Keir Hardie, calling for a general strike in the event of war. Mrs Fawcett's Suffrage Society protested against war on 4 August, while an equal number of patriots cried 'Down with Germany' in Parliament Square and Trafalgar Square.

The divided Cabinet finally agreed on intervention on the plea of the German invasion of 'Little Belgium'. Once war was declared, opposition crumbled. The majority supported the call to fight for victory. For those who had long predicted war with Germany, and who firmly believed in the inevitability of that war in the defence of Britain's interests, the declaration of war came as a relief. Northcliffe's comment to Wickham Steed, his Vienna correspondent, was 'Well it's come!' to which Steed replied 'Yes, thank God!'[29]

Chapter Three

The Machinery of Propaganda

Propaganda is the task of creating and directing public opinion. In other wars this work has not been the function of government . . . but . . . in a struggle which was not of armies but of nations, and which tended to affect every people on the globe, this aloofness could not be maintained. Since strength for the purposes of war was the total strength of each belligerent nation, public opinion was as significant as fleets and armies . . .

The Organisation and Functions of the Ministry of Information,
Cmnd 9161, 1918.

That was said after four years of war. At the beginning, however, the government had an imperfect grasp of the significance of manipulating public opinion. In a nation converted to the idea of war but seeking articulation of its cause, the government relied on the speeches of politicians to explain the duty to accept and fight the war.

Establishing control of public opinion was a gradual process brought about by *ad hoc* methods. The government did not have a conscious policy for propaganda until later in the war, when it appeared to them that a small section of the population who dissented from the war aims were gaining influence among a war-weary population. For the most part, until then, they relied on the propaganda activities of the press, which amplified their call for national unity, and on the activities of a large number of voluntary patriotic organizations, mostly in private hands, who responded to the call to duty by propagating support for the war. Control of public opinion came about through a gradual adaptation to the new circumstances of total war.

It was part of a wider recognition of the new wartime role of government, which entailed the extension of state control into all aspects of national life. Liberal laissez-faire doctrines which prevailed at the outset were eroded under the pressure of war. The principle of voluntaryism, which was equated with individual liberty, died hard. State control was anathema to the Liberals. Yet by the end of the war, the wartime administration, headed by two successive Liberal Prime Ministers, Asquith and Lloyd George, had centralized control of manpower, recruitment and munitions production, and was well on the way to controlling food supplies – and public opinion.

With the country on its side, the government had no need to establish formal propaganda machinery to the home front. No national newspaper opposed the war. In parliament on 6 August, nobody voted against the government, though a few, like Phillip Snowden and Ramsay Mac-Donald, abstained and later formed the nucleus of pacifist opinion. Dissent in the Liberal Party dwindled rapidly. Five Cabinet ministers threatened resignation, but only Lord Morley and John Burns carried out the threat. The others, John Simon, Jack Pease and Lewis Harcourt, espoused the widely held Liberal view that the best way to support the country was to fight for an early victory.

Those groups which had been the focus of pre-war discontent and civil conflict: the official trades union movement, the Labour Party and the women's movement, notably Mrs Pankhurst's Women's Social and Political Union and Mrs Fawcett's National Union of Women's Suffrage Societies, rallied to the call for national unity and actively supported the war. Only a small group of socialists, Liberal backbenchers and trades unionists continued their opposition, working with small support in the Independent Labour Party, the Union for Democratic Control and, later, in the No Conscription Fellowship and in Workers' Committees.

Government propaganda was necessary, however, to justify the war and encourage recruitment. Justification of the war was the corollary of the call for volunteers. The appeal to sacrifice was inseparable from the image of a just war – the crusade which, it was claimed, Britain was fighting in the name of civilization.

Britain's justification for the war lay in the cause of 'Little Belgium'. Until the invasion of Belgium, the government and the press were divided about Britain's moral obligation to support France in the event of German attack. Only a handful of people were, in any case, aware of the exact terms of Britain's obligation to support France under the Entente Cordiale of 1904, because diplomacy had been shrouded in secrecy. Germany's violation of Belgian neutrality provided the moral argument necessary to unite the Liberal Party and the nation.

The government took the lead in defining the terms of an idealistic war. They were formulated by Asquith, the Prime Minister, on 6 August 1914 with the words: 'We are fighting to vindicate the principle that small

NO THOROUGHFARE

Punch, 12 August 1914

Figure 3 *Bravo, Belgium!*

Britain's main justification for going to war was the defence of 'Little Belgium'

nationalities are not to be crushed in defiance of international good faith, by the arbitrary will of a strong and overmastering power.' Britain was fighting in a moral crusade for righteousness – 'not for the maintenance of its own selfish interests, but . . . for principles the maintenance of which is vital to the civilized world.' He emphasized Germany's war guilt and Britain's conscientious attempts to keep the peace. 'The war,' he said, 'has been forced upon us', and 'it was only when we were confronted with the choice between . . . the discharge of a binding trust and a shameless subservience to naked force that we threw away the scabbard.'[1]

Lloyd George, Chancellor of the Exchequer, justified the war as a matter of national honour. His conversion from neutrality was typical of the change of attitude of many Liberals. His record with the Pro Boer Liberal Group, and his consistent opposition throughout the previous decade to increases in naval and military expenditure led many to anticipate his support for neutrality. The outbreak of war forced his hand. At the Queen's Hall in September he argued:

There is no man in this room who has always regarded the prospect of engaging in a great war with greater reluctance, with greater repugnance than I have during the whole of my political career . . . There is no man either inside or outside of this room, more convinced that we could not have avoided it without national dishonour . . . If we had stood by when two little nations were being crushed and broken by the brutal hands of barbarism our shame would have rung down by everlasting ages.

Further vindication of the government's action was provided by rumours of German atrocities in Belgium and France. Newspapers gave wide coverage to these, and Asquith exploited them in October:

We could not stand by and watch the terrible unrolling of events – public faith shamelessly broken, the freedom of small peoples trodden to the dust, the wanton invasion of Belgium and then of France, by hordes who leave behind them at every stage of their progress a dismal trail of savagery, of devastation and of desecration worthy of the blackest annals of the history of barbarism.[2]

The lead given by the government was taken up by private and voluntary organizations. An unquestioning acceptance of the terms of Britain's justification was echoed in the speeches and writings of numerous individuals and by patriotic organizations which sprouted daily to spread propaganda about the war. It was amplified by the patriotic press which instantly rallied to the call to justify the war and aid the recruiting campaign.

Literary men were to have an important impact in formulating opinion. An extraordinarily large number of eminent literary figures succumbed to the prevailing mood. One voice, that of George Bernard Shaw, was all the more conspicuous for withholding wholehearted support for the war. In a pamphlet 'Commonsense and the War', he argued that the government used Belgium as a pretext, and that the real reason was to destroy a dangerous rival. His behaviour was so unusual that a question was asked about the possible suppression of the pamphlet, though no action was taken against it.

Others publicized their patriotism. On 18 September 1914, fifty-three writers signed a public statement in *The Times* supporting a war in which 'destiny and duty . . . call upon us to defend the rights of small nations and to maintain the necessary law-abiding ideals of Western Europe against the rule of "Blood and Iron" and the domination of the whole Continent by a military caste'. Signatories included H. G. Wells, Thomas Hardy, Arthur Quiller-Couch, John Masefield, Arnold Bennett, Gilbert Murray, Rudyard Kipling and Arthur Conan Doyle. Conan Doyle also wrote a recruitment pamphlet 'To Arms' which was widely advertised in *The Times*.

Another group of writers, including Edmund Gosse, John Buchan, Thomas Hardy, Henry Newbolt and Gilbert Murray joined the 'Fight for Right Movement', founded by Sir Francis Younghusband, which had as its slogan 'To Fight for Right till Right be Won'. Their manifesto, evangelical in tone, demonstrates the flight from reason to which even leaders of the literary world succumbed when dealing with war:

The spirit of the Movement is essentially the spirit of Faith: Faith in the good of man; Faith therefore in ourselves, Faith in the righteousness of our Cause, Faith in the ultimate triumph of Right; but with this Faith the understanding that Right will only win through the purification, the efforts and the sacrifices of men and women who mean to *make* it prevail.[3]

Their talents were later used by the government when it set up official propaganda, at first only to neutral and allied countries, later to the enemy and the home front. Gilbert Parker headed propaganda to America at the Secret War Propaganda Bureau. H. G. Wells worked with novelist Colonel John Buchan at the Department of Information formed in 1917, and later with Lord Northcliffe on propaganda to enemy countries at the Ministry of Information formed in 1918. Rudyard Kipling directed propaganda to colonial countries at the Ministry, and Hugh Walpole was responsible for propaganda to Russia at the War Propaganda Bureau and later at the Ministry. Arnold Bennett conducted propaganda to France at the Ministry and eventually became acting Head when Lord Beaverbrook, the Minister, resigned in October 1918.

It was not without a struggle that some writers came round to total support for the war and its aims, and then lent their pens to furthering the cause. Gilbert Murray, a distinguished classical scholar, expressed the dilemma of a number of Liberal intellectuals in his pamphlet, 'How Can War Ever Be Right?'. He had signed a plea for neutrality published in the *Daily News* on 5 August 1914, and was a member of the Neutrality Committee. In the pamphlet, written in August 1914, he argued that, in war 'you are simply condemning innocent men, by thousands and thousands to death, or even to mutilation and torture', but he also had to agree that 'honour and dishonour are real things'. The Belgian issue had convinced him and he believed that 'the government, in deciding to keep its word at the cost of war, has rightly interpreted the feelings of the average citizen'. Despite his personal hatred of war, he found some comfort in the thought that 'War is not all evil. It is a true tragedy, which must have nobleness and triumph in it as well as disaster', and, though war is painful and horrific, yet 'to have something before you, clearly seen, which you know you must do, and can do, and will spend your utmost strength and perhaps your life in doing, is one form at least of a very high happiness, and one that appeals – the facts prove it – not only to saints and heroes, but to average men'.

Other pamphlets came from equally distinguished pens. H. G. Wells, whose support for the war aims waned later, expressed the belief, in his pamphlet 'The War that will End War', that war would eradicate Prussian militarism. In the *Daily News*, he wrote: 'We are, I believe, assisting at the end of a vast intolerable oppression upon civilization. We are fighting to release Germany and all the world from the superstition that brutality and cynicism are the methods of success, that Imperialism is better than free citizenship.'[4]

From six members of the Oxford Faculty of Modern History came the pamphlet 'Why We Are At War: Great Britain's Case' (10 October 1914) which used historical argument to prove that Germany was the aggressor. Even reasoned argument, it appeared, could only assess the situation in propagandist terms. Chapter six summed up the war as 'a struggle between two nations, one of which claims a prerogative to act outside and above the public law of Europe in order to secure the "safety" of its own State, while the other stands for the rule of public law'. The 'Oxford Pamphlets' on the war followed. A. D. Lindsay contributed one on 'The War to End War', a title which became something of a catch phrase. Sir Edward Cook, later head of the Press Bureau, contributed 'How Britain Strove for Peace', which again set out to prove Germany's war guilt.

Poets played an important part in propaganda. Patriotic verse was published in daily newspapers and in small anthologies and was widely read at the time. For instance, the National Relief Fund produced an anthology sold for charity which included work by John Masefield, Rudyard Kipling, William Watson, Alfred Noyes, Henry Newbolt and Robert Bridges. Most of the poems comprised a clarion call to arms, like Kipling's bellicose piece 'Hymn Before Action':

The earth is full of anger
The seas are dark with wrath
The nations in their harness
Go up against our path;
Ere yet we loose the regions –
Ere yet we draw the blade
Jehovah of the Thunders
Lord God of Battles, aid.

The most influential of the voluntary patriotic organizations, which sponsored and distributed these pamphlets, was the Central Committee for National Patriotic Organizations. It was set up in August 1914 as a coordinating body for patriotic activities with Asquith as president and Balfour and the Earl of Rosebery as vice-presidents, and it was run by H. C. Cust and G. W. Prothero. Their aims were described as educational, but the line between education and propaganda in wartime is a fine one. They drew on respectable academic talent – the Oxford pamphlets were commissioned by them – and encouraged support from educational institutions at home and abroad. In the belief that knowledge breeds commitment, their aim, through literature and meetings, was to establish 'such an abiding foundation of reasoned knowledge among all classes by emphasizing the righteousness, the necessity and the life and death character of the struggle, as shall sustain the wills and sacrifices of the British people through the blackest days of weariness and discouragement'.[5]

In addition there were the relief organizations and charities which fed on the wartime mania for sacrifice and added their voice to the cause, while providing both a practical outlet for patriotic energies and a method of filling up leisure time and giving the satisfaction of 'doing one's duty'. Many were concerned with relief of Belgian refugees. One such was the Belgian Relief Fund, formed in August 1914 by Lady Lugard, the Hon. Mrs Alfred Lyttleton, Lord Hugh Cecil and H. E. Morgan, with a view to 'extending hospitality to destitute women and children'. Another was the National Relief Committee in Belgium, formed in early 1915, and chaired by the Lord Mayor of London. During its first year it received £160,000 in contributions and was involved in the distribution of nearly a million Belgian flags, 185,000 posters and 200,000 medallions of King Albert of the Belgians. The posters were commissioned from established artists like the Dutch cartoonist Louis Raemaekers, John Hassall and Frank Brangwyn.

Yet another was the National Relief Fund, started by the Prince of Wales on 6 August in anticipation of unemployment and food shortages. Within two weeks the fund accumulated one and a quarter million pounds.[6]

Charities were getting out of hand. People were asked to contribute right, left and centre – not only money, but every type of comfort for the soldiers. Tobacco Funds, Food Funds and Clothes Funds mushroomed. Queen Alexandra issued a special appeal to women to help relieve the distress of war amongst the families of soldiers and sailors. Queen Mary's Needlework Guild provided patriotic work for women at home. People set about knitting and sewing, making and mending and donating money for every conceivable eventuality. (It was typical of the spirit of voluntary-ism that the volunteer patriots failed to notice how unemployment among women in the garment trade was rising and creating new destitution among some former employees.) *The Times* ran a daily column of 'Practical Patriotism – How to be useful in Wartime' which listed home defence organizations and an expanding number of charities to which gifts could be sent. Voluntaryism had run riot, and in March 1916 the situation became so impossible that a group of established charities sent a deputation to the Home Office demanding that a licence should be given before charities could collect money.

The politicians noted these activities with relish. Lloyd George exploited the wartime mania in September at a recruiting meeting, when he appealed to

something infinitely greater and more enduring which is emerging already out of this great conflict – a new patriotism, richer, nobler, and more exalted than the old . . . It is bringing a new outlook to all classes.

The great flood of luxury and sloth which had submerged the land is receding, and a new Britain is appearing. We can see for the first time the fundamental things that matter in life . . .[7]

Lloyd George's message to civilians was that the spirit of sacrifice was not confined to soldiers. The war was being fought on the home front too. His appeal to the nation to become better people in the just cause of war was part of that fostering of self-righteousness and hatred, based in fear, which overtook the civilian sensibility.

Voluntary patriotic activity had some impact on public opinion, but it was the press which had the greatest influence in moulding attitudes towards the war. The influence of the press was to be greater in this war than in any previous one. For one thing, there were more newspapers. In 1870, there were six London daily papers, four evening papers, and four Sunday papers. By 1900, the number of London dailies had risen to thirteen, evening papers to nine, and Sundays to ten, while by 1914, there was a total of sixteen London dailies, five of which had been established since 1900. They had bigger circulations. There was now a mass reading public, the product of the 1871 Education Act, which influenced the sales not only of the newer papers, but of old established ones as well. In 1886, *The Times* sold 45,754 copies, whereas in 1914 the circulation was 183,196. The new *Daily Mail* was selling at just under a million copies in both 1900 and 1914, while the *Daily Mirror*'s first edition in 1903 sold 276,000.

The introduction of mechanical typesetting and the fall in wood pulp prices had resulted in a considerable reduction in the cost of printing, which made large circulation newspapers an economic possibility.

The man who exploited this possibility was Lord Northcliffe, who had been primarily responsible for establishing popular journalism. He appealed to the tastes of ordinary people, and changed the appearance of newspapers by using bolder typeface and two-column headlines, a tactic which paid off in circulation figures, especially in wartime. He moved away from the traditional party allegiance of the press to take on the role of political commentator independent of party, thus giving himself a political freedom which he used extensively in the war. By 1914 Northcliffe was the most powerful man in Fleet Street, controlling, in addition to his popular journals, *The Times*, which he had acquired from the Walter family in 1908 – thereby realizing his greatest ambition. The *Daily Mail* and *The Times* worked as a balancing act: *The Times* retained a respectable degree of objectivity and serious political comment, while the *Daily Mail* was not only a platform for Northcliffe's views, but provided a more sensational presentation of news and comment.

The press was controlled through censorship, and the government's relationship with the press was not always a happy one. In this war of novelties, one novelty which the government had to come to terms with was the extent to which it was dependent on public opinion, and it was some time before it recognized this dependence.

Meanwhile, censorship worked as a form of 'negative propaganda', because, by restricting access to information about the war, a false picture was built up and disseminated among the civilian population. Although all newspapers supported the national cause once war was declared, their patriotism was not rewarded with the confidence of either the government or the military leaders.

Government control of information was established through the Press Bureau, announced on 6 August by Winston Churchill as a machine to ensure that 'a steady stream of trustworthy information supplied both by the War Office and the Admiralty can be given to the Press'.[8] The government had no clear policy on how to do this. The Press Bureau was hurriedly improvised – 'It was never constituted at all – "it growed",' commented Sir Edward Cook, its director from 1915, and the officials were 'left to work out its scope and methods as experience might suggest'.[9]

'Experience' suggested a twofold function for the Bureau – to provide information and to exercise censorship. An issuing department channelled information from the War Office and the Admiralty, and supplied Allied news bulletins, communiqués from the front, and, later, communiqués from all other departments. (The navy had a separate branch and a separate navy censor.) Press articles were surveyed by the Censorship Department. Censorship was compulsory for cables, including press cables, but otherwise press censorship was voluntary, that is, editors were given the freedom to decide which articles to submit to the censor. The Defence of the Realm Acts provided the basis for editorial decisions. DORA, as she was known, was introduced at the beginning of the war to give the government wide powers of control over aspects of national security. The omnibus regulations affecting the press stated that 'No person shall without lawful authority collect, record, publish or communicate, or attempt to elicit any information . . . of such a nature as is calculated to be or might be directly or indirectly useful to the enemy' (Regulation 18 [12]). Further clauses prohibited information on movements of troops, ships and aircraft, or location or description of war material, and there were regulations prohibiting false statements, statements 'likely to cause disaffection to' the success of His Majesty's Forces or those of his Allies, or his relations with foreign powers, and statements 'likely to prejudice recruiting' or undermine public confidence in bank notes or government financial measures (Regulation 27).

The organization of the Press Bureau might have worked in the interests of the civilian population, the government and the press, had it not been for stubbornness on the part of the War Office, and indecisiveness on the part of the government with regard to information. Certain indiscretions by the press merely compounded the muddle. What actually happened was that so little information was released that the home front was left in a state of bewilderment about the nature of the war. Much of the information which did get through was exaggerated, distorted and misrepresented. Of the real nature of trench warfare and the horrific effect of modern weapons, the country remained largely in the dark. For the home front the glamour of war stayed untarnished for a long time. Restriction on information about all aspects of the war eventually led to a gap in understanding about what it was being fought for at all. In an attempt to prevent information reaching the enemy, the War Office and the government succeeded in blinkering the public and creating a myopia about the very nature of the war.

Some indication of the extent of restriction of information is given by the instructions issued by the Press Bureau for the guidance of editors. These instructions originated from the service departments or from the ministries, and editors used them as a basis for deciding whether to submit articles for censorship. Altogether 700 such instructions emanated from the Bureau, covering all aspects of security. During 1915, only twelve suggested prosecutions were referred to the Director of Public Prosecutions, but the Press Bureau was asked to admonish individual editors for indiscreet publications as often as three times a week.[10]

Weather reports were stopped because they might have been useful to the enemy, and from April 1916, chess problems were banned 'unless [editors] are absolutely satisfied that the senders are of British nationality and perfectly reliable', the suspicion being that they might have been coded messages to spies. Zeppelin raids, which caused a great stir, were at first freely reported, and news of the damage confirmed prevailing convictions about German 'frightfulness'. But in September 1916, a Press Bureau instruction severely restricted information on the grounds that 'the military damage has been slight, but at the same time, so long as

the Germans think that the raids have great effect, they will be continued, and long accounts tend to produce the impression both in
England and abroad that they are of greater importance than they are in
reality'.[11] Information was confined to brief official communiqués from
the Press Bureau.

Dangers from submarine attack after 1915 caused the news of movements of merchant ships to be banned at various times. Later, publication
of names of ships was banned, then the number of ships, and finally only
the tonnage of ships lost was published. The circulation of Lloyd's
Register and all reference books dealing with mercantile tonnage was
severely restricted, and no photographs of British ships were allowed to
be published unless they had been 'doctored' by the Censor.

News from the front and the movement of troops was the subject of
a very large number of instructions. Details of units or battalions were
prohibited in the press as they might have given away the order of battle.
Advance predictions of troop movements were checked against secret
information and censored if they were accurate. If they were wrong, they
could get passed – the Press Bureau never guaranteed the accuracy of the
reports it approved, and was not averse to creating mischief for German
intelligence.

The War Office, which took the traditional view that wars were the
prerogative of the military establishment, acted as the main obstruction
to the gathering of information. At the outbreak of war, all newspapers
appointed accredited correspondents, but these were not allowed anywhere near the front, and those of them who went to France were so
controlled in their movements and deprived of facilities that they had all
returned by the end of 1914. Despite a campaign by Lord Riddell,
Chairman of the Newspaper Proprietors' Association, and Lord Northcliffe, correspondents were not allowed at the front until May 1915. The
government aquiesced in this policy of obstruction. As a concession to
the press, an 'Eye Witness' was appointed in September to report on the
war as part of his military duty. He was attached to the staff of the
Commander-in-Chief, and his reports, after censorship at G.H.Q.,
were passed on to Lord Kitchener for his personal approval. 'Eye
Witness' was Lt Col. Sir Ernest Swinton, whose personal guidelines for
his reports for the home front were 'to tell as much of the truth as was
compatible with safety, to guard against depression and pessimism, and
to check unjustified optimism which might lead to a relaxation of effort'.[12]
Not much truth got through those barriers.

Kitchener's policy, as stated in November 1914 in the House of Lords, was that 'it is not always easy to decide what information may or may not be dangerous, and whenever there is any doubt, we do not hesitate to prevent publication'. He alleged that General Joffre, as Commander-in-Chief of the Allied armies, was responsible for this attitude, but Basil Clarke, one of the last correspondents to leave France, believed that 'the persistence of the British government in putting difficulties in the way of newspaper correspondents, while other allied countries were but luke-warm in the matter, tends to confirm the view that the British were leaders in this crusade'.[13] Asquith attributed Kitchener's indifference to the demands of the press to an 'undisguised contempt for the "public" in all its moods & manifestations'.[14]

The explosive dispatch from Amiens in *The Times* of 31 August 1914 highlights some aspects of the relationship between press and government. A *Times* correspondent, Arthur Moore, had managed to make contact with British troops on their retreat from their first engagement in France at Mons. The report he sent back was published under the sensational headlines: FIERCEST BATTLE IN HISTORY. HEAVY LOSSES OF BRITISH TROOPS. BROKEN BRITISH REGIMENTS. The text described how 'the broken British Army fought its way desperately with many stands, forced backwards and ever backwards by the sheer incon-querable mass of numbers', and it was coloured by interviews with soldiers in disarray. It convinced Northcliffe, who published it, of the urgent need for more recruits. F. E. Smith, Head of the Press Bureau, who could have been expected to tone it down, was also convinced. He revealed later that he had not only passed it, but recommended an additional paragraph emphasizing the need for 'men, men and yet more men'. It was an extraordinary thing for the Head of the Press Bureau to admit.

The report was considered a bombshell to national morale. But when, on 5 September, Churchill wrote to Lord Northcliffe: 'I think you ought to realise the harm that has been done . . . I never saw such panic-stricken stuff written by any war correspondent before; and this served up on the authority of *The Times* can be made, and has been made, a weapon against us in every doubtful state', Northcliffe pointed out that in view of the additions made by the official head of the Press Bureau, 'There was no other possible conclusion except that this was the govern-ment's deliberate wish.'[15]

There was an outcry at home. The *Morning Post* came out in defence of a Press Law, the *Daily Sketch* advocated stronger censorship on the grounds that 'it is the view of the mothers of the soldiers' and the *Daily Telegraph* protested against 'highly alarmist stories . . . not justified by the facts'. A Press Bureau statement was issued, associated with Kitchener but written by Churchill, which did what Asquith described as 'dish up for [the public] with all his best journalistic condiments the military history of the week'.[16] It stated that a battle had indeed taken place in which the troops had 'offered a superb and most stubborn resistance', and warned that reports from unauthorized correspondents should be treated 'with extreme caution'. The government was consolidating its forces and bringing down the veil again.

The next day, Asquith gave a vague assurance that arrangements were being made about the supply of news, referring to the appointment of 'Eye Witness'. *The Times*, undeterred by criticism, launched an attack against

the lack of comprehension in high places of the right use of the Press in wartime . . . The idea prevails apparently, that the Press wants news solely for its own purposes. No conception could be more foolish or obsolete. In a time of great crisis the Press has a great and patriotic duty to perform. It has to stimulate deeper public interest in a struggle which is bound to last a very long time and on which the fate of the Empire depends. It cannot do so if it is kept in the dark.

Some indication of Asquith's attitude to the press is provided in his correspondence about this issue. He wrote to Churchill on 5 September 1914:

My dear Winston,
    The papers are complaining, not without reason, that we keep them on a starvation diet.
    I think the time has come for you to repeat last Sunday's feat, & let them have thro' the Bureau an 'appreciation' of the events of the week; with such a seasoning of condiments as your well-skilled hand can supply.
    For all that the public know, they might as well be living in the days of the prophet Isaiah, whose idea of battle was 'confused noise & garments rolled in blood'.

A number of points emerge from this episode. Firstly, the government's answer to press discontent was not to increase information, but to season what information there was already to make it palatable, that is, filter it beyond any connection with reality. Secondly, it reveals a complete lack of concern about informing the public of the course of a war which was to involve civilians on an unprecedented scale. Lastly, it throws light on the way disasters were treated, namely, as far as possible preventing news of them from being published.

Churchill was a master in this last respect. During the Dardanelles campaign he exercised his art with particular care. Churchill was primarily responsible for this campaign which provoked considerable opposition from his own staff at the Admiralty and from some Cabinet members. When it was abandoned, the government abandoned Churchill. Churchill's concern for public morale, and indeed for his own career led him to take certain liberties with information. Douglas Brownrigg, his Chief Naval Censor, described how he worked:

> He was, of course, a master of language and had a *flair* for framing communiqués . . . He was also a bit of a gambler, that is, he would hold on to a bit of bad news for a time on the chance of getting a bit of good news to publish as an offset, and I must say that it not infrequently came off! On the other hand there were days when it did not, and then there was a sort of 'Black Monday' atmosphere about – a bad 'settling day' sort of look on all our faces.[17]

Secrecy in military and naval matters was, however, excessive. Some thought the danger of too much secrecy was that public confidence in the truth-telling capacity of the government would be damaged. Douglas Brownrigg argued that the issue of public confidence sometimes out-weighed military considerations, citing one particular episode as an example. On 27 October 1914 the battleship *Audacious* was sunk by a mine off the Irish coast in full view of the liner *Olympic* carrying a number of American passengers who took photographs of the sinking ship. Lord Jellicoe immediately cautioned Churchill at the Admiralty that the loss of the ship should be kept secret for as long as possible, because the information would be very valuable to the enemy at a time when the margin of British naval supremacy was small. Elaborate plans were formulated under Churchill to keep the *Olympic* at Lough Swilly until another ship could be kitted out at Belfast as an exact replica of the *Audacious*. Publicity was given to her 'repair', and then her rejoining the Fleet. *The Times* criticized the Admiralty for refusing to reveal the facts. No official confirmation appeared until after the war, on 13 November 1918. Brownrigg was in no doubt that 'the continued suppression of the loss of that ship cost us the confidence of the public both here and abroad, and gave the Germans a useful bit of propaganda to use against us'.[18]

ANOTHER ATROCITY.

Figure 4

Concern about suppression of information was taken up by the
Opposition in November 1914. Bonar Law, Leader of the Opposition,
challenged the government that 'the Press is more muzzled than is
necessary for military reasons and consequently, if that be so, it is dis-
advantageous from the point of view of every other interest in this
country'. He demanded assurance that military considerations were the
sole reason for withholding information. Asquith reiterated that information was only withheld 'lest it should give the enemy an advantage
he would not otherwise have had'.[19]

Agitation continued in the press. Northcliffe believed that absence of
information about the stirring episodes of war was not only damaging to
recruitment but detrimental to a proper appreciation at home and
abroad of the efforts of the British troops. This constant pressure had its
effect, but not until April 1915, when the government finally came to an
agreement with Lord Riddell permitting war correspondents to go to the
front. The first correspondents reached the front in May. The tense
relationship created by the government's attitude to the press inevitably
influenced the press attitude to the government, and Northcliffe became
more conspicuous in his outspoken criticism of the Asquith government's
lack of forcefulness in running the war.

Greater freedom in war reporting lifted the veil a little bit, but censorship was still severe. The home population had very little real idea of the
nature of the war. This ignorance facilitated the task of propaganda, since
information on which to base real assessment was limited, which made
exploitation of fear and patriotism easier.

The government had taken ten months to come to terms with the
responsibilities of controlling information. They were even slower in real
coordination of propaganda. There was no coordinated propaganda to
the home front until 1917. The only government propaganda agency, the
Secret War Propaganda Bureau, was established in September 1914 to
counter German propaganda and gain neutral countries' support for the
Allied cause. A certain amount of material produced by the Bureau was
distributed to the home front. It also worked out principles of influencing
public opinion which were later developed and used on the civilian
population.

The Bureau's first director was Charles Masterman, a Liberal
Christian Socialist, former literary editor of the *Daily News* and first
director of the National Insurance Commission. He and his colleagues
lacked either the Lloyd George flair for rhetoric or the journalistic flair

for sensation. For instance, Masterman insisted that atrocity stories should be authenticated to avoid the possibility of being proved wrong. He objected to 'the demand that his department should lose all integrity or sense as a condition of the work they were doing'.[20] Masterman's guiding principle was 'to present facts and arguments based on these facts'. His dilemma was that in wartime facts were not always readily available, and were often unpalatable. His policy paid off. The publication of the Bryce Report (see p. 93) was the supreme propaganda achievement of the department. Its apparent authenticity succeeded in eradicating doubts about the truth of German atrocity stories.

The Bureau produced pamphlets commissioned from well-known writers and published politicians' speeches and articles and interviews from the press; these were translated into seventeen different languages and distributed mainly through personal contacts throughout the world. The Bureau started illustrated newspapers, including the *Illustrated War News*, and propaganda newspapers for specific areas: *El Espelho* for Portugal and Brazil, *America Latina* for Spanish-speaking South America, and *Hesperia* for Greece. They supported the clandestine Belgian paper *L'Indépendance Belge* by providing picture blocks, and generally distributed pictorial matter, posters, films and lectures, while providing resources for the press of neutral countries to put across a favourable view of Britain.

Propaganda to the Allies emphasized the British role in the war, in particular to counteract 'an undercurrent of uneasiness found manifesting itself in France and, to a lesser extent, Russia, as to whether the efforts and sacrifices being made by England were comparable with those of the Allies, or commensurate with the importance of the struggle'.[21] In America, Gilbert Parker, who headed the American section, operated a policy of stealth, in contrast to the bombardment tactics of German propaganda there. He used only personal contacts and personally authenticated documents for distribution in America. American visitors had the Allied point of view put to them in strong terms, and British representatives in America persuaded influential Americans to publicize their case. Opinion in America was by no means entirely pro-Allies. There was a strong group of pro-German propagandists and a large German population. Opposition to the Allies intensified when the British blockade policy seriously affected neutral, especially American, shipping. In 1916, President Wilson was re-elected as the man who would keep America out of the war, and he saw his role as peace-maker between

10. The caption below the picture reads, 'Although in April 1917 our cavalry had not the full opportunity for which one correspondent said "they burn and are ready", they had many occasions to tighten their girths for a gallop and try conclusions with enemy patrols and rearguards. They rode into the burning ruins of villages and found scattered Germans, left behind to snipe or to complete the work of devastation, and at these they charged full tilt, so hot with wrath that they hoped the wretched creatures would not be too terrified to put up some sort of resistance, and would not answer to the shout of "Surrender!" with a whimpered "Kamerad!" '

Surrender! British Cavalry Beat and Cow the Hun

'We ran the gamut of all emotions which make men risk their lives and all the forces which deter them from doing so . . .'   Eric Field, Caxton's Advertising Agency

11

13

11 & 12. The image of war heroes who reminded Britain of past glories had the power to inspire new loyalty and a new spirit of sacrifice

13 & 14. The appeals to do one's duty and to conform were among the most naive forms of persuasion

15, 16 & 17. How images of womanhood were used in the appeal to get men to enlist

15

16

17

18. The war as a modern crusade. Old emblems in a new war

19 & 20. After conscription was introduced in 1916, the target of persuasion became the women, who were called upon to help the war effort on the home front

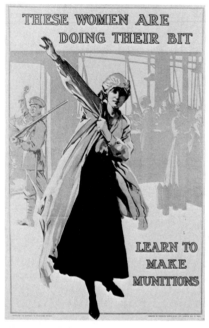

18

1

20

belligerent nations. His equivocations led fervent patriots in Britain to conclude that he was in the pay of the Germans. The propaganda effort built a nucleus of favourable opinion in the country, though America did not actually enter the war until 1917.

German propaganda to neutrals was, in general, less efficient than British. The Germans were not so effective at simplifying the issues of the war into right against wrong, and failed to establish any coordinated machine for propaganda. They were also put at a particular disadvantage when, on 15 August 1914, the Allies cut the transatlantic cable, thus cutting off Germany's main line of communication to America. Germany's main propaganda effort was through press conferences organized by the army and a press service which reported military operations and was responsible for censorship and control of information from the front. Like Britain, Germany failed to realize that in a long war enthusiasm for fighting would wane, but she failed to seize the initiative, not only in counteracting Allied propaganda to neutrals about German war guilt, but also in exploiting in the simplest terms, using simple images, those events which could denigrate the enemy.

The English Secret War Propaganda Bureau was doing exactly this. But there was considerable overlap with other government departments which began to realize the value of propaganda. The Foreign Office was distributing news to neutral countries, and the Foreign Office, Admiralty and War Office had intelligence departments monitoring public opinion abroad. It was an uneasy alliance which, in 1917, was partly resolved with the formation of the Department of Information.

By 1917, the conditions of war had changed. Morale in all countries was deteriorating. The naïve patriotism which fed the early war fever had abated. Three years of attrition produced only stalemate. The toll on human life was undermining civilian morale.

The government had increased its control of most crucial aspects of national life, abandoning laissez-faire methods under the pressure of war. Conscription, introduced in 1916, rationalized recruitment procedures and facilitated control over industrial manpower. Control of munitions production was established under the Ministry of Munitions in 1915. A Food Controller was appointed in January 1917 to cope with food shortages and rising prices, which had produced allegations of profiteering. Rationing was finally introduced, on a restricted basis, in July 1918. Control of public opinion was the next area for government attention.

In reaction to the mood of discontent and war weariness, the government, under Lloyd George (who replaced Asquith in December 1916), began to organize propaganda as an official government activity. A Department of Information, headed by the novelist John Buchan, was set up in February 1917 on an official basis. Sir Edward Carson, a minister in the War Cabinet, was given responsibility for propaganda activities, though he was not altogether a success at the job. The Department took over the work of Wellington House (The Secret War Propaganda Bureau) and helped to coordinate some of the intelligence activities of the service ministries. Its work was primarily concerned with propaganda to Allied and neutral countries.

The Department of Information had sections dealing with the origination and distribution of literature, with monitoring foreign news (in conjunction with the Foreign Office, the Admiralty and War Office Intelligence), with providing news and press articles at home and abroad, and with the production and distribution of film. For the first time journalists were officially involved in propaganda – through an Advisory Committee which included Robert Donald, editor of the *News Chronicle*, C. P. Scott, editor of the *Manchester Guardian*, and Lord Northcliffe. Sir George Riddell, proprietor of the *News of the World*, joined later, and Lord Beaverbrook, who later headed the Ministry of Information, replaced Northcliffe when he went to America to set up the British War Mission, a propaganda agency for America.

On the home front, a new organization came into being, the National War Aims Committee (NWAC), to direct the first propaganda aimed specifically at the home front. Its main function was directly to counteract pacifist propaganda, which the government believed to be exploiting unrest and causing strikes which could jeopardize the whole running of the war.

The NWAC was formed in June 1917 under an all-party executive with Asquith as president, Bonar Law and G. N. Barnes as vice-presidents and the two Chief Whips, Lt Col. R. A. Sanders and F. E. Guest, as joint chairmen. This all-party arrangement was designed to allay fears that a propagandist body on the home front could be used for party political gain, fears which were at the root of opposition to the unfamiliar activity of home front propaganda.

From the start, the Committee had a slightly amateurish air about it. It was dependent on voluntary donations and contributions from party funds until November 1917, when £240,000 was voted out of public funds, the largest sum ever spent on home front propaganda. In July 1917 the Committee took over the Central Committee for National Patriotic Organizations (CCNPO), and used their branches for propaganda. The educational spirit of the CCNPO survived within the National War Aims Committee.

The two main aims of the Committee were to 'counteract and, if possible, render nugatory the insidious and specious propaganda of pacifist publications' and to exhort the population to 'inflexible determination to continue to a victorious end the struggle in maintenance of those ideals of Liberty and Justice which are the common and sacred cause of the Allies'.[22] The Committee's general aim was to 'strengthen the national morale and consolidate the national war aims as outlined by the executive government'. Support for these objectives was by no means unanimous. It was precisely the *lack* of clear government war aims which was the focus for discontent, suspicion and criticism of the government. Thus in October 1917 the Brighton and District Trades Council not only turned down a request for cooperation, but voted to burn the Committee's documents and return the ashes. The government's lack of war aims prompted the Labour Party, at its special Conference in August 1917, to draw up a separate Labour Memorandum on War Aims; this memorandum provided the basis for Lloyd George's first major speech on the subject, delivered to a trades union audience at Caxton Hall in January 1918, which was itself a propaganda exercise designed to deflect further criticism.

To counteract pacifist propaganda on the industrial front, the NWAC collected specimens of all types of pacifist literature for analysis, and resolved

to dwell on the democratic development and improvement of the lot of the working classes which State control and other war changes have already secured; to suggest the prospect of further improvement and greater freedom when the war is over . . . [and] to inspire all workers at home with . . . a living sense of their responsibility and share in the great task; to give them tangible proof of the government's appreciation; so to brace and hearten them that, however long the war may last, its crusading character may be their dominating thought.[23]

To this end, the Committee concentrated operations in areas of unrest. For example, when a drop in iron ore production was reported in Cumberland, the Committee mounted a special campaign there. Other spheres of operation were Wigan, described by an investigator as 'the worst place for pacifists that I have ever had any experience of, the common allegation being that the war was a capitalist quarrel',[24] and Hull, where it was reported that the men were prepared to 'down tools' on any trifling excuse. NWAC speakers in dockyard areas were advised to hold their meetings away from the dock, and 'to limit themselves to war aims not trade disputes'.[25] When it was observed that women were particularly prone to war-weariness special meetings were set up for them.

The NWAC used the constituency party organizations and local committees of patriotic organizations to arrange meetings and distribute literature. Local meetings and large patriotic rallies were held in in-dustrial areas like one in Birmingham, called 'Win the War Day' (21 Sept. 1918) in which a tank led a procession through the town, while the whole area was bombarded with leaflets and pamphlets: distributed from stalls, handed out by boy scouts, and in the case of 250,000 leaflets, showered from an aeroplane. Between September 1917 and October 1918, 899 meetings were recorded and full-scale campaigns were carried out in 345 out of a total of 468 constituencies. The NWAC head-quarters provided speakers, arranged visits to the front, and engaged music hall artists to lighten the proceedings with patriotic songs, and eye-witnesses from the front to recount their experiences. A travelling cinema even toured the country. Speakers at NWAC meetings included politicians, authors and volunteers who were paid a nominal fee, while writers were commissioned to compose some of the fifty pamphlets and articles for the press which emanated from the Committee. Other products included posters, like one entitled 'Huns Ancient and Modern', picture postcards, cigarette cards, banners, cartoons, Christmas cards and twenty-five sketches which were sold at £10 each.

The aim was to persuade the population to continue fighting the war by warning against the dangers of a negotiated peace with Germany, usually by reiterating the horrors of German frightfulness. This was the main theme of the lantern lectures set by the Committee, and the subject of one of their more specious products 'The German Crimes Calendar', which summarized the war in terms of German barbarities. Activities like these did a great deal to fan anti-Germanism, and incurred the hostility of H. G. Wells, at least, who was working on enemy propaganda at Crewe House, and who complained that the Committee was doing nothing except 'antagonizing our people against anything and everything German', while being 'totally unconstructive about the war aims or what was to happen after the war'.[26]

The government was also engaged in propaganda in more specific areas connected with the national interest. Various government departments set up committees to publicize their work and encourage public participation in the government's aims. The propaganda of these bodies was as pervasive as recruitment propaganda had been before conscription. A Ministry of National Service was set up which spent most of its time appealing for National Service Volunteers especially women, to take on civilian jobs and release men for active service. A War Saving Committee was also created to encourage support for National Savings Schemes and the various government War Loan Schemes. It used a nationwide network of 1,530 local committees, who devoted their energies to promoting thrift.[27] In December 1917, a tank bank was set up in Trafalgar Square which earned £319,640 in one week by selling War Bonds and War Savings Certificates. The first ten customers were girls who had lost their sweethearts in the war.[28]

In this new appeal to sacrifice, the various government committees employed imagery which highlighted the idealistic aims of the war and denigrated the enemy. In January 1917 subscription to the War Loan Scheme was equated with a personal contribution towards the fight for 'mankind's right to march forward towards the dawn of a new life on earth'.[29] Film was used later, including one animated sketch with the slogan 'Every Child Can Help to Stamp out the Hun', showing National Savings stamps obliterating the face of a German soldier, and another with the slogan, 'It's the Last Shilling Which Will Break the Kaiser's Back' with an appropriate simple illustration.

Campaigns to save food in the absence of compulsory rationing prompted a great deal of voluntary propaganda. The government took the lead, with the Director-General of Food Economy, Kennedy Jones, asserting that the public should

look well at the loaf on your breakfast table and treat it as if it were real gold, because the British loaf is going to beat the German . . . Women have done nobly in the war, but they must do still more . . . today the kitchen is the key to victory and is in the fighting line alongside our undying heroes of the trenches and our brave men of the sea.[30]

Altogether 30,000 associations and 1,200 committees were working on propaganda to promote food economy. London was plastered with posters claiming 'Eat less Bread and Victory is Secure'.[31] Rationing, on the basis of 'loose voluntarism' was introduced by the end of 1917. An SOS League was formed which pledged not to exceed the rations laid down by the Food Controller, Lord Rhondda. Three million people joined.

Equally popular was the demand to turn over all available land to cultivation. The King contributed the symbolic gesture of turning over the flower beds round the Queen Victoria memorial to vegetables, and dividing the Royal Parks up into allotments. 'Idle Land for Food' was the slogan. Rowland Prothero, Minister of Agriculture, observed solemnly that 'It is my sincere conviction that it may be on the cornfields and potato lands of Great Britain that victory in the Great War may be lost or won.'[32]

The main government propaganda effort was still, however, directed at neutrals, allies, and the enemy. In February 1918, the Ministry of Information was set up under Lord Beaverbrook. It replaced the failing organization of the Department of Information which, under Sir Edward Carson, had been suffering from inter-departmental squabbles and had lost much of its dynamism. Carson, according to Beaverbrook, was 'hostile to the Prime Minister, critical of the government and nursing a grievance. His enthusiasm for the cause of propaganda was not apparent.'[33] Lord Beaverbrook's enthusiasm, on the other hand, had already been proved by his success at organizing Canadian propaganda during the war.

His appointment sparked off a row in parliament about the ethics of newspapermen becoming members of the government – which became more strident when it was learned that Northcliffe, then a friend of Lloyd George, was to be appointed Director of Propaganda to enemy countries, and was to have direct access to the Cabinet. Austen Chamberlain, of the Unionist War Committee, led the attack, arguing that the presence of newspapermen in government administration made the government responsible for what appeared in the press; at the same time, with uncharacteristic concern for the press, it was argued that newspapers would lose their freedom if proprietors lost the right to comment on government actions. Spencer Hughes observed that journalists were in an ideal position to conduct propaganda, since 'they are not hampered by what Dr Johnson termed "needless scrupulosity"'. This hostility petered out when the government became involved in other activities.

Though most of the Ministry's work was with foreign propaganda, it did explore new methods of propaganda for the home front. The use of war artists, started under Masterman's Wellington House operation, and also used by Beaverbrook during his Canadian propaganda experience, was expanded. Official war artists had been allowed to the front in 1916, the first being Muirhead Bone. More were commissioned, and regular exhibitions were held of the work of Bone, Paul Nash, Nevinson, and others.

The most important development was in film, which was used for the first time as a medium for propaganda. At the beginning of the war, although cinema audiences for Charlie Chaplin and D. W. Griffith films totalled twenty million, the official view of film was of 'an instrument for the amusement of the masses: the educated classes thought of "the pictures" as responsible for turning romantic shop boys into juvenile highwaymen, as a sort of moving edition of the "Penny Dreadful".'[34] In the course of the war, and particularly under the Ministry of Information, the role of 'the pictures' changed from an instrument for the amusement of the masses into an instrument for the manipulation of the masses. Northcliffe observed in September 1918: 'Speaking as a newspaperman, I hate to confess it, but the motion picture is doing more for the Allied cause than any other means of thought transmission. Not everyone reads the newspapers, and those who do forget what they have read, but no one can forget what he has seen happen on the screen.'[35]

The government took some time to appreciate the power of film. Like war correspondents, cameramen were not allowed to the front until autumn 1915. Masterman pioneered the use of film when, despite resistance from the service departments, he managed to get film of the Grand Fleet, the New Armies in training, and the army in Flanders. With film lent by Vickers Maxim, he put together the propaganda film *Britain Prepared*, which was shown in neutral countries in December 1915. Wellington House released the first major actuality film of the war, *The Battle of the Somme*, in August 1916. It had 2,000 bookings in the first two months and raised about £30,000 for military charities.[36]

Earlier on, independent film companies, as anxious to prove their patriotism as anyone else, had made up for the absence of factual film with old travelogues of Belgium and hurriedly-produced patriotic dramas like the Hepworth film fantasy titled *Unfit* (or *The Strength of the Weak*) which opened in October 1914 with the billing: 'Both brothers wish to enlist, only the older is accepted. The younger is "unfit". He goes to the front as a war correspondent and in the end gives his life to save his brother for the sake of a girl they both love.'[37] Recruiting films like *England's Call* were shown accompanied by military bands and girls in khaki singing patriotic songs.

The music hall lightning cartoon sketch was transposed successfully on to film by independent film companies like Neptune Films. Lancelot Steed produced numerous witty and patriotic long cartoons which glorified Britain's war effort and encouraged Hun-hating through the simple and prevalent method of ridiculing the enemy.

The first cooperation between the government and the film industry came with the establishment of the War Office Cinematograph Committee in 1916. It took over the Trade Committee which had already been showing actuality film taken at the front by such cameramen as Geoffrey Mallins and Lt J. B. McDowell. The Committee was chaired by Beaverbrook, with William Jury representing the trade, Reginald Brade from the War Office, and later Sir Graham Greene from the Admiralty. They cooperated with the Department of Information's cinema division, which made films for distribution in neutral countries. Regular biweekly news films were started in British cinemas in 1917.

The Ministry of Information officially adopted film, and set up its own studios staffed by professional film-makers in order to produce short propaganda films. These films were made for other government departments, using actresses like Ellen Terry to dramatize a message which aimed, for instance, to recruit women into munitions factories or the land army, or to encourage food economy by providing hints on alternative menus or how to grow your own food. Frequently, the dramatizations were intended to show how moral censure would fall on people who failed to do their duty. After the success of the French film, *Mothers of France*, starring Sarah Bernhardt, film-makers stressed the stirring human angle rather than the purely military aspects of the war. In 1917, the War Office partly sponsored D. W. Griffith's, spectacle, *Hearts of the World*, which was released in 1918.

The Ministry also invented the 'film tag', a short film of about two minutes embodying in story form some useful moral such as 'Save Coal' or 'Buy War Loans'. It was attached at the end of the newsreels and often took the form of a witty lightning sketch cartoon by Lancelot Steed and others. By 1918 film had arrived as a medium of propaganda.

Most of the Ministry's work was with foreign propaganda, however. Northcliffe headed propaganda to enemy countries, Rudyard Kipling directed colonial propaganda, and Lord Rothermere, Northcliffe's brother, directed propaganda to neutral countries. Despite a great deal of hostility from the Foreign Office, which had its own propaganda machine and intelligence branches, the Ministry set up a structure for acquiring information and disseminating propaganda. Propaganda in enemy countries worked to undermine morale and foment revolution amongst dissident groups in the Balkans and the Habsburg Empire. Devices were perfected for dropping leaflets behind enemy lines and generally destroying morale amongst German troops by emphasizing the magnitude and strength of the Allies and the effects of the blockade on Germany. General Ludendorff, after searching around for an excuse for the German defeat, found the answer in the effectiveness of British propaganda. This was also an admission of the failure of German propaganda, especially in neutral countries, where, Ludendorff wrote, 'We were subject to a moral blockade', as a result of Allied propaganda there.

Meanwhile the French conducted their propaganda through the Maison de la Presse, set up under the Ministry of Foreign Affairs in 1916, which dealt with intelligence, provided news, information and literature for propaganda in neutral countries, and laid particular stress on the religious nature of the war, on an appeal to avenge the humiliation of 1871, and on the fight for justice and freedom from oppression. This organization produced propaganda about atrocities in France in order to influence neutral opinion. France, too, had been slow to coordinate propaganda, since the main effort was concentrated at the beginning on the military offensive against the enemy, and it was the military which took over control of the press. There was a great deal of voluntary propaganda, and by March 1917, 30,000 societies with more than eleven million members in France and overseas had banded together in the Union des Grandes Associations Contre La Propagande Ennemie, which worked in neutral countries and at home. After a more or less abortive attempt by Northcliffe to coordinate Allied propagande in March 1918, the French reorganized their various propaganda agencies under the Centre d'Action de Propagande Contre L'Ennemie which utilized the organization and agents in neutral countries, and assisted in undermining morale behind the German lines with its own leaflets and pamphlets.

When America entered the war in 1917, the whole propaganda effort was immediately made official under George Creel's Committee on Public Information, which consisted of the Secretaries of State and the Secretaries for the Army and Navy. In its overseas propaganda effort aimed at destroying German morale the Committee emphasized the strength the addition of American troops had given to the Allied forces. In particular, it portrayed President Wilson as a man who embodied the ideals of freedom and democracy, an image which was particularly useful in the Committee's appeal to the ordinary German to detach himself from the power of the Prussian Junker class, which had brought so much misery to the world. At home, recruitment propaganda stressed in particularly vivid posters the barbarity of the Germans and their 'frightfulness'.

By 1918, British propaganda to the home front, no less than propaganda abroad, was established as an essential aspect of modern warfare. The realization, slow to dawn, that efficiency at the front was dependent on efficiency and morale at home was crucial to the development of government propaganda machinery to manipulate the civilian response to war. By 1918, the home front was fighting its own war: against the 'enemy in our midst' and against the phantom fears roused by war and exploited by propagandists in order to inflame hatred against enemy aliens and pacifists, as much as against Germans. Wartime propaganda generated fear, hatred and illusion, and confused more than clarified the issue for a nation which was undergoing one of the greatest tragedies of modern history.

Soldiers returning from the war found an England which they did not recognize:

England was beastly in 1918; it was in the hands of the dismal and incompetent. Pessimism raged among those who knew nothing of the war; *défaitisme*, the desire to stop the war at all costs, even by the admission of defeat, broke out among the fainthearts; while those at home who still had the will to fight preferred to use the most disgusting means – to fight by lying propaganda, and by imitating the bad tradition of the German Army which consistently made war against civilians. No wonder that a genuine and silent pacifism was rising in the breast of the war-weary populations. Envy, hatred, malice and all uncharitableness, fear and cruelty born of fear, seemed the dominant passions of the leaders of the nations in those days. Only in the trenches (on both sides of No Man's Land) were chivalry and sweet reasonableness to be found.[38]

Chapter Four

Getting the Troops

The populace caught the war fever. In every capital they clamoured for war . . . On Monday afternoon I walked with Mr Asquith to the House of Commons to hear Grey's famous speech. The crowd was so dense that no car could drive through it . . . It was distinctly a pro-war demonstration. I remember observing at the time: 'These people are very anxious to send our poor soldiers to face death; how many of them will ever go into battle themselves?' It was an unworthy doubt of the courage and patriotism of the demonstrators. A few days later recruiting stands were set up in the Horse Guards Parade, and that great open space beheld a crowd of young men surging around these stands and pushing their way through to give their names for enlistment in the Kitchener Armies.

D. Lloyd George, *War Memoirs*, vol. I, pp. 64–5.

The first necessity of war was men to fight it. The recruitment campaign was the most concerted propaganda exercise of the first half of the war. It combined persuading men to fight with providing justification for the war which gave them the reason for fighting. In the initial euphoria, thousands of men joined up. In the beginning, far from having to use persuasion, the War Office recruiting stands were inundated with people already persuaded of their duty to fight. As the hopes of a short war faded, the supply of recruits dwindled, while the demands of the war machine for an unlimited number of men increased.

At first the government relied on the voluntary principle to get the men. It was only after a long and acrimonious debate that the Liberal government, pledged to doctrines of laissez-faire and the freedom of the individual, was persuaded to introduce conscription in January 1916. In the meantime, they relied on the propaganda campaigns conducted by the War Office, by the Parliamentary Recruiting Committee and by a host of unofficial recruiting bodies to bombard the young men of Britain with persuasive arguments for sacrificing their lives.

The need for recruits was vital. Britain had less than a quarter of a million regular troops, most of them stationed on duty in various parts of the Empire, an Army Reserve of 150,000, a Special Reserve of 63,000 and a Territorial Force of 63,000. Under the terms of the Entente Cordiale, Britain was committed to support the French left flank initially with an Expeditionary Force of 60,000.

Lord Kitchener, who took over as Secretary of State for War, came to two important conclusions. First, that it would be a long war, three years at least – an insight which contradicted all the popular assumptions. Second, that this war needed a mass army to fight it. But how were the men to be got?

Conscription was out of the question. Neither Kitchener nor the Liberals, nor the majority of the population, supported it, despite the activities of Lord Roberts' National Service League campaign before the war. Britain had for centuries relied on a small volunteer force to fight its wars, and rejected the Continental pattern of large conscript armies.

Lord Kitchener's first military decision was to by-pass the Territorial Force, which he disparagingly called 'weekend soldiers' and 'a town clerk's army' in favour of creating the New Armies, consisting of volunteers who would be raised and trained from scratch.

This decision opened the flood gates for the propaganda of persuasion. Such was the moral pressure and ferocity of the campaign that by the time conscription was being debated, even staunch Liberals had to agree that the bullying, highly pressurized methods of some recruiting bodies amounted to what Conservatives called the tyranny of illegal conscription. In addition, recruitment propaganda had a more fundamental effect. It glamourized war in order to exhort men to enlist. It distorted the nature of war so effectively that the soldiers' war – the real war – became unrecognizable to the civilians who had been fed on the images and symbols of propaganda and starved of the real facts.

Voluntaryism certainly worked initially. Kitchener's appeal for the first 100,000 went out on 6 August. Northcliffe's papers, *The Times* and the *Daily Mail*, were the first to carry the War Office's quarter-page type-script advertisement headed 'Your King and Country Need You', which invited men between the ages of nineteen and thirty to enlist 'for three years or the duration'. It was reproduced on posters, and, shortly after, the other national newspapers followed Northcliffe's lead. By 25 August the first 100,000 had joined up. Three days later came the call for the next 100,000, and the upper age limit was increased to thirty-five. In a

Figures 5a and 5b

single day, 1 September 1914, the day after news of the retreat from Mons appeared in the Amiens Dispatch in *The Times*, a record of 30,000 enlisted.

Recruitment was brisk until, by late September, the first 500,000 had enlisted. From then on the numbers dwindled. By November the Parliamentary Recruiting Committee was reporting a marked decline in enthusiasm. 'Business as Usual' took over as the catch phrase of the moment. By December 1914, the stream of recruits was down to about 30,000 a week, and remained at that level for most of 1915. By July 1915 two million men had enlisted.

Initially, the appeal of propagandists to naïve patriotism and the call of duty to King and Country was sufficient. But as enthusiasm abated, more and more sophisticated techniques were employed to stir the conscience of those men who had not yet joined up.

War Office recruitment methods consisted of typescript advertisements and posters advertising the country's needs on the one hand, and the activities of recruiting sergeants on the other. Since 1913, the army authorities had been employing the Caxton Advertising Agency, run by Hedley Le Bas, to give a face lift to recruitment advertising. With a budget of £6,000 the Agency had come up with modern typescript advertisements headed 'What the Army Offers' and consisting of enticing descriptions of a soldier's life. These were novel methods, and they were continued into the war. Caxton's produced the first advertisements headed 'Your King and Country Need You'.

When the rate of recruitment began to fall off the advertising agencies pumped new life into recruitment advertising. Eric Field, who worked at Caxton's, wrote 'Pure patriotism as a recruiting appeal soon lost its initial force . . . We ran the gamut of all emotions which make men risk their lives and all the forces which deter them from doing so.'[1] One method was to appeal to the people who were employing men eligible to volunteer, as in 'Five Questions to Those Employing Male Servants':

1. Have You an able bodied groom, chauffeur, gardener or gamekeeper serving you who, at this moment, should be serving your King and Country?
2. Have You a man serving at your table who should be serving a gun?
3. Have You a man digging your garden who should be digging trenches?
4. Have You a man driving your car who should be driving a transport wagon?
5. Have You a man preserving your game who should be helping to preserve your Country?

    A great responsibility rests on You. Will You sacrifice your personal convenience for your Country's needs?[2]

Another method was to appeal to women to send out their men, as in such posters as 'Women of England! Do Your Duty! Send your man today to join the Glorious Army'.

Recruiting officers operated in all towns, holding meetings in town halls, at street corners and outside makeshift recruiting booths. They were assisted by the patriotic efforts of voluntary bodies and individuals. For instance, Lord Derby, the future Director of Recruiting, arranged War Office support for raising local 'pals' battalions which were to be trained and housed not by the War Office, which was creaking under the strain of the indiscriminate recruiting, but by local municipalities and private individuals. It was an effective way of exploiting local pride. In Liverpool, a meeting addressed by Lord Derby on 28 August 1914 called on the clerks of Liverpool to form their own battalion, an action which resulted in 4,000 recruits. On Tyneside, an individual recruiter got War Office permission to raise one local battalion on 28 October. By 18 November he had succeeded in raising four.[3] Altogether 304 units were raised in this way, including, in Liverpool, a dockers' battalion which subjected itself to military discipline and was available to handle any pressing government work.[4]

The other arm of official recruitment was the Parliamentary Recruiting Committee (PRC). It was an all-party group with Asquith, Bonar Law, the leader of the Opposition, and Arthur Henderson, the leader of the Labour Party, as joint presidents. It grew out of the activities of the National Liberal Federation, which circularized its constituency bodies with the call to 'render such services as each can best perform in movements which know no Party distinctions'. A meeting was held on 31 August 1914 between the Chief Whips and Sir Henry Rawlinson of the War Office to discuss 'how the grave issues of the war should be fully comprehended by the people and thereby give a powerful impetus to recruiting'.[5] The PRC was formed to do just that.

It was financed by a small grant from the War Office and supplemented by voluntary contributions. The constituency organizations distributed its pamphlets and leaflets, carried out a house-to-house recruitment canvass and compiled a Householders Return to estimate the number of potential recruits. Nightly meetings and patriotic rallies were addressed by speakers provided by the Committee, often accompanied by music hall artists, the singing of patriotic songs, and much flag waving. In constituencies it was a source of local pride to match recruiting figures with the national average. For instance, in Guildford, regular processions were held through the town, led by boy-scout torch-bearers and the Lord Mayor in his robes, while the list of volunteers was published regularly in the local newspaper, all of which excited tremendous interest.[6]

The bulk of the Committee's work, apart from pamphlets, was the production of over 200 posters. In the First World War, the poster, which had emerged as a respectable art form in the late nineteenth century, was transformed into a medium of propaganda on a scale never used before. Though most of the PRC posters did not reflect modern developments in design, there was one exception, their first and most famous, the Lord Kitchener poster. The design, by Alfred Leete, first appeared on the front cover of the London weekly magazine *London Opinion* of 15 September 1914. The Committee took it over and added 'God Save the King' to Kitchener's face. The original spawned numerous variations. It was the most successful poster of the war, and it established Kitchener's image as the embodiment of the nation's resolution and strength. He recalled Britain's imperial victories. Even government leaders who later

Imperial War Museum

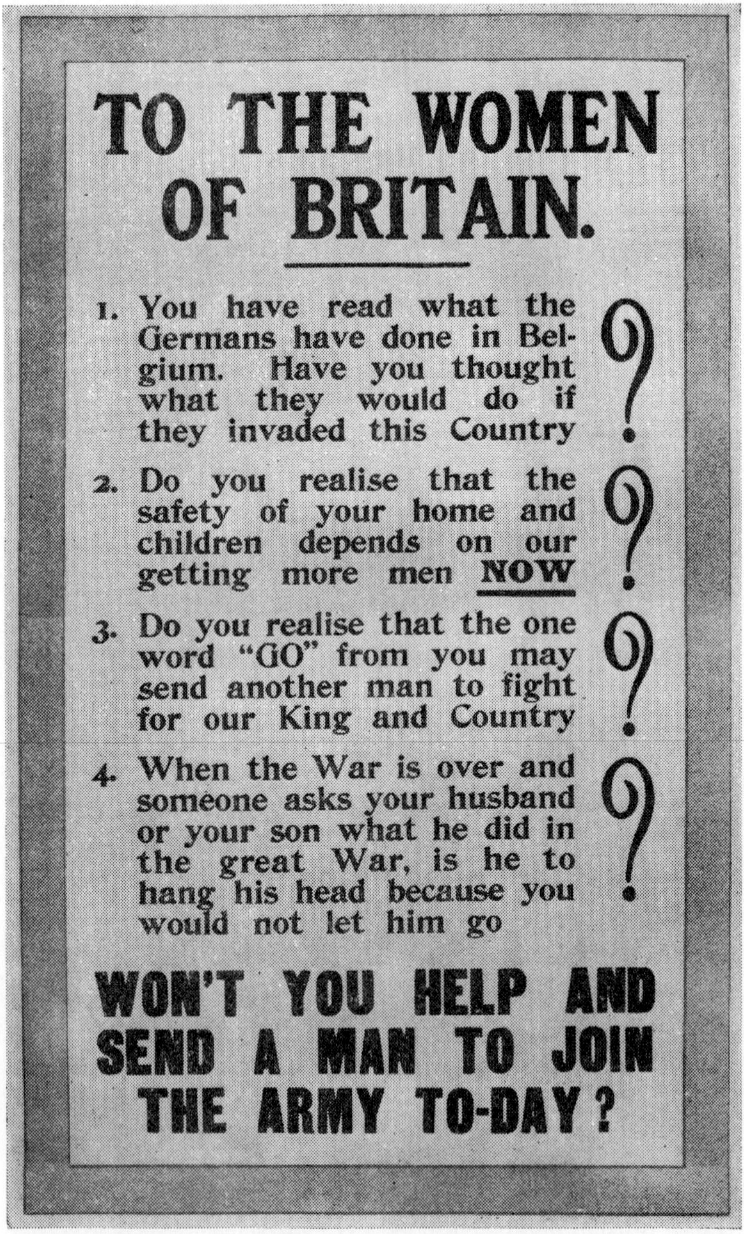
TO THE WOMEN OF BRITAIN.
1. You have read what the Germans have done in Belgium. Have you thought what they would do if they invaded this Country?
2. Do you realise that the safety of your home and children depends on our getting more men NOW?
3. Do you realise that the one word "GO" from you may send another man to fight for our King and Country?
4. When the War is over and someone asks your husband or your son what he did in the great War, is he to hang his head because you would not let him go?
WON'T YOU HELP AND SEND A MAN TO JOIN THE ARMY TO-DAY?

Figure 6 The appeal to women to become recruiting agents

doubted his capacity to manage the war paid tribute to the success his image had in inspiring confidence at the beginning. Miss Elizabeth Asquith called Kitchener himself 'The Great Poster'.

Subsequent PRC posters were less well-designed, the product of haphazard production and design methods. Most of them were designed by printers' artists after a suggestion, lacking detailed thought, had been made by the PRC. Conscious advertising expertise was absent. The appeal was to naïve patriotism, and the message was simple, direct, and often sentimental. 'Line Up Boys', 'Step into Place' and 'There's Room for You' are typical. Some posters used German outrages as a plea to enlist, as in 'Remember Belgium' and 'Remember Scarborough', though both were remarkably mild compared with the crude hate propaganda posters used in America and Australia for recruitment. Others appealed to women to send their men to war, as 'Women of Britain Say – Go', or attempted to shame men with a poster of a woman saying 'Will You Go – or Must I ?'

By January 1915, *Times* journalist Michael MacDonagh described the scene in London as 'vibrant with the call to arms'.

Posters appealing to recruits are to be seen on every hoarding, in most shop windows, in omnibuses, tramcars and commercial vans. The great base of Nelson's Pillar is covered with them. Their number and variety are remarkable. Everywhere Lord Kitchener sternly points a monstrously big finger, exclaiming 'I Want You'. Another bill says: 'Lord Kitchener wants another 100,000 men'. ('My word,' remarked a lonely spinster according to a current joke, 'one would do me!') 'Rally Round the Flag; Every Fit Man Wanted', 'Forward to Victory; Enlist Now'. Consequently, khaki is to be seen everywhere, and the voice of the drill sergeant is to be heard from morning until night in the Royal Parks, the gardens of the Inns of Court and in several of the squares.[7]

The feature which was most noticeably absent from all recruitment posters was any explicit description of the war. The details were partly excluded because they would deter men from enlisting, but also because few of the artists had been anywhere near the front. Gerald Spencer Pryce was almost exceptional in having a distinguished career as a dispatch rider in Belgium, and winning the Military Cross. Frank Brangwyn, one of the more realistic artists, was criticized on several occasions for being 'too artistic' and for 'showing the seamy side of war'. Of his famous poster 'To Arms', one commentator wrote,

The motives that make a man enlist nowadays are many and varied.

3

Those that keep back the man who *ought* to enlist are, I believe, first, lack of knowledge of the need and second, *fear* in some form or another – not so often actual fear of death, I believe, as fear of the discomforts and hardships of the soldier's life. Such a poster as this one by Mr Brangwyn tends to emphasize the latter rather too much.[8]

All recruitment failed to be explicit about the war. It was not the intention to be explicit. The object was to pressurize men into enlisting by evoking the familiar images and symbols of war and thus exploiting the emotions of potential recruits.

In the end, any appeal was justified. The unofficial recruiting bodies were even more active than the official ones. Some were quite moderate. For instance, Frank Pick, general manager of the London Electric Railway Company commissioned a series of posters of particularly high quality from artists like Frank Brangwyn and Gerald Spencer Pryce.

Others were quite fanatical. One of the strongest appeals used by unofficial recruiting bodies was the moral censure of men who did not enlist. 'The Order of the White Feather' was one particularly hysterical group. Launched by Admiral Penrose Fitzgerald from the bandstand at Folkestone, it consisted of squads of patriotic women whose sole object was to hand out white feathers, the sign of cowardice, to any young man they came across out of uniform. It was a sign of the hysteria produced by war. Michael MacDonagh commented: 'The bellicosity of these females is almost as terrible to the young man who has no stomach for fighting as an enemy with banners and guns. At the sight of them he is glad of the chance of being able to hide anyhow his diminished head.'[9] The campaign was responsible for some appalling mistakes, since the difficulty of distinguishing a 'shirker' from a man on leave in no way deterred these women from doing their duty. Hence the story circulated of a man who, fresh from receiving a VC from the King at Buckingham Palace, was handed a white feather while he was smoking a cigarette out of uniform in Hyde Park. Within a week of his return to the front, he was killed. White feathers handed to men with serious though not visible physical disabilities caused acute embarrassment.

Women were themselves the target of a great deal of moral pressure to send their men to fight. One particularly appalling example of this was an advertisement 'To the Women of London':

Is your 'Best Boy' wearing Khaki? If not don't YOU THINK he should be?

If he does not think that you and your country are worth fighting for –
do you think he is *worthy* of you?

Don't pity the girl who is alone – her young man is probably a soldier
fighting for her and her country – and for YOU

If your young man neglects his duty to his King and Country, the time
may come when he will NEGLECT YOU.

Think it over – and then ask him to

JOIN THE ARMY – TODAY

Other posters proclaimed 'Do you realize that if you keep back a Son
or Sweetheart, You are prolonging the War and adding to the peril of
those who have gone?' and 'Women of England. Release Men to Fight',
while a PRC poster showed an old woman talking to a young man with
the caption 'Go – It's Your Duty, Lad'.

Women's organizations which were actively involved in the recruitment drive included Emmeline and Christabel Pankhurst's Women's
Social and Political Union and Mrs Fawcett's National Union of Women's
Suffrage Societies. The Pankhursts argued that the active participation of
women in the 'national emergency' would further their campaign for the
vote and for women's equality. They supported the recruitment campaign
and the war. 'Everything that we women have been fighting for and
treasure,' argued Christabel Pankhurst, 'would disappear in the event of
a German victory. The Germans are playing the part of savages, over-
riding every principle of humanity and morality . . .'[10] In 1916 their
magazine the *Suffragist* was renamed *Britannia* as a sign of their patriotic
allegiance, though this did not prevent occasional outspoken criticism of
the Asquith government's conduct of the war.

Other women took a more robust line. Baroness Orczy, a fashionable
romantic novelist, formed the Women of England's Active Service
League, whose manifesto read

Your hour has come! . . . You know me, don't you? Together we have
laughed and cried over that dauntless Englishman the Scarlet Pimpernel,
and thrilled over the brave days of his League. Now we shall form ourselves into an Active Service League, whose sole object will be that of
influencing our men to offer themselves at once to the nearest recruiting
officer.

She called for 100,000 volunteers to sign a pledge 'to persuade every man
I know to offer his service to his country' and 'never to be seen in public
with any man who, being in every way fit and free for service, has refused
to respond to the country's call'.[11] 20,000 women responded to her call.

THE GREATER GAME.

MR. PUNCH (*to Professional Association Player*). " NO DOUBT YOU CAN MAKE MONEY IN THIS FIELD, MY FRIEND, BUT THERE'S ONLY ONE FIELD TO-DAY WHERE YOU CAN GET HONOUR."

Figure 7

Sarah MacNaughten, another novelist, observed 'There is a peculiar brutality which seems to possess everyone. Always I am reminded of birds on a small ledge pushing each other into the sea. The big bird that pushed another one over goes to sleep comfortably.'[12]

Other patriots were railing against any young man who carried on 'business as usual' to the extent of going to any form of entertainment. Football was an early target. Football, it was argued, like drink, sapped the energies of the young. The *Daily Mirror* took up the campaign against slackers in August 1914 with a front page picture of a soldier standing over a wounded comrade contemplating a crowded football stadium under the caption 'Will they *never* come?' Michael MacDonagh described the scene at football matches:

> Going to football matches in the old days we used to be confronted with evangelical posters greatly concerned for our eternal welfare, asking us, among other questions: 'Are you prepared to meet your God?' and bidding us 'Repent for the Time is at Hand'. In these days the posters carried by a line of sandwichmen, walking up and down before the gates of the Chelsea football ground, ask the crowd such questions as 'Are You Forgetting that There's a War On?', 'Your Country Needs You', 'Be Ready to Defend Your Home and Women from the German Huns' . . .[13]

The Football Association put its facilities at the disposal of recruitment bodies, who thereby gained access to vast working class audiences. Grounds were used for drilling, and offices for army storage, and well-known speakers addressed the crowds before matches. Footballers them-selves set the lead by volunteering in front of the crowd, and a poster appeared:

Do you want to be a Chelsea Die Hard?
If so
Join the 17th Battalion
Middlesex Regiment
'The Old Die Hards'
And follow the lead given
By your favourite Football Players.

By the end of 1914, an estimated 500,000 men had joined via foot-balling organizations, and crowds had diminished considerably. After eight months of war, football ended, with Lord Derby presenting the trophy after the 'khaki final' between Chelsea and Sheffield United, with the words 'You have played with one another and against one another for the Cup; play with one another for England now.'[14]

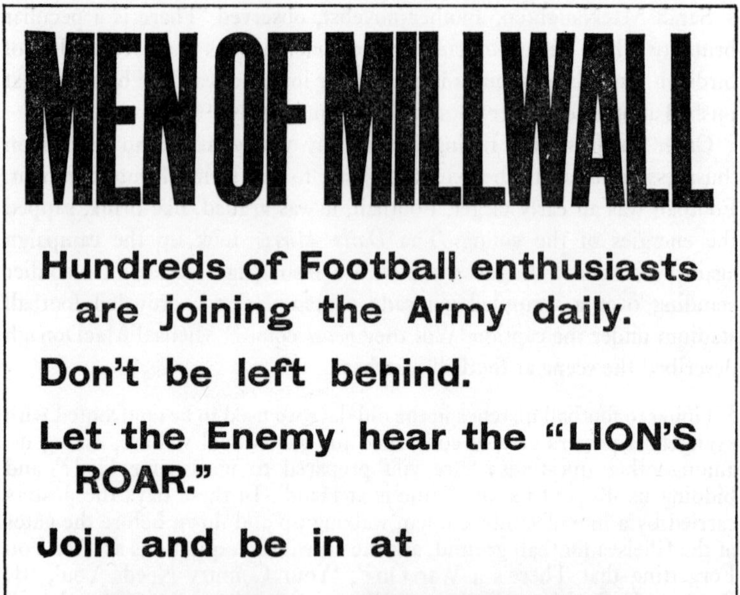
MEN OF MILLWALL
Hundreds of Football enthusiasts are joining the Army daily.
Don't be left behind.
Let the Enemy hear the "LION'S ROAR."
Join and be in at
THE FINAL
and give them a
KICK OFF THE EARTH
Apply:
West Africa House, opposite National Theatre, Kingsway.

Imperial War Museum

Figure 8

Rugby, a game played mainly by public schools, was cancelled at the beginning of the war, though the sporting spirit provided a useful basis for a plea for enlistment in *The Times*, for instance, which read: 'All Varsity men, Old Public School Boys – men who are hardened to a soldier's life by strenuous pursuit of sport should enlist at once.'

Other unofficial recruiters, like Horatio Bottomley, were motivated by a craving for self publicity, and by the opportunity which the most popular cause of the war provided for making money. Horatio Bottomley was the most famous unofficial recruiter of the war. Before the war he was known as the most colourful swindler and bankrupt in Britain and was once complimented by counsel at one of his bankruptcy trials as 'the cleverest thief in Europe'. He was a former MP for South Hackney and editor of the scurrilous magazine *John Bull*. In both roles he masqueraded as the champion of 'the little man', which earned him enormous popularity. When war broke out, he turned his extravagant rhetorical talents to the cause of patriotism.

A brief lapse in the editorial line of *John Bull* a week before the war, which expressed the sentiment 'To Hell with Serbia', and praised Austria's 'just demands', was made up for by the torrent of aggressive patriotic chauvinism which Bottomley pumped into *John Bull* for the rest of the war, directed against 'Germhuns' (enemy aliens), 'traitors', especially Ramsay MacDonald and 'Kur' Hardie, and 'shirkers'. It earned for *John Bull* the title 'Tommy's Bible', and for Horatio Bottomley a place in comedy verse of the period as 'the gentlemen's friend' who's

Noted today for seeing fair play
In a country that claims to be free.

Bottomley was a businessman. His political platform was for a 'Businessman's Government'. It was as a businessman that he strayed on to the stage of recruitment propaganda, where he remained fixed throughout the war.

Patriotism paid. He described himself as 'an oratorical courtesan. I sell myself to the man with the most money.' His speeches varied according to the fee. He could command up to £1,000 – for a week at the Glasgow Pavilion. He was always entertaining. In Bournemouth he played prosecuting counsel against the Kaiser and the German nation on the charge of wilful murder of civilization – for the sum of £200.

His first recruiting rally was held six weeks after the outbreak of war at the London Opera House. By 8.00 p.m. 25,000 people were queueing for seats for 5,000. It was a pageant, with a play specially written by Seymour Hicks (*England Expects*) and music hall turns. Phyllis Dane sang 'We don't want to lose you but we think you ought to go' for the first time.

His most famous and expensive offering, his 'Prince of Peace' speech was first delivered there. It showed a fine blend of rabble-rousing chauvinism and evangelical rhetoric:

If the British Empire resolves to fight this battle clearly, to look upon it as something more than an ordinary war, we shall one day realize that it has not been in vain, and we, the British Empire, as the chosen leaders of the world, shall travel along the road of human destiny and progress at the end of which we shall see the patient figure of the Prince of Peace, pointing to the Star of Bethlehem that leads us on to God.

Bottomley embarked on country-wide tours where his popularity increased to the tune of popping champagne corks. In *John Bull* and his weekly *Sunday Pictorial* column, he duplicated his particular brand of journalism. Bottomley visited the front and dispatched his impressions: 'I have been in Hell – and from its depths have seen the striking splendour of Heaven. In the scorched and blackened track of the Devil, I have met with God.' *John Bull* was scattered with alliterative headlines like 'The Potty Potentate of Potsdam' and, later 'No Mercy for the Berlin Butcher'.

For some he represented the extreme of hysterical and ugly patriotism, but his meetings drew far larger crowds than those of the political leaders, a fact which prompted the *Daily Mail* to suggest he be included on official platforms 'to add a little zest to their meetings'. He claimed for himself the title of Chief Unofficial Recruiting Agent, though the government declined to authorize it for him. He was so successful in public that one serious commentator could write 'Next to Kitchener, the most influential man today is Horatio Bottomley.' His influence was being used for interests other than the country's, however.

While his fine phrases were echoing round the recruiting halls, the 'gentleman's friend' was manipulating a gigantic fraud on subscribers to a patriotic scheme, organized through *John Bull*, for the purchase of War Loan Stock, War Savings Certificates, and Victory Bonds. The proceeds were traced directly to Bottomley's pocket, but not until 1921, when he was convicted of larceny and sentenced to six years' imprisonment. The ends to which he would exploit patriotic emotions appeared to be limitless. He was the hero of the die-hard patriots and the 'little man', but he manipulated the emotions of both because the profits for Bottomley's pocket and for his self-esteem were enormous. Nevertheless, he was effective as the most popular unofficial recruiter of them all.

The effects of all this indiscriminate propaganda were numerous. It intensified war fever because it involved the whole population in a moral obligation, not only to support the war but to do something about it or to persuade others to do something about it. The atmosphere even affected lifelong pacifists like Arnold Bennett, who wrote in his diary: 'When one sees young men idling in the lanes on Sunday, one thinks: "Why are they not at war?" All one's pacific ideas have been rudely disturbed. One is becoming militarist.'[15]

The effects of free enterprise propaganda on the military machine was chaos in the short term and disruption of essential industries in the long term. The massive drain on skilled men from essential occupations who enlisted in the first euphoria contributed to a shortage of industrial manpower which was to affect the production of munitions for the front. A 'starring system' to keep back men in essential occupations was not introduced until the formation of the Ministry of Munitions in 1915. More crucial in the short term was the total incapacity of the War Office to cope with the volume of recruits. Supplies of uniforms and arms were rapidly used up. The New Army recruits had to 'make do' with sticks for rifles and bayonets, and civilian clothes and old navy-blue uniforms instead of khaki. Most of the officers needed to train recruits had been sent off to France in the first emergency. Makeshift accommodation was often sufficiently bad to dampen the enthusiasm of even the most ardent recruits. Altogether Britain's mobilization during the first months of war presented a picture of amazing inefficiency in which only a dogged optimism about the favourable outcome of the war could have sustained morale. Propaganda played a considerable part in sustaining that morale.

There is no doubt also that propaganda succeeded in getting the troops. Propaganda justifying the war, and recruitment propaganda had provided the recruits with a reason for fighting the war. Britain was fighting for freedom from aggression, and for the defence of small nations. Britain was fighting for the honour of Britain. It was a moral crusade on behalf of the weak. It became the struggle for 'civilization against barbarism', for the 'rule of Right against Might'. Politicians and patriots presented the war as an idealistic one, and appealed to idealism in the population. C. E. Montague described how the recruitment propaganda had affected the men, at least at the beginning:

Figure 9 The power of moral censure used in recruitment propaganda

Most of those volunteers of the prime were men of handsome and boundless illusions. Each of them quite seriously thought of himself as a molecule in the body of a nation that was really, and not just figuratively, 'straining every nerve' to discharge an obligation of honour . . . All the air was ringing with rousing assurances. France to be saved, Belgium righted, freedom and civilization re-won, a sour, soiled crooked old world to be rid of bullies and crooks and reclaimed for straightness, decency, good nature . . .[16]

That idealism was expressed by some soldiers in the hope that war itself would bring about a revolution in values, that the war was the dawning of a new age. Rupert Brooke expressed this in his poem 'Peace':

Now, God be thanked Who has match'd us with His hour,
    And caught our youth and wakened us from sleeping,
With hand made sure, clear eye and sharpened power,
    To turn, as swimmers into cleanness leaping,
Glad from a world grown old and cold and weary . . .

Others joined up because they saw the war as a challenge to their manhood; men like J. B. Priestley, who described this challenge as

almost like a conscription of the spirit, little to do really with King and Country flag waving and hip-hip-hurrah, a challenge to what we felt was our untested manhood. Other men who had not lived as easily as we had, had drilled and marched and borne arms – couldn't we? Yes, we too could leave home and soft beds and the girls and soldier for a spell, if there was some excuse for it, something at least to be defended. And here it was.[17]

Propaganda appealing to the individual's obligation to King and Country and to defend Britain's honour clearly struck a naïve chord of patriotic response. But, as the unofficial volunteers found, the widespread fear of moral censure also had its effect. Charles Sorley, a soldier poet who was killed in 1915 at the age of nineteen, repudiated Brooke's idealistic motives for going to war when he wrote of him: 'He is far too obsessed with his own sacrifice, regarding the going to war of himself (and others) as a highly intense, remarkable and sacrificial exploit, whereas it is merely the conduct demanded of him (and others) by the turn of circumstances, when non-compliance with this demand would have made life intolerable.'[18]

The pressure to conform led many to enlist just because everyone else had; Edwin Routledge, for instance, who joined the Border Regiment in May 1915 at the age of sixteen and a half. He described his experience.

We were in Aspatria and there was a recruiting drive there, and there was a man from the Seaforth Highlanders recruiting on Brand Row. He said that for every recruit he got, he got an extra day's leave, and he had been at home for about six months then persuading people to join the army. There was a crowd of us, and some were drunk and some were over emotional, and some saw the glory of it all, but they were all anxious to go. And I said, well you're just a lot of fools. I said it's not what he's telling you; they kill people where you're going. I said, well you get yourself joined if you like, but I'm off . . . and just as I was getting back into Aspatria, there's this gang coming down the street. 'Oh we've all joined up, we've all joined the Army' and 'Come on, come on, you'd better go with us.' Well I says 'I think you're a lot of fools but I suppose I might as well, if you're going', but I says 'I think we're doing wrong.'[19]

Others joined for more hard-headed reasons, to escape unemployment or, like Edwin Routledge's brother, a miner, who said to him 'Well, with miners and the death tolls high in the pits – and it was in those days, it used to kill over a thousand people a year in the coal mines – well, it's just a bit bigger risk than that.'[20]

If anyone had any doubts about what the war was being fought for, it was erased in army training. All the propaganda about the righteousness of the war, and all the propaganda denigrating the enemy boiled down to one objective – to kill the Boche. Siegfried Sassoon described one episode in his training:

The sergeant, a tall sinewy machine, had been trained to such a pitch of frightfulness that at a moment's notice he could divest himself of all semblance of humanity. With a rifle and bayonet he illustrated the Major's ferocious aphorisms, including facial expressions. When told to 'put on a killing face' he did so, combining it with an ultra vindictive attitude. 'To instil fear into the opponent' was one of the Major's main maxims. Man, it seemed, had been created to jab the life out of the Germans. To hear the Major talk, one might have thought he did it himself every day before breakfast. His final words were: 'Remember that every Boche you fellows kill is a point scored to our side; every Boche you kill brings victory one minute nearer and shortens the war by one minute. Kill them! Kill them! There's only one good Boche and that's a dead one.'[21]

Another effect of recruitment propaganda was, of course, that it glorified war, both to the recruits and to the civilian population. The difference between the recruits and the civilians was that the recruits, when faced with first-hand experience of the war, found very rapidly that it was not the jovial picnic which they expected. The civilians never quite came to terms with the real facts of the appalling slaughter on the western front.

This was not entirely surprising at the beginning. Few people had any idea of what modern warfare would be like. Britain had not been involved in a Continental war for more than half a century, and the new generation's experience was of wars fought in far-off outposts of the Empire. The glory of war was still intact. As one young writer put it:

War to my generation implied campaigns on the Indian Frontier, in Egypt or in South Africa. My ideas of a European war were derived from panoramas of the Franco–Prussian conflict to be seen in continental cities. It was the war of tradition. Cavalry charged at the foe. When death came it was a heroic death brought about by heroes on the other side.[22]

Recruitment propaganda emphasized the heroic and glorious nature of war, and this idealization persisted even after soldiers at the front realized that it bore no relation to the reality of modern warfare. It persisted because it was an integral part of the recruitment drive. And after conscription was introduced in 1916 and the recruitment campaign became less urgent, this idealized image remained fixed for civilians on the home front, because it was necessary for propagandists to retain it in order to sustain morale.

The press, as a main source of information from the front and a vehicle for recruitment propaganda, assisted in this distortion. For one thing illustrated newspapers, histories and part works, mostly owned by the national newspapers, were almost the sole source of visual information from the front until cameramen were allowed there in 1916. They were particularly prone to glamourize war. Imaginative drawings took the place of photographs. These were done mostly by artists who had never been anywhere near the front. They based their drawings on truncated reports, and drew on the imagery of previous wars for their inspiration. Heroic cavalry charges virtually never took place throughout the entire war, but the pages of illustrated newspapers were full of them. These pictures were action-packed portrayals of Good versus Evil, in a style which bore a distinct resemblance to boys' comics.

The other reason why the press assisted in the distortion was because they were initially starved of information from the front and lacked the means to form an accurate perspective on events. Because of the War Office embargo on war correspondents till 1915 the press was dependent on dry official communiqués from the Press Bureau. During the press campaign to get correspondents to the front, one of Lord Northcliffe's newspapers claimed: 'Our Government tries to throttle its Press, and seems to be totally unaware that in the process it is chilling enthusiasm for the war.'[23] Lord Northcliffe believed that the stirring episodes of war would encourage recruitment. In the absence of such episodes, the press, in their role as recruiting agents, carried out exaggerated and sustained hate propaganda against the enemy to emphasize the magnitude of the threat from Germany. Starved newspapers pounced on any copy they could get, in particular, interviews with wounded soldiers from the front, who eagerly described fiery hand-to-hand battles, situations in which they had charged through and through the enemy 'until they broke like frightened hares in terror of the hounds', knocked 'all the stuffing out of the German cavalry' and, generally had a 'grand time . . . and I wouldn't have missed it for lashings of money'. To newspapers pre-occupied with exhorting men to enlist, they were presented as returning heroes. To show the real facts of the war of attrition would be to deter men from enlisting, a fact which became increasingly evident as more news seeped through.

As the facts of the war became clear, the question of sustaining morale assumed increasing importance. The glorification persisted, because the worst aspects of war were left out of published reports. Newspaper proprietors were conscious of this, correspondents developed a style which was essentially optimistic, and the soldiers themselves felt constrained to keep their experiences locked away from civilian view.

Newspaper proprietors knew that a great deal of distortion of the truth was going on, but had a duty to keep up morale. For instance, Lord Rothermere once commented to J. L. Garvin

You and I, Garvin, we haven't the pluck of those young lieutenants who go over the top. We're telling lies, we know we're telling lies, we daren't tell the public the truth, that we're losing more officers than the Germans, and that it's impossible to get through on the Western Front. You've seen the correspondents shepherded by Charteris, they don't know the truth, they don't speak the truth and we know they don't.[24]

Correspondents selected information for their dispatches, excluding the worst. As Philip Gibbs, of the *Daily Chronicle*, explained:

My dispatches tell the truth. There is not a word, I vow, of conscious falsehood in them . . . But they do not tell all the truth. I have had to spare the feelings of the men and women who have sons and husbands still fighting in France. I have not told all there is to tell about the agonies of this war, nor given in full realism the horrors that are inevitable in such fighting. It is perhaps better not to do so, here and now, although it is a moral cowardice which makes many people shut their eyes to the shambles, comforting their souls with fine phrases about the beauty of sacrifice.[25]

The soldiers found that they, too, were incapable of exposing the civilians to the shock of warfare. 'This isn't war as the world understands it,' wrote one soldier, 'the truth of the matter is that everyone out here considers it only fair to one's womankind to hush up the worst side of the war and make light of it.'[26] Siegfried Sassoon recorded 'an inability to reveal anything crudely horrifying to civilian sensibilities', and found himself suppressing 'all unpalatable facts about the war'. By this subtle process of exclusion, the image of the heroic soldier persisted in civilian minds. As one private in the West Kents recalled: 'Some people wondered how it was that I was not a happy slayer of Germans, as I told them on most occasions it was a case of seeing the enemy didn't get us, let alone trying to kill him. People at home thought all the time that we were continually fighting hand-to-hand from morn till night.'[27]

Soldiers recorded the stark contrast between the image of the war which was presented at home and their own experience. C. E. Montague noted in the average correspondent's reports – there were notable exceptions – a 'cheerfulness in face of vicarious torment and danger' that 'roused the fighting troops to fury against the writer'. The image presented was that

regimental officers and men enjoyed nothing better than 'going over the top'; that a battle was just a rough jovial picnic; that a fight never went on long enough for the men; that their only fear was lest the war should end on this side of the Rhine ... The most bloody defeat in the history of Britain ... might occur on the Ancre on 1 July 1916, and our Press come out bland and copious and graphic, with nothing to show that we had not had quite a good day – a victory really. Men who had lived through the massacre read the stuff open-mouthed.[28]

Sassoon noted the contrast bitterly in 1916: 'Bellicose politicians and journalists are fond of using the word "crusade". But the "chivalry" (which I'd seen in epitome in the Army School) had been mown down and blown up in July, August and September, and its remnant had finished the year's "crusade" in a morass of torment and frustration.'[29]

The image of war presented by the soldiers themselves is different. At the beginning they also were imbued with idealism. 'How eager we were to get to the front,' wrote Private Kemp. 'At the time we thought war was such a wonderful thing and were so keen to be doing something.'[30] The soldiers' poetry was also used as propaganda on the home front.

Rupert Brooke's poetry crystallized that idealism. His death in 1915 (from blood poisoning) coincided with the publication of his poem 'The Soldier' in *The Times*. He caught the imagination of a nation which was seeking heroes and martyrs. He became a legend, the personification of youth sacrificed in the cause of liberty. Winston Churchill's obituary in *The Times* was itself a piece of propaganda.

A voice had become audible, a note had been struck, more true, more thrilling, more able to do justice to the nobility of our youth in arms engaged in this present war, than any other – more able to express their thoughts of self surrender, and with a power to carry comfort to those who watched them so intently from afar. The voice has been swiftly stilled. Only the echoes and the memory remain; but they still linger . . .[31]

That note – the chord of patriotism, the willingness for sacrifice – was struck in 'The Soldier':

If I should die, think only this of me:
That there's some corner of a foreign field
That is for ever England. There shall be
In that rich earth a richer dust concealed
A dust whom England bore, shaped, made aware,
Gave, once, her flowers to love, her ways to roam,
A body of England's, breathing English air,
Washed by the rivers, blest by suns of home.

Julian Grenfell also wrote early in the war in a spirit of idealism about its glories and his poems were similarly used in recruitment propaganda. He was killed in action in May 1915. In October 1914 he wrote in a letter home: 'I *adore* war. It is like a big picnic without the objectlessness of a picnic'; and in November, 'It is all *the* best fun . . . It just suits my stolid health and stolid nerves and barbaric disposition. The fighting – excitement vitalizes everything, every sight and action. One loves one's fellow man so much more when one is bent on killing him.'[32] That enthusiasm came out in his poetry. 'Into Battle', written in April 1915, reflects an optimism about war which was absent in later poets:

The naked earth is warm with spring
  And with green grass and bursting trees
Leans to the sun's gaze glorying
  And quivers in the sunny breeze;
And life is Colour and warmth and Light
  And a striving evermore for these;
And he is dead who will not fight
  And who dies fighting has increase.

The fighting man shall from the sun
  Take warmth, and life from the glowing earth
Speed with the light foot winds to run,
  And with the trees to newer birth;
And find, when fighting shall be done
  Great rest, and fullness after dearth.

Grenfell's relish for war, in which he sees the positive aspects of growth and change, reveals an innocence about its nature, and its effect on men. The innocence of later poets was tempered by experience.

The New Army's first big offensive at Loos in 1915 was an abysmal failure. For very small gains, casualties totalled 50,000. The artillery bombardment which opened the offensive failed to destroy the German defences and men went over the top to be mown down in their thousands. Raw recruits in reserve arrived too late. On the Somme, on the first day, July 1916, there were 60,000 casualties, though the published figure was nowhere near that. The battle was presented as a victory. Between July and November 1916, the British lost some 420,000 casualties for an advance of six miles. Three British died for every two Germans. For both sides it was a turning point. 'By the end of 1916,' Lloyd George wrote, 'losses were greater than [Britain] had sustained in the aggregate of all her wars put together since the Wars of the Roses.'[33]

The idealism of 1914 could not withstand the reality of trench warfare. It drained away with the blood of so many comrades. The complexity of the situation, and the sheer discomfort and horror of the conditions gave the lie to the clear-cut, black and white image of war which prevailed at home.

More complex emotions replaced exhilaration for the soldiers in the 'zone of human havoc'. The poetry which came later reflected this. Sassoon, who later made a protest against the continuation of the war, wrote an epitaph to the soldier's innocent view of the war in his 'Suicide in the Trenches':

I knew a simple soldier boy
Who grinned at life in empty joy
Slept soundly through the lonesome dark
And whistled early with the lark.

In winter trenches, cowed and glum
With crumps of lice and lack of rum,
He put a bullet through his brain.
No-one spoke of him again.

. . .

You smug faced crowds with kindling eye
Who cheer when soldier lads march by,
Sneak home and pray you'll never know
The hell where youth and laughter go.

Wilfred Owen used the image of the horrific effects of gas warfare to express his loss of idealism about the war in 'Dulce et Decorum Est', written after a gas attack.

If in some smothering dreams, you too could pace
Behind the wagon that we flung him in,
And watch the white eyes writhing in his face,
His hanging face, like a devil's sick of sin;
If you could hear, at every jolt, the blood
Come gargling from the froth-corrupted lungs,
Bitter as the cud
Of vile, incurable sores on innocent tongues –
My friend you would not tell with such high zest
To children ardent for some desperate glory,
The old lie: Dulce et decorum est
Pro patria mori.

The preoccupation with nature and rural delights which characterized Georgian poetry took on a new meaning in war. The scale of destruction increased an awareness of nature. Julian Grenfell made a correspondence between nature's blossoming and the soldier's exhilaration. Charles Sorley, by contrast, saw only the alienation of the soldier from nature. 'All the Hills and Vales Along' illustrates this:

Earth that never doubts nor fears,
Earth that knows of death, not tears,
Earth that bore with joyful ease.
Hemlock for Socrates,
Earth that blossomed and was glad
'Neath the cross that Christ had,
Shall rejoice and blossom too
When the bullet reaches you.

Wherefore, men marching
On the road to death, sing!
Pour your gladness on earth's head,
So be merry, so be dead.

Private Kemp, who was at the front from 1915 to early 1917, recorded his disillusion with war, which he felt for the first time during the Battle of Loos in September 1915:

We began to see many wounded being taken back and remnants of regiments passing out as fresh troops had taken their place. These fellows were covered in chalk and mud and their drawn haggard faces made an impression on us which caused us to be much quieter. From that date I never heard the soldiers singing whilst on the march, and our picnic war had vanished. This was going to be a war with a vengeance, and, worse still, we had lost that hatred of the enemy which had prompted us to enlist. All we had to hope for now was 'a blighty one', as a wound was called, or a hard winter of bitterness in the trenches.[34]

Though many soldiers did believe the war was being fought to prevent the 'huns' ever starting another war, Hun-hating evaporated when the soldiers faced the enemy daily, sometimes only twenty yards away. The difficulty of breaking through the German lines induced something akin to respect for the military prowess and endurance of the enemy. 'As we lost our friends and pals,' wrote Private Kemp, 'the desire to destroy the enemy grew less, and we began to be more cautious and to respect the enemy more.'[35]

The image of the enemy as a devil faded somewhat when, as Montague described, if you took over his trench, 'Incarnate Evil had left its bit of food half-cooked, and the muddy straw, where it lay last, was pressed into a hollow by Incarnate Evil's back as by a cat's.' And if you went over his pockets, 'they never contained the right things – no poison to put in our wells, no practical hints for crucifying Canadians; only the usual stuffing of all soldiers' pockets – photographs and tobacco and bits of string and the wife's letters . . .'[36]

A common feeling was that both sides were helpless in a war which seemed to be controlled not by men but by machines. One soldier commented on the contrast with the home front '. . . the spirit of the trenches was more humane than the spirit behind the lines. Atrocity stories were not fabricated on the front. That duty which compels you to kill a man does not compel you to hate him. Of the two, hating is the worst lapse from humanity.'[37]

It was not so much hatred or the burning flame of duty which helped many soldiers to endure, but 'comradeship and mutual support without which the men in the trenches could not have survived a single day'.[38] Charles Edmonds commented: 'The strain of war was more likely to break the civilians who were not disciplined, not united and sustained by *esprit de corps*. Luckily they were not put to so severe a test as the soldiers; but what they endured, they endured singly, man by man. And they knew only the horrors of war, only the fear, the hatred, the pain and discomfort.'[39]

Not all the ranks felt this way, however. Private Kemp commented of comradeship: 'It is all bosh in my opinion, as men who were decent in civil life were decent in war, and men who were selfish in civil life were selfish in war, and most times it ended up with everyone being selfish . . . To look after oneself . . . that was what this inhuman war taught me as well as many other decent fellows to do.'[40]

Finally the prevailing mood at the front was dogged endurance. Soldiers just stuck it out. Private Kemp described how he felt when he was shelled at the Battle of Loos:

From that day we loathed and detested war as something worse than barbarism, and its very brutality was hateful to think about. To see men smashed to pieces with their heads and limbs blown off, and to feel the very ground rock with the concussion of shells, combined with the sickening smell of burnt powder and the smell of blood – that was what war was. Just hell broke loose. And men had to face it hungry, thirsty, cold and absolutely fed up.[41]

After the Battle of the Somme, he wrote:

War, where is the glamour of you, that we had been told was so splendid, and which we found to be so damned rotten and inhuman? It was unfit for rats to live in, let alone human beings, and even the rats were absent from this terrible Somme of shells, and mud, mud and rain, and mules plunging trace high through it to feed the guns with those cursed shells . . . By this time I didn't care two hoots who won the war and I think I am safe in saying that was the opinion of many more who served in the ranks. Our grub was wangled, our fag issue was stolen and sold . . . War by this time had turned men into savages and heathens.[42]

The cartoonist Bruce Bairnsfather captured the image of war as dogged endurance. An officer who went out in 1914, Bairnsfather drew humorous cartoons which portrayed the fed-up, sceptical soldier. He was epitomized in the character 'Old Bill', who was constantly up to his waist in water, being blown up by shells, and living entirely on plum jam and damp biscuits. He was immensely popular, in the trenches and at home. The humour took the edge off the reality. As Phillip Gibbs wrote:

Our men in the trenches . . . with just a fluke of luck between life and death, seized upon any kind of excuse for laughter, and many times in ruins and in the trenches and in dug outs, I have heard great laughter. It was the protective armour of men's souls. They knew that if they did not laugh, their courage would go, and nothing would stand between them and fear.[43]

Very little of this image of war reached the home front in 1915 and 1916. The propagandist view of war was given to the general public for as long as recruitment propaganda was necessary. By mid-1915, however, assumptions about the running of the war were being questioned on the home front.

Centralized government control, particularly, in 1915, control of munitions production, was making inroads into private effort. Faith in voluntaryism was being eroded. At the same time, criticism of the government's handling of the war, because of deadlock at the front, the inactivity of the navy, and the failure of the Dardanelles operation produced a crisis leading to demands in the press and among Conservatives for a more forceful hand at the helm, and the abolition of Asquith's 'wait and see' methods.

In addition, the voluntary recruitment campaign, not only because of the vulgar methods which were employed to scrape out more and more men, but also because some people believed it took the best men and left the 'shirkers', led a substantial section of the Conservative Party, including Curzon and Milner, who were prominent in the National Service League, some Liberals, notably Lloyd George and Churchill and a section of the press to the conclusion that conscription was essential. Conscription was to provide the issue on which the Conservatives chose to discredit the Asquith Liberals for their mishandling of the war.[44] What forced the issue was the combination of internal dispute about the failure of the Dardanelles campaign and the question of munitions shortage. Matters came to a head in May 1915, when Admiral Fisher, the First Sea Lord under Winston Churchill at the Admiralty, resigned over Churchill's handling of the Dardanelles campaign. This gesture forced the formation by Asquith of a Coalition government which included a number of Conservative supporters of conscription.

Two days later, on 21 May, Northcliffe made the first of his public attacks on Kitchener, the country's undisputed idol, for his conduct of the war. This attack reflected feeling in the inner circles of government, but not in the country. In the *Daily Mail*, under the headline the SHELLS SCANDAL: KITCHENER'S TRAGIC BLUNDER, Northcliffe exposed the disastrous shortage of high explosive shells which made successful offensive operations virtually impossible, and concluded that Kitchener was becoming a hindrance to the military success of the war. Far from smashing the nation's faith in its idol, the attack resulted in the *Daily Mail* being burnt on the Stock Exchange and being banned from the

Service Clubs of Pall Mall. Its circulation dropped from 1,386,000 to 238,000 and advertisers cancelled their contracts. Demonstrations at the Baltic Exchange and in Cardiff protested at this unpatriotic attack, and a plaque was hung over the *Daily Mail* offices which read 'Allies of the Hun'. It did nothing to dent public faith in Kitchener, though it contributed to a sense of crisis about the running of the war. Kitchener was indispensable to national morale. His propagandist image made him impregnable. As Lloyd George said: 'The trouble in war . . . was that you had to create for the people a dazzling hierarchy of Gods of War, the Generals. When you found out privately that they had feet of clay, you still had to go on with their public worship – or else the people would lose faith. So would the ordinary soldiers.'[45]

The conscription campaign was conducted mainly by Conservatives supported by the Northcliffe and Tory press, and, among Liberals, Lloyd George and Winston Churchill. (Most Liberals opposed it, and one Cabinet member, Sir John Simon, resigned when it was introduced.) They led a campaign in the press to convince the country that conscription was the only way to 'get out' the estimated 600,000 'shirkers' and 'slackers', and that the measure was not after all 'anti-democratic', and in parliament to get measures introduced which led up to conscription, but which also put the Liberal government in a fix whereby they had to accept conscription against all their traditional principles.

The National Registration Bill of 15 July 1915, which enabled the government to collect accurate information on the number of men available for military service, was followed by the appointment in October of Lord Derby, a conscriptionist, as Director of Recruiting, and the initiation of the Derby Scheme.

Lord Derby's scheme was to get men to attest their willingness to enlist, while Asquith pledged that married men would not be called up until all the single men had been 'got'. It was the first step in the rationalization of recruiting and turned out to be the first step towards conscription. The Derby Scheme was supported by Asquith, who believed that men would respond to the call, and by the Labour Party, even more opposed to conscription, who believed it would save the voluntary system. Two and a half million men attested, but the figures revealed the existence of 316,464 single fit men who were not 'starred', but who had not enlisted.

On 28 December the broad outlines of a bill which applied to single men between the ages of eighteen and forty-one was accepted by Asquith, who claimed that he was redeeming his pledge to the married men. McKenna, Runciman, Simon and Grey in the Cabinet threatened to resign, though only Simon carried out his threat. On 6 January 1916 the voting on the first reading of the Bill was 403 for, 103 against and 150 abstentions – which revealed that Asquith had seriously over-estimated the extent of opposition, and also that the Conservative campaign had proved remarkably successful.

The Act produced fewer men than anticipated. In the first six months the average monthly enlistment was around 40,000 a month, much the same as it had been under the voluntary system. By April it was clear that further measures were necessary if the government was going to meet the Allied military commitment. After a secret session of the House of Commons, when the Dublin Rebellion and the surrender of British troops in Mesopotamia had created a renewed upsurge of patriotism (29 April 1916) new measures to include all men, married or single, up to the age of forty-one were accepted and introduced in May.

From then on, recruitment propaganda was reduced to a trickle. It was replaced by other forms of propaganda. Women, who had been the target of a great deal of recruitment propaganda, were now being called upon to enlist for work in the munitions factories and on the land. For instance, at an enormous rally organized by Mrs Pankhurst and Mrs Fawcett's women's organizations, under the banner 'We demand the right to work' (17 July 1915), Lloyd George made the memorable statement: 'Without women, victory will tarry, and the victory which tarries means a victory whose footprints are footprints of blood.'[46]

The call to sacrifice life was replaced by the call to sacrifice money – for the Government War Loan and War Savings Schemes. Posters appealing for food economy replaced the recruitment posters as the submarine war bit deeper into food supplies and the drive to save food intensified. Later, when war-weariness beset the nation, the halls which had echoed with the voice of recruiting sergeants rang with the voices of patriotic organizations who were keeping up morale, salvaging the tarnished image of sacrifice for a righteous cause, and re-clarifying the warm aims which had by then become obscured by the facts of war.

The demand for men did not cease with the Military Service Acts. The drain on men at the front was incessant, and the demand of the military machine relentless. In January 1918, Sir Auckland Geddes, Lloyd George's Director General of National Service, announced that it was necessary to comb out another 420,000 to 450,000 men from those

now in civil life or in essential industries. The stark alternatives were to
call up their fathers, to send out those who had been wounded again and
again to the trenches or to stop leave for the men at the front. The fact
was that there were insufficient reserves at the front. The Battle of Arras
(9–14 April 1917) claimed 142,000 men, Passchendaele 324,000. 'The
government,' said Sir Auckland Geddes, are now 'determined that reck-
lessness with regard to human life, and thoughtlessness with regard to
casualties, shall be stamped out wherever it appears.'[47] It was a little late
to come to that conclusion. Lloyd George wrote later:

> Every nation was profligate of its manpower in the early stages of the
> war and conducted its war activities as if there were no limit to the
> number of young men who were fit to be thrown into the furnace to feed
> the flames of war. The Allies, who had an enormous superiority in
> numbers of fit men available, nearly threw away their advantage by the
> reckless prodigality of their military leaders . . . The idea of a war of
> attrition was the refuge of stupidity and it was stupidly operated, with the
> consequence that the overwhelming superiority in manpower which the
> Allies enjoyed at the beginning of the War had by the fourth year been
> melted down to the dimensions of dubious equality.[48]

This disastrous state of affairs called for a new round of propaganda –
propaganda to sustain morale, propaganda to fight to the finish and
propaganda against a negotiated peace. Very little was left now of the
image of war which the home front had absorbed in the first two years
before the Somme. Very little was left for the soldiers of the glory of war,
and less was left of the idealism which had inspired the first hundred
thousand to fight in the moral crusade.

Chapter Five

The Evil Hun

A coarse patriotism, fed by the wildest rumours and the most violent appeals to hate and the animal lust of blood, passes by quick contagion through the crowded life of cities, and recommends itself everywhere by the satisfaction it affords to the sensational cravings. It is less the savage yearning for participation in the fray than the feeding of a neurotic imagination that marks Jingoism. The actual rage of the combat is of a different and more individual order. Jingoism is the passion of the spectator, the inciter, the backer, not of the fighter; it is a collective or mob passion which, in as far as it prevails, makes the individual mind subject to a control that joins him, irresistibly, to his fellows.

J. A. Hobson, *The Psychology of Jingoism*, pp. 8–9.

That was written in 1900 about jingoism.

Throughout the war, a campaign of hate was waged against Germany. It affected the civilian population most of all. All the fears of a nation at war with its strongest rival came to the surface in response to exactly those 'violent appeals to hate and the animal lust for blood'. The first task of propaganda was to 'mobilize the animosity of the community against the enemy'.[1]

The essence of propaganda is simplification. In wartime, the intricate patterns of politics are refined into simple and crude images of right and wrong. Germany was the aggressor, Britain the crusader for the rights of small nations, for democracy and freedom. The British view of Germany was reduced to a stereotype. Michael MacDonagh, diarist of the Great War, summed up that stereotype: 'Germany has always been disliked and distrusted for her bullying policy of sabre rattling, the mailed fist, the goose step, and the spiked helmet – symbols of violence and brute force. Indeed she has been suspected for years of looking forward to war with Great Britain.'[2]

Wickham Steed, Foreign Editor of *The Times*, saw the conflict in terms of opposing ideologies:

Figure 10 *The Triumph of 'Culture'*

German 'frightfulness' – as an aspect of German culture

Some saw, indeed, that behind the moral issue lay not only a question of life and death for England and the Empire, but a struggle between two incompatible conceptions of civilization, between the Prusso–Napoleonic and the Christian, between the Militarist and the Liberal. Germany had become virtually pagan, worshipping a deity more akin to Odin than to Christ. For many years I had revolted inwardly against the doctrines which had come to be her effective creed . . . Hence the almost joyous relief with which I, like other ardent spirits, learned that the die was cast and the battle fairly joined.[3]

Rudyard Kipling more succinctly caught the flavour of popular mythology about Germany when he wrote: 'However the world pretends to divide itself, there are only two divisions in the world today – human beings and Germans.'[4]

Initially the motive for anti-German propaganda was to justify the war and Britain's part in it. The drive for recruitment, which used the appeal to revenge, helped to fan the flames of hatred. Eventually, the campaign took on an impetus of its own. Hatred became an indispensable part of civilian morale, as Arthur Conan Doyle made clear in 1918:

Hatred, or, if my critics prefer it, righteous wrath, is the means to attain invincible resolve and it is as such that I have recommended it. Lukewarm feelings can give only half-hearted results. If our workers could actually see the vile things which have been perpetrated upon our people, they would be filled by such feelings, call them what you may, that they would work with redoubled heart and vigour. Since they cannot see them they should be brought home to them in every way, verbal or pictorial, that is possible . . .[5]

No one group or government agency was entirely responsible for this. It was part of a gradual process, a slow filtering of fact and opinion which eventually deposited a unified image. The 'campaign' kept hate alive throughout the war by denigrating the enemy and eventually transforming him into a monster, even a devil. Information which gave a sympathetic picture of Germany was controlled, sometimes to a ludicrous extent. When a correspondent described 'good German cigars' the editor insisted on deleting the word 'good' since this was not a word which could be applied to anything German. Relevant information necessary to give a balanced and accurate picture was frequently withheld in reports, often on the grounds of security, but more often because it was bad propaganda to complicate the issue. Any information which could denigrate the enemy was distorted and exaggerated. Rumour was frequently presented as fact to a civilian population which was starved of information about the war. Truth was reconditioned to fit the prevailing image of the enemy.

The campaign to discredit the enemy focused on its methods of warfare, its people and its Kaiser. 'Frightfulness' was the word coined to describe German methods of warfare, and applied particularly to the use of modern weapons, especially submarine and gas. The German people using these were the 'evil Huns' with all the attributes of the barbarian, and the chief barbarian was the Kaiser.

It was atrocity stories which crystallized the image of the evil Hun in the minds of the civilian population. Stories of rape, murder and mutilation accompanied the fall of all the towns in Belgium and France as the Germans advanced. Atrocity stories occur in every war. What distinguished the atrocity stories of this war was the speed at which the stories spread, and the number of stories which circulated. The press were partly responsible through their wide coverage. Reading the newspapers of the time, it is very difficult to disentangle what was actually happening in Belgium from all the rhetoric which aimed to blacken the view of Germany. There was no room for the German version.

For instance, when Rheims Cathedral was bombarded on 22 September 1914, the act was dubbed 'The Kaiser's Crowning Infamy' by the *Daily News*. The impression was given that the Cathedral had been totally destroyed, though in fact only a small part had been seriously damaged. The Cathedral held a prominent place in French history: it was a shrine, where, for generations, the Kings of France had been consecrated. Legend had it that the oil was brought down by a dove from heaven. In 1914, it was a marker for artillery fire and an observation post for the enemy, i.e. a military target. The military significance of the building was totally ignored in reporting the incident.

By 1916, the soldiers knew that the bombardment of any buildings, including churches, was a commonplace of war. One writer described the soldier's view in fictionalized documentary style:

When the German star shell had spent itself they crossed the road to the rear of the redoubt, and marked the other two emplacements – in comparative safety now.

'The only trouble with this place,' said Ayling, as he surveyed the last position, 'is that my fire will be marked by that house with the clump of trees behind it.'

The Engineer produced a small note book, and wrote in it by the light of a convenient star shell.

'Right-o!' he said, 'I'll have the whole caboodle pushed over for you by tomorrow night. Anything else?'

Ayling began to enjoy himself. After you have spent nine months in an unprofitable attempt to combine practical machine gun tactics with a scrupulous respect for private property, the realization that you may now gratify your destructive instincts to the full came as a welcome and luxurious shock.

'Thanks,' he said, 'You might flatten out that haystack too.'[6]

The primary authoritative sources of information about the war were the government and the press. Politicians were circumspect about the details of atrocities in their wartime speeches, though they used them to arouse emotion when they spoke about recruitment. 'The new philosophy of Germany is to destroy Christianity,' said Lloyd George on 19 September 1914. 'The Prussian Junker is the road-hog of Europe. Small nationalities in his way are flung to the roadside, bleeding and broken; women and children thrust under the wheel of his cruel car . . .' Asquith, in October 1914, spoke of the Germans as 'the hordes who leave behind them at every stage of their progress a dismal trail of savagery, of devastation and of destruction worthy of the blackest annals of the history of barbarism.' Politicians were wisely cautious about giving credence to the crude details of atrocities, but used their emotional charge to make larger points about liberty and sacrifice.

The press were under no such constraint, and gave great prominence to atrocity stories. In the absence of factual information – there was general criticism about the 'fog of war' – atrocity stories provided much-needed copy. The motives of the press were mixed: understandable patriotism mingled with sensationalism. The patriotic newspapers took on the role of recruiting agents. Lord Northcliffe wrote to Asquith in 1914 complaining that they could not fulfil this role:

I have been asked by the head of the Recruiting Department of the War Office to use my many newspapers as an aid to recruiting. I think it is my duty, however, to tell you that, having for some time been engaged in careful enquiries throughout England and Germany, I find that whereas there is in Germany immense enthusiasm for the War, there exist in parts of this country, apathy, ignorance, or ridiculous optimism, more especially in the provinces.

The chief hindrance to recruiting is that whereas the German public are supplied with the work of photographers, artists, cinematograph operators and war correspondents, our people have nothing but the casualty lists and mutilated scraps with which it is quite impossible to arouse interest or follow the War intelligently.

The public *cannot* be aroused by present methods.[7]

Atrocity stories filled the gap. There was, however, a lack of discrimination about the stories which were published, and little attempt
was made to verify details. The characteristic atrocity story came from 'a
correspondent' some distance behind the scene of operations. It was
invariably a supposedly verbatim account by an unidentified Belgian
or French refugee. Even these accounts were usually second-hand, as
were the reports gleaned by eager correspondents from refugees arriving
in Britain. These stories were sensational news. No effort was made to
spare readers of the vivid gory details – they were, indeed, 'violent
appeals to hate and the animal lust for blood'.

Such lack of discrimination did, of course, produce mistakes. One of
the earliest atrocity stories concerned a nurse from Dumfries. The
Dumfries Standard of 16 September 1914 carried the story of a twenty-
three-year-old nurse, Grace Hume, who had gone to serve in the camp
hospital at Vilvorde in Belgium at the outbreak of war. The report stated
that the invading Germans had attacked the hospital, killing wounded
men. The Germans had then cut off Nurse Hume's breast, leaving her
to die in agony. A scribbled note was sent to her sister, Kate, in Dumfries,
dated 6 September, which said: 'Dear Kate, this is to say goodbye. Have
not long to live. Hospital set on fire. Germans cruel. A man here has had
his head cut off. My right breast has been taken away. Give my love
to –. Goodbye. Grace.' Versions of this story appeared in other newspapers including the *Evening Standard*, *Pall Mall Gazette* and *Westminster Gazette*. In the *Star*, the headlines read: 'A NURSE'S TRAGEDY.
DUMFRIES GIRL VICTIM OF SHOCKING BARBARITY.' Another letter
was delivered by a Nurse Mullard, who was with Nurse Hume when she
died. It told of Nurse Hume's heroism in shooting a German who
attacked a wounded soldier, and of how her left breast had also been cut
off. On 18 September, however, *The Times* leader reported results of
inquiries into the affair, which revealed that Nurse Hume was actually in
Huddersfield and had never been to Belgium, that no Nurse Mullard
existed, and that the whole story was the fabrication of Nurse Hume's
seventeen-year-old sister, Kate. On 30 September she was charged with
forgery, and later convicted. There were no headlines in the newspapers
to announce the forgery. The press had swallowed the story whole.

Some stories were questioned by readers after publication. On 12
September 1914 *The Times* published a letter from a London vicar
containing an 'extract from a letter addressed to his son from an officer
serving in the British Expeditionary Force'. The headline read: 'BRITISH

TROOPS AT THE FRONT. PERSONAL NARRATIVE. VICTIMS OF
GERMAN BARBARISM', and the letter ran: 'We have got three girls in
the trenches with us who came to us for protection. One had no clothes
on, having been outraged by the Germans . . . another poor girl has
just come in having had both her breasts cut off. I caught the Uhlan
officer in the act, and with a rifle at three hundred yards, killed him . . .'
Lord Selborne was stirred to protest to *The Times* that 'such statements
as these cannot possibly be allowed to rest on anonymous authority'. A
discussion followed in the columns of the *Daily News* about the tech-
nicalities of shooting Germans at three hundred yards under heavy fire,
but no authentication was provided.

The majority of stories passed unchecked either by editors or the Press
Bureau. The *Sunday Chronicle* of 2 May 1915 told the story of a 'charitable
great lady' who, while visiting a home for Belgian refugees in Paris, saw
a little girl who kept her hands in 'a pitiful little worn muff', though the
room was hot. When the child asked her mother to blow her nose for her,
the lady protested that 'surely such a big girl could use her own handker-
chief'. The mother replied in a 'dull matter-of-fact tone', 'She has not
any hands now, ma'am.' The theme of mutilation of children was so
familiar that a *Times* correspondent on 2 September 1914 could quote a
French refugee as saying: 'They cut the hands off little boys so there will
be no more soldiers for France.' In October 1914, a clergyman told the
Manchester Geographical Society: 'You will hear only a hundredth part
of the actual atrocities this war has produced. The civilized world could
not stand the truth. It will never hear it. There are, up and down England
today, scores – I am understating the number – of Belgian girls who have
had their hands cut off. That is nothing to what we could tell you.' Later
that month, the same man wrote to the *Daily News*, asking 'Will anyone
who has actually *seen* such cases here in England send me particulars?'
No one replied.

Many of the atrocity stories had been circulated in previous wars. The
Daily News of 1 October 1914, carried the story of a boy scout who was
shot by Uhlans for refusing to give information about the French Army.
A similar incident of a small boy using a wooden gun was reported in the
Franco–Prussian War. A German atrocity story described the discovery
of buckets full of eyeballs which had been extracted by the enemy. The
story dates back to the Crusades when it was used against the Turks.[8]
Norman Angell, sociologist and philosopher, took a broad view of the
repetition of atrocities when he wrote, in 1926:

From *The Kaiser's Garland*

Figure 11 'The Gentle German' by Edmund J. Sullivan

The moral dangers inseparable from the assumption of tribal and collective responsibility, which is implied in the wartime exploitation of atrocities, are as plainly writ in the history of every war as is the fact of atrocities themselves. The atrocity phenomenon is so invariable that one could, with perfect assurance, on the first day of every war, say exactly what accusations would be made continually by one side against the other.[9]

But the fact was that atrocity stories were still believed, and all this evidence contributed to the hatred which continued to replace sense till the end of the war. The question was – how could one not believe the stories? Robert Graves was as taken in by them as many others:

It never occurred to me that newspapers and statesmen could lie. I forgot my pacifism – I was ready to believe the worst of the Germans. I was outraged to read of the cynical violation of Belgian neutrality. I wrote a poem promising vengeance for Louvain. I discounted perhaps 20 per cent of the atrocity details as wartime exaggeration. That was not, of course, enough.[10]

He quotes an interesting account of the genesis of an atrocity story:

'When the fall of Antwerp got known the church bells were rung.' [i.e. at Cologne and elsewhere in Germany] – *Kölnische Zeitung*.
'According to the *Kölnische Zeitung*, the clergy of Antwerp were compelled to ring the church bells when the fortress was taken.' – *Le Matin* (Paris).
'According to what *The Times* has heard from Cologne via Paris, the unfortunate Belgian priests who refused to ring the church bells when Antwerp was taken have been sentenced to hard labour.' – *Corriere della Sera* (Milan).
'According to information in the *Corriere della Sera*, from Cologne via London, it is confirmed that the barbaric conquerors of Antwerp punished the unfortunate Belgian priests for their heroic refusal to ring the church bells by hanging them as living clappers to the bells with their heads down.' – *Le Matin* (Paris).

Exaggeration and distortion played a constant part in the atrocity stories. Factual evidence was invariably lacking. Despite the widespread reports of mutilation of civilians, there were no photographs as evidence, a fact which few seem to have questioned. Lord Northcliffe offered £200 for an authentic photograph, but the prize was never claimed.[11] The *Daily Chronicle* published a book of fifty-eight photographs of towns after bombardment, but felt obliged to comment, after detailed descriptions of outrages against civilians: 'It will be understood that one cannot, however, produce photographs of these cruelties as in each case, the fiends

4

who committed them were careful enough to cover up all traces of them.'[12]

Faked photos were used, however. A photograph in the *Daily Mirror* (25 August 1915) showed three cavalry officers grinning as they held up trophies. The caption read: 'Three German cavalrymen loaded with gold and silver loot.' It was in fact a photo published before the war in the *Berliner Lokalanzeiger* (9 June 1914) showing the three men who had won cups in the Army steeplechase in the Grunewald.

Illustrated newspapers filled in the gaps left by the absence of photographs. They specialized in drawings of the reported incidents, with captions underlining the message of German 'frightfulness'. Many of these illustrated papers were owned by the proprietors of the dailies. Part works, such as *The Great War*, which advertised themselves as illustrated histories of the war, were not averse to the use of sensational captions. Needless to say, most of the drawings were done in Britain, many by people who had never seen foreign soil, and they were the products of fertile imagination rather than observation.

In the confusion of war, many of the incidents were open to differing interpretations, depending on which side you were on. By a process of eliminating some pieces of relevant information and exaggeration of other aspects of the story, propaganda worked towards the suppression of any information sympathetic to the enemy. On 25 August 1914, the Germans bombarded Louvain. This ancient town had a medieval library containing priceless manuscripts, which was destroyed. The press reported the massacre of civilians in the main square, mutilation by drunken soldiers, deportation of civilians, looting and rape. It was presented as an unprovoked attack on civilians. On 4 September *The Times* headlines ran: 'FATE OF LOUVAIN. WANTON SHOOTING AND BURNING. BODIES BURIED BY DRUNKEN GERMAN TROOPERS.', and on 5 September: 'THE INFAMY OF LOUVAIN. INCREDIBLE BARBARITY. CITIZEN'S TERRIBLE JOURNEYS. GERMAN SAVAGERY RUN RIOT.' Conflicting reports arrived in Britain. A few days after the Germans had invaded Louvain, fighting broke out. The Germans claimed that the fighting had been started by *francs tireurs* – guerrilla fighters. The Belgians claimed that the fighting had been started by drunken German soldiers. The German justification was that they retaliated against the *francs tireurs* by shooting hostages and burning part of the town. The British press embroidered the story to include the destruction of the whole town, and were especially outraged by the destruction of the ancient historical manuscripts and the library, which was presented as a deliberate act of barbarism by the Huns.

The effects of an invading army using modern weapons and heavy bombardment were appalling, and produced high casualty figures: 5,000 civilians died in Belgium. The Germans did take hostages and were particularly harsh on civilians who showed any form of resistance. Throughout the invasion the same pattern prevailed as they advanced on the towns. The Germans claimed that their actions were reprisals against resistance fighters, who had haunted the Germans since the Franco–Prussian War. General Ludendorff wrote:

It was the sort of thing which aroused that intense bitterness that during those first years characterized the war of the Western Front . . . the Belgian government took a grave responsibility on itself. It had systematically organized civilian warfare. Such action was not in keeping with the usages of war; our troops cannot be blamed if they took the sternest measures to suppress it. For my part, I had taken the field with chivalrous and humane conceptions of war. This *franc tireur* warfare was bound to disgust any soldier. My soldierly spirit suffered bitter disillusion.[13]

In the British press no credit was given for any German justifications. This is not surprising. But while the British press was praising the heroic resistance of Belgian civilians, with illustrations, they were at the same time pouring scorn on German protestations of organized civilian resistance. In Germany stories were circulating which matched British atrocity stories. They claimed that 'It is proved beyond doubt that German wounded were robbed and killed by the Belgian population and indeed were subject to horrible mutilation, and that even women and young girls took part in these shameful actions. In this way, the eyes of German soldiers were torn out, their ears, noses, fingers and sexual organs cut off or their body cut open.'[14] These statements were supplemented in the German press by stories of priests gunning down German soldiers from behind their altars[15] and civilians gouging out the eyes of wounded German soldiers.

The exclusion of relevant information, which would have qualified the response, was particularly clear in the case of Edith Cavell. The 'martyrdom' of Edith Cavell caught the imagination of artists and newspapers alike. But a great deal of factual information was withheld from the readers. As a nurse running a training hospital in Brussels, she had, since early in the war, been involved in an underground network helping

Allied prisoners to escape. She knew well enough that the penalty for this was death, and, within the conventions of war, the Germans were perfectly 'entitled' to shoot her. The French shot two nurses in 1915 for exactly the same offence, helping the Germans. Nevertheless, Nurse Cavell's execution in October 1915 produced an outcry. 'The cold-blooded murder of Miss Cavell, a poor English girl, deliberately shot by the Germans for housing refugees, will run the sinking of the *Lusitania* close in the civilized world as the greatest crime in history,' proclaimed the Bishop of London in Trafalgar Square, committing, as most of the press also did, the factual error of mistaking – or misrepresenting – her crime. Concern for her death was most wildly expressed at home. From the front, F. H. Keeling wrote:

I see from the papers that the silly sentimental agitation about Nurse Cavell still goes on at home. A good many soldiers out here don't think much of it. I have discussed it with many and found all of my opinion – while admiring the woman immensely, I think the Germans were quite within their rights in shooting her. The agitation reveals the worst side of the English character.

The legend of German frightfulness included not only stories of German maltreatment of allies and neutrals, but also of barbarous methods used by Germans on their own people. The story of the corpse factory was one. It had a brief life but, though it was rapidly denied, denials did not kill the story. *The Times* of 17 April 1917 carried a report from Herr Karl Rosner, correspondent of the *Berliner Lokalanzeiger*, which was claimed as the first definite German admission of the way Germans used their dead bodies:

We pass through Everingcourt. There is a dull smell in the air as if lime were being burnt. We are passing the great Corpse Exploitation Establishment (Kadaververwertungsanstalt) of this Army Group. The fat that is won here is turned into lubricating oils and everything else is ground down in the bone mill into powder which is used for mixing with pigs' food and as manure – nothing is permitted to go to waste.

On 17 April *The Times* pursued the subject with a report from *La Belgique*, via *L'Indépendance Belge*, of 10 April, giving a detailed account of a factory near Coblenz where trainloads of stripped bodies of German soldiers, wired into bundles, arrived, and were simmered down in cauldrons for stearine and refined oil. *The Times* of 20 April published a story from a Sergeant B of the Kents who heard an account of the corpse factories from a German prisoner: 'This fellow told me that Fritz calls his margarine "corpse fat" because they suspect that's what it comes from.'

A German Army Order was produced as evidence, which led to questions about whether the German word *Kadaver* was ever applied to human corpses. Lord Robert Cecil evaded questions about the authenticity of the story in the House of Commons with the reply that '*The Times* is a reputable newspaper.' A leaflet appeared, apparently from within the Department of Information, though Mrs Masterman claims that Charles Masterman at Wellington House considered it and rejected it. The leaflet publicized the case:

Attila's Huns were guilty of atrocious crimes, but they never desecrated the bodies of dead soldiers – their own flesh, as well as the fallen of the enemy – by improvising a factory for the conversion of human corpses into fat and oils, and fodder for pigs.

That is what the autocrats of Prussia have done – and admitted. 'Admitted' is too mild a word. They have boasted of it. It is an illustration of their much vaunted efficiency! A sign of their pious *Kultur*! Proof of the zeal to waste nothing! Further evidence of the Kaiser's self imposed deification! 'There is one law, mine!'

How was the discovery made? Quite simply. Herr Karl Rosner, the Special Correspondent of the *Berliner Lokalanzeiger* on the Western Front, made the announcement in his published dispatch of 10th April.

By 3 May, however, *The Times* was reporting that the French were treating the story as a misunderstanding, and on 17 May the German Minister Herr Zimmern officially denied that human bodies were used and the story died. But the smell stuck.

In October 1925, a speech by Brigadier General Charteris, who headed Intelligence at G.H.Q. in France, re-opened the discussion. The *New York Times* reported Charteris as saying that the story had started as propaganda to China and that he had transposed the captions of two German photographs to give the impression that the Germans made dreadful use of corpses. On his return to England, Charteris claimed that the report of his speech was incorrect, and that he was referring only to speculations published in a book about the possible origin of the story. In reply to a Commons question in November 1925, the Secretary of State for War, Sir L. Worthington Evans, reiterated that the War Office had no reason at the time to disbelieve the story or the evidence, adding that the War Office had checked the use of the word *Kadaver* and found that it was used for German corpses. The suspicion was raised that this was

Punch, 31 May 1916

Figure 12 *Injured Innocence*

*The German Ogre: 'Heaven knows that I had to do this in self-defence;
it was forced upon me.' (Aside) 'Fee, fi, fo fum!* [*According to the Imperial
Chancellor's latest utterance Germany is the deeply-wronged victim of
British militarism*]

not a complete denial of War Office complicity in the story, but the case was allowed to rest there.

Once the seeds of atrocity stories were sown, they germinated rapidly in the war-fevered brains of the civilian population, who were being encouraged at every point to place the whole guilt of the war behind Germany's frontiers. The case against Germany in the early months of the war, however, rested not only on the dubious evidence of newspaper correspondents, but also on a remarkable series of reports produced by a Belgian Committee of Inquiry. This was set up under the Belgian Minister of Justice in August 1914 and published eight reports between August 1914 and early 1915, which gave details of atrocities in different areas of Belgium from 'eye-witnesses' and refugees. They were clearly a propaganda exercise and were published widely in Britain, France and America. The evidence was used as the basis for articles in dailies and periodicals, and books and anthologies of writings on the war.

Evidence from the Belgian Committee was also used in the major British propaganda exercise – the publication of the Bryce Report on Alleged German Atrocities. This was a government-backed enterprise, set up by Asquith in December 1914 in response to a call for authentic evidence. Lord Bryce, who was highly respected in America and Britain as former Ambassador to Washington, chaired the committee, which consisted of lawyers and historians. Charles Masterman, at the Secret War Propaganda Bureau, was responsible for the Report's translation into thirty languages. This was Masterman's answer to those critics who claimed that his restraint about publishing unverified stories indicated his lack of patriotism. Masterman's view had always been that authenticated stories were more powerful than the rumour and distortions of the popular press.

The Bryce Report was the first real attempt by an official government body to influence opinion at home, and its influence was enormous because of the seal of respectability and authenticity which it carried. It was based on 1,200 depositions by Belgian refugees, and came out in May 1915, seven days after the sinking of the *Lusitania*. The evidence was collected in Britain by a team of lawyers. The witnesses were not under oath, and they were unidentified in the final report. Many of them were under strain when they arrived, and much of the evidence was second-hand. The committee did not go to Belgium, and its members were relieved of much of the labour of actually interviewing. Although the depositions were meant to be kept in custody at the Home Office until after the war, no trace of them has been found. It would appear that, in general, the information used in the report was taken without much checking of references and sources, and most of it must be seen as influenced by the same rumour and exaggeration which was evident in previous journalistic reports of atrocities, and by the reports from the Belgian Committee of Inquiry.

While it is the case that modern warfare produced casualties and mutilation on an enormous scale, and that the Germans were hard in their treatment of civilian resistance, there is very little evidence from German sources to support the assumption of large-scale organized terrorization and incendiarism as part of German military policy. The Report concluded, however, that 'a deliberate campaign of terrorization' had been carried out by the Germans in Belgium. It accused the Germans of 'deliberately and systematically [organizing] massacres of the civilian population' whereby 'innocent civilians, both men and women, were murdered in large numbers, women violated and children murdered'. They concluded that 'elaborate provision had been made for systematic incendiarism at the very outbreak of war' and 'that burnings and destruction were frequent where no military necessity could be alleged, being indeed part of a system of general terrorization'. Embodied in its final conclusion was the authentication of all the numerous reports which came out of Belgium from a variety of sources, namely that 'Murder, lust and pillage prevailed over many parts of Belgium on a scale unparalleled in any war between civilized nations during the last three centuries.'

The Report contained records of incidents which contravened the Rules and Usages of War (Hague Convention) – 'particularly by the using of civilians, including women and children as a shield for advancing forces exposed to fire, to a less degree by killing the wounded and prisoners and in the frequent abuse of the Red Cross and the White Flag'. It gave details of incidents which had occurred, providing some interpretations of their significance, though objectivity was inconsistent in the Report. For instance, referring to the mutilation of children, they concluded that in some cases this might have resulted from 'a cavalry charge up a village street, hacking and slashing at everything in the way'. But they neither explained nor commented on the emotive story of a two-year-old child who stood in the way of the soldiers: 'The man on the left stepped aside and drove his bayonet with both hands into the child's stomach, lifting the child into the air on his bayonet and carrying it away on his bayonet, he and his comrades still singing.'

The committee quickly disposed of the suggestion that *francs tireurs* had attacked soldiers:

There may have been cases in which such firing occurred, but no proof has ever been given, or, to our knowledge, attempted to be given in such cases. The inherent improbability of the German intention is shown by the fact that after the first few days of the invasion every possible precaution had been taken by the Belgian authorities by way of placards and handbills to warn the civilian population not to interfere in hostilities.

Taken as a refutation of German claims this is strikingly flimsy.

The most important effect of the Bryce Report was the influence it had on public attitudes in Britain, and more especially in America. Charles Masterman's department sent over representatives to speak at the publication of the Report – only a week after the sinking of the *Lusitania*. Masterman's department had a declared concentration of propaganda in America, and these two incidents together amounted to a double first for the propaganda effort to bring America into the war on the Allied side.

In Britain, the report strengthened the case against Germany. To question the validity of atrocity stories was considered unpatriotic. The committee's Report was the final answer to civilian doubts about atrocities. Lord Bertie, British Ambassador in Paris, said, in May 1915: 'I began by not believing in German atrocities, and now I feel that I myself would, if I could, kill every combatant German that I might meet.' The findings were used as source material for propaganda agencies like the Parliamentary Recruiting Committee, the Central Committee for National Patriotic Organizations and the numerous committees for relief in Belgium.

Several days after the publication of the Bryce Report, the Germans brought out their White Book on atrocities committed by Belgian civilians against German soldiers. Their report concluded that the Belgian government had systematically organized armed civilian resistance against the Germans, and had committed outrages against German soldiers. The evidence for these conclusions was based on a number of depositions from soldiers and eye-witnesses.

*

While atrocity propaganda was gradually taking effect, Germany revealed another aspect of itself to the British civilian population. In December 1914 German warships shelled the peaceful coastal resorts of Scarborough and Hartlepool, damaging property, killing 137 people and injuring 592, including a party of schoolchildren. The stupidity of this act was appalling. As a show of strength, it misfired badly. It was interpreted as an unprovoked attack on innocent civilians – yet another act of 'frightfulness'. And this was on Britain's shores! Fears of invasion magnified the incident out of all proportion. The Parliamentary Recruiting Committee exploited those fears with posters on the theme 'Remember Scarborough'. And then, on 24 December – Christmas Eve – the first aeroplane raid took place over Dover.

The bomb on Dover killed no one. In the New Year, the Germans staged their first Zeppelin raid on England, over Yarmouth and Sheringham, killing four people. Horror was combined with awe and fascination at this monster from the skies which dropped destruction on – again – innocent civilians. The first Zeppelin, which had bombed Antwerp in August 1914, had been greeted with outrage in the newspapers. When it was Britain's turn, the reaction was magnified.

Zeppelin raids continued intermittently during the spring. Newspaper reporting was unrestricted until in June 1915, under DORA, the Press Bureau confined reports to brief official communiqués for security reasons. In June, outlying London was bombed, killing twenty-four people,[16] and again in October 1915 there were raids in Norfolk, Suffolk, the Home Counties and London, with casualties of 199. Alarm was combined with criticism of the inadequacy of defences against air attack. In June 1915, the police for the first time introduced instructions about what to do in an air raid, and later that year blackouts were organized. DORA was used to enforce regulations about street lighting.

Zeppelin raids, and later, aeroplane raids, continued throughout the war, making death, casualties, damage to property and inconvenience a part of normal civilian life. Inevitably, the attacks on civilians, resulting often from terrible inaccuracy in the bombing attempts, contributed to the legend of German frightfulness. Total figures for civilian casualties amounted to 5,611: 1,570 civilians were killed during the war – 1,413 of them in air attacks.[17] There were on average two air raids a month from 1915 onwards. There was no outcry against the Allies, when, on 22 September 1915, Allied bombers raided Karlsruhe, killing 103 civilians; or when on 26 June 1916 bombs dropped on the same city killing or wounding twenty-six women and 124 children.[18]

In Britain, it was the civilians' main taste of war at first hand. Siegfried Sassoon, back from the front, described one such attack from the soldier's point of view:

Bombs had been dropped on the station and one of them had hit the front carriage of the noon express to Cambridge. Horrified travellers were running away . . . while I stood wondering what to do, a luggage trolley was trundled past me; on it lay an elderly man, shabbily dressed and apparently dead. The sight of blood caused me to feel queer. This sort of danger seemed to demand a quality of courage dissimilar to front line fortitude. In a trench one is acclimatized to the notion of being exterminated and there was a sense of organized retaliation. But here one was helpless; an invisible enemy sent destruction spinning down from a fine weather sky; poor old men bought a railway ticket and were trundled away dead on a barrow; wounded women lay about in the station groaning.[19]

Despite the self-righteous outpourings of the newspapers, the civilians, when faced with death, acted with humanity. When a Zeppelin was brought down near a Sussex village, the local population gave the mutilated pilot a decent burial in the local church.

Some sense of military logic did occasionally seep through the barrier of propaganda. In July 1917, Lord Montagu said in the House of Lords:

It was absolute humbug to talk of London being an undefended city. The Germans had a perfect right to raid London. London was defended by guns and aeroplanes and it was the chief centre for the production of munitions. We were therefore but deluding ourselves in talking about London being an undefended city, and about the Germans in attacking it being guilty of an act unworthy of a civilized nation. That might not be a popular thing to say at the moment, but it was the actual fact of the situation. The right line for the government to take was: 'This is a war of nations, and not alone of armies, and you must endeavour to bear the casualties you suffer in the same way as the French and Belgian civil populations are bearing the casualties incidental to this kind of warfare.'

At the front, also, new methods of warfare were being used which were to shock civilian sensibilities further. On 22 April 1915, the Germans used poison gas for the first time. The Times of 29 April responded in its leader column:

This atrocious method of warfare . . . this diabolical contrivance . . . the wilful and systematic attempt to choke and poison our soldiers can have but one effect upon the British peoples and upon all non-German peoples of the earth. It will deepen our indignation and our resolution, and it will fill all races with a horror of the German name.

What was ignored was that the Allies were just as prepared to use that weapon 'as a necessity of war'. It was not the refined sense of a code of war which prevented them, but sheer practicality. Colonel Maude wrote:

All shells, all fires, all mining charges, give out asphyxiating gases and from some shells the fumes are poisonous. The use of these has been discussed for years, because the explosive that liberates the deadly gas is said to possess a quite unusual power; but the reason why many of these types was not adopted was because they were considered too dangerous for our gunners to transport and handle, not that when they burst they would have poisoned the enemy. At this time, this quality of deadliness was defended on the grounds of humanity, as the death inflicted would be absolutely certain and painless, and hence there would be no wounded.[20]

By the end of the war the American Chemical Warfare Service, established in June 1918, was engaged in sixty-five 'major research problems' including the development of eight gases more deadly than any used to date – one rendered the soil barren for seven years.[21]

The world after the Vietnam war is unfortunately familiar with the technology of chemical warfare, and its abuses; in 1915 it was yet another unspeakable horror – which the Germans had the temerity to use first. While it is questionable whether the use of poison gas (on soldiers or civilians) is ever justified, the point is that at the time, the moral outrage which accompanied news of its use completely ignored its military significance. The use of poison gas by the Allies shortly afterwards was justified on the grounds of retaliation. One diabolical contrivance deserves another. That is apparently the 'logic of war'.

German submarine warfare, of all modern warfare techniques, had the most far-reaching effects on civilian lives and produced the greatest outcry, after Belgium. Here again, the logic of the political and military situation was sacrificed for the sake of denigrating the enemy. Submarine warfare was an attack on the nerve centre of the Empire. In exposing the vulnerability of Britain's defences it shocked a nation which had been accustomed to domination of the seas for centuries.

On 4 February 1915, the German government announced their intention, as from 18 February, to carry out unrestricted submarine warfare. All enemy vessels, armed or unarmed, found in British waters, would be destroyed. The British press presented this as a blatant attack on unarmed vessels. The events leading up to the German decision are an example of how violence escalates in wartime. Also, German submarine warfare was an important link in the political manoeuvrings which forced America into the war.

Churchill's policy as First Lord of the Admiralty from the outbreak of war was to *deter* the Germans from surface attack. Admiralty orders were issued to the masters of ships making it an offence to obey the U-boat

order to surrender a ship. Further orders stated that all U-boats were to
be fired on. Captured German crews were to be treated as 'felons' without
the rights of prisoners of war, and 'survivors should be taken prisoner or
shot – whichever is the most convenient'.[22] In December 1914, an
Admiralty order stated that: 'In all action, white flags should be fired
upon with promptitude'[23] – an order which, whatever the justification,
was a blatant contravention of the rules of war.

At the same time, British ships were ordered to paint out their name
and port of registry, and in British waters to fly a neutral flag – the
Cunard order contained a further directive: 'Pass the word around that
the flag to use is the American.'[24] In February 1915, Churchill endorsed
the policy of 'mystery ships' or 'Q' ships. Apparently unarmed merchant
vessels carried concealed armaments and a naval crew dressed as
civilians. The regular steamer from Portsmouth to St Malo was disguised
in this way. The net result of these tactics was that the Germans had no
idea whether ships were armed or unarmed.

The aim of these tactics was to protect British shipping routes across
the Atlantic. They caused considerable opposition in America. Britain
was dependent on American munitions and wartime supplies of food-
stuffs. During the first eighteen months of the war, American trade in
munitions totalled $508,269,245.[25] But inevitably American ships were
lost in submarine attacks.

Britain's intention was also to prevent supplies getting to Germany and
other enemy countries. Shortly after the outbreak of war, Britain declared
a blockade on Germany. This affected American trade fundamentally.
American ships had to get full approval from British authorities to ship
material to Britain's allies, and Britain also put an embargo on the export
of raw materials from the Empire for use in American manufacture, until
contracts had been signed guaranteeing that there would be no re-export
of the manufactured goods to Germany. On 2 November 1914 Britain
declared the whole of the North Sea a military zone, thus enabling herself
to stop and search American ships in the Straits of Dover, and so establishing the right to detain ships for indefinite periods of time at neutral
ports. This was a serious interference with American freedom of the seas.
Protests passed across the Atlantic about the treatment of American
merchant vessels and about the misuse of the American flag. There were
periods when US relations with the Allies were worse than with the
Central Powers, and seemed to be 'within an ace of producing a rupture
of diplomatic relations'.[26]

Churchill's policy at the Admiralty can be seen as an exercise in propaganda brinkmanship. While the immediate aim of propaganda to America, conducted through the War Propaganda Bureau, was to persuade American opinion to the Allied cause, clearly it extended to pressure on America to come into the war. Colin Simpson in his book *Lusitania* has argued that Churchill's policy was not only to protect British shipping, but also to involve America so much in the submarine war that it became increasingly difficult for her to remain neutral. He finds a clue to Churchill's attitude in *The World Crisis*:

The distinction between politics and strategy diminishes as the point of view is raised. At the summit true politics and strategy are one. The massacre which brings an ally into the field is as serviceable as that which wins a great battle. The manoeuvre which gains an important strategic point may be less valuable than that which placates or overawes a dangerous neutral.

In the context of the submarine war, by arming merchant vessels and misusing the American flag, the chances were increased that American ships would be sunk by U-boats. Indeed Churchill urged Runciman to arrange favourable insurance rates for neutral shipping in order to increase it. On 12 February 1915 he wrote to Runciman:

It is most important to attract neutral shipping to our shores in the hope especially of embroiling the United States with Germany. The German formal announcement of indiscriminate submarining has been made to the United States to produce a deterrent effect on traffic. For our part we want the traffic – the more the better; and if some of it gets into trouble, better still. Therefore do please furbish up at once your insurance offer to neutrals trading with us after 18 February. The more they come, the greater our safety and the Germans' embarrassment.[27]

However, America was not to be so easily involved in the war. President Wilson saw himself as the peacemaker amongst the belligerent nations. When, in February 1915, the Germans proclaimed unrestricted submarine warfare, stern warnings were sent to Britain against using the American flag to confuse the issue, and Germany was held strictly accountable for any loss of American life.

Unrestricted submarine warfare resulted in the sinking of twenty-five merchant vessels from 18 February to 28 May 1915. Twenty of these twenty-five ships suffered no loss of life. Protest in Britain and America, nevertheless, centred on the methods used by the Germans, of which Admiral Tirpitz came to be associated as the chief exponent. They included sinking without warning, killing crew members instead of taking prisoners, ignoring neutral flags, and sinking unarmed vessels.

Germany justified submarine warfare as retaliation against the Allied blockade. Germany, like Britain, was dependent on the import of raw materials. The flow of these determined the respective nations' capacity to continue the war. For Britain, the navy was considered the mainstay of defensive power, but when it became a war of armies, the importance of the navy in strategy dwindled. The economic war took on unprecedented strategic importance. The blockade was justified as much by tradition as by necessity:

The attack on seaborne commerce was deep-rooted in the tradition of the British Navy, and thus the transition to an indirect attack on the life of the enemy nation – her supplies of food and raw materials – was an almost imperceptible progress. When this pressure was exercised against herself in a novel form and by a new weapon – the submarine – it was human, if illogical, that she should decry it as an atrocity.[28]

The other side of the issue was raised in America after the British liner *Falaba* was torpedoed in the Irish Sea. One American was drowned. This produced anti-German reaction in America. In a debate on the issue, Secretary Bryan, who opposed American intervention, raised the entirely valid point that 'Why should we be shocked at the drowning of a few people if there is no objection to the starving of a nation?'[29] In fact, there was surprisingly little support for this view, despite considerable pro-German propaganda in America. Partly this was due to a natural sympathy with the Allies, and partly to the fact that British propaganda directed to the US was very carefully planned by the Secret War Propaganda Bureau, but above all because the sinking of a ship was a far more definite and fertile focus for protest and propaganda than the slow starving of a nation.

The most dramatic example of this was the sinking of the Cunard liner, *Lusitania*, on 7 May 1915 off the Irish Coast by a U-boat. 1,195 lives out of a total of 1,959 on board were lost, 124 of them American. The ship went down in eighteen minutes; the main explosion was followed by a second which sealed its doom.

There was every expectation both in Britain and the US that this would bring America into the war. The sinking was portrayed as a ruthless attack on an unarmed vessel carrying civilian passengers. A fact which was not disclosed at the time was that the *Lusitania* was carrying

5,400 cases of ammunition. The *Daily Mail* specifically denied this on
11 May: 'It is untrue that the *Lusitania* was carrying ammunition on its
final voyage . . .' A week before the ship sailed, warnings about the
dangers of travelling on the *Lusitania*, signed by the Imperial German
Embassy, though originating from a pro-German group in America,[30]
were published in newspapers in America, including a warning placed
directly alongside the shipping advertisements. This fact was also
ignored at the time.

The propaganda opportunities of the sinking of the *Lusitania* were not
missed. A medal was struck, purportedly in Germany, glorifying the
deed. The medals had wide circulation in Allied countries. In fact, a
medal was designed by Herr Goetz, a Munich craftsman, and forty-four
copies were originally produced, intended as a satirical comment on the
German government's allegation of contraband being carried by the
Lusitania.[31] 300,000 more medals were later struck on the instruction of
Captain Reginald Hall, Director of British Naval Intelligence, and made
by Mr Gordon Selfridge of department store fame.[32] Leaflets with
pictures of the medal were also distributed by the CCNPO, with
captions like 'Another triumph for our glorious Navy' which were aimed
at whipping up hatred of Germany.

Eight days later the Bryce Report was published simultaneously in
Allied and neutral countries, apparently by coincidence, but with the
effect of confirming still further the image of the Evil Hun.

America did not enter the war. The sinking of the *Lusitania* resulted
in US agreements with Germany to spare large vessels (6 June) and sink
no passenger ships without warning (17 August). However, ships were
frequently sunk, including American ships, and it was not until May 1916,
after the worst month of submarine warfare, when one in four British
ships leaving port did not return, that the Germans agreed with America
that merchant vessels could not be sunk without warning and without
saving lives. After the Allied refusal to consider German peace proposals
in early 1917, the Germans again declared unrestricted submarine warfare. This was the end of notes of protest from America. Germany knew
that their action was likely to bring America in on the Allied side. After
several incidents, and on the pretext of the Zimmermann telegram, the
Americans declared war on 6 April 1917.

Submarine warfare shocked Britain. The fact that the blockade was
producing far worse hardships for innocent civilians became a point of
jubilation for patriotic die-hards. Any information which betrayed

Broken pledges, treaties torn,
Your first page of war adorn.
We on fouler things must look
Who read further in that book.
Where you made—the deed was fine !—
Women screen your firing-line ;
Villages burned down to dust ;
Torture, murder, bestial lust,
Filth too foul for printer's ink,
Crimes from which the apes would shrink.
Strange the offerings that you press
On the God of Righteousness !
*—*Barry Pain.

In the Trail of the Hun

There were many proved instances of Germans using women and children as battle-screens.

22. The sinking of the *Lusitania* was portrayed by the Allies as one of the foulest atrocities of the war

23. The Kaiser in league with the devil

24. Italian propaganda spared no imaginative detail in the representation of 'William the Bloody'

25. Australian artist David Lindsey depicted the German as a brutal and savage monster

A GREAT NAVAL TRIUMPH.

German Submarine Officer. "THIS OUGHT TO MAKE THEM JEALOUS IN THE SISTER
SERVICE. BELGIUM SAW NOTHING BETTER THAN THIS."

THE ELIXIR OF HATE.

Kaiser. "'FAIR IS FOUL, AND FOUL IS FAIR;
HOVER THROUGH THE FOG AND FILTHY AIR.'"

22

GUGLIELMO IL SANGUINARIO
GUILLAUME LE SANGUINAIRE

24

'A violent appeal to hate and the animal lust for blood' – *J. A. Hobson*

27

28

The caption to the picture reads, 'There are already, thanks to William the Bloody, in Europe more than 5,000,000 corpses and nearly 7,000,000 wounded. What will the victorious nations do to this man?' – *Le Matin*

[*Drawn by S. C. Bailie.*

sympathy with Germany was given short shrift. The cry on the recruiting posters was 'Avenge the *Lusitania*'.

Losses from submarine attack were severe. In autumn 1917, convoys were introduced which cut down losses by about a third. But Britain had to tighten her belt to survive. Food prices were rising, and there were allegations of profiteering, though the usual course was to blame the submarines. In early 1917 a Food Controller was appointed, but voluntaryism prevailed, with the drive to produce food on every available square yard of land. The Board of Agriculture was authorized to take possession of all available land, including commons and parks, and use it for allotments. The government called for voluntary rationing of meat, bread and potatoes, aided by the King who read a proclamation to that effect from the steps of the Royal Exchange in May 1917. In September 1917, the state provided a subsidy to millers and bakers and the price of bread was fixed – an unprecedented interference in individual liberty. This upsurge in propaganda to the civilian population to do their bit gave further opportunities for poster artists to elaborate on the image of the Evil Hun.

But who was responsible for all this? The scapegoat for all 'frightfulness' was the Kaiser. On his head fell the guilt of all German war crimes and atrocities. His son, the Crown Prince, came in for a great deal of ridicule and was portrayed as chinless and ineffectual. After *Lusitania*, the Kaiser was indicted for murder – a theme which was to be taken up at the end of the war with all the fury of a victorious nation. On 6 August 1914 the *Evening News* christened him 'The Mad Dog of Europe' which encouraged such comments as 'The only way to treat the mad dog is to shoot it.'[33] At his feet was thrown the sole responsibility for systematically organizing terrorization in Belgium, for poison gas, and for the submarine campaign, despite the fact that he had opposed unrestricted submarine warfare in 1917 (on the grounds that it would bring America into the war).

He was a great gift for British cartoonists and film-makers who used the ancient method of ridiculing the enemy to boost morale at home. His alleged reference to the British army as 'that contemptible little army' was turned on its head and became a catch phrase for morale-boosting and recruitment.

He was portrayed as the greatest practitioner of brutal militarism. The image of 'sabre rattling and the mailed fist' which had been built up in the period before the war, was embroidered and expanded throughout the

Punch, 28 Ootober 1914

Figure 13 *A Gargoyle of Nôtre Dame De Paris*

war. Scapegoats were needed, and much of what was said about the Kaiser was ridiculous. In solemn essays attempts were made to prove that the Kaiser was mad.

'Madness has always dogged the steps of the Hohenzollerns,' asserted one author in a book provocatively entitled *The Unspeakable Prussian* (October 1914). Another writer found argument for insanity in the facts that 'hereditary cancer and muscular paralysis are in the Kaiser's blood from the male side, that the Kaiser's father died of cancer in the throat, and that at this moment the Kaiser is tormented with ear trouble which medical experts say not only affects the bronchial channels but seriously distempers and heats the brain', and, as if realizing that this was hardly medical evidence of insanity, went on: 'The Kaiser's treatment of his mother, England's Princess Royal, showed all the refined brutality of a youthful lunatic.'[34]

He was held responsible for leading the German nation into the war of aggression and for, apparently, every act committed during the war. He became a hated symbol of the German nation. 'Everything he touched he vulgarized . . . he has turned Berlin into a sink of debauchery . . . The only thing he gave to German manhood is the Imperial moustache and "Kaiser Champagne",' wrote Austin Harrison.[35] Sir Theodore Cook, editor of the *Field*, described him as 'the incarnation of ruthless evil' who 'by the worship of the Moloch-fetish, changed his people from seventy million souls who formed a state into seventy million soulless serfs who worshipped Machinery at the State's bidding . . . who gave themselves up to a hate inspired savagery that belongs to the twilight ignorance of the prehistoric savage.'[36]

In a letter to the *Daily Mail* (22 September 1914) after the bombardment of Rheims Cathedral, Sir W. B. Richmond wrote:

This last act of the barbarian chief will only draw us all closer together to be rid of the scourge the like of which the civilized world has never seen before.

The madman is piling up the logs of his own pyre. We can have no terror of the monster; we shall clench our teeth in determination that if we die to the last man the modern Judas and his hell begotten brood shall be wiped out . . . Our great England will shed its blood willingly to help rid civilization of a criminal monarch and a criminal court which have succeeded in creating out of a docile people a herd of savages.

Such impassioned hysteria characterized the brute instincts which were aroused during the war. Scorn was poured on the Kaiser's assertion

Figure 14 *The Kaiser's Birthday: 27 January 1915*
Death: 'Happy Birthday, Sir!'

that God was on his side. God was, after all, on the Allies' side – or
what was the war about? The Kaiser was compared with the Devil
and with the barbarian chief, Attila the Hun. 'The modern Attila respects
neither the laws of God nor the laws of man,' proclaimed *The Times*
leader, after the bombardment of Rheims Cathedral. The rabble-
rousing orator, Horatio Bottomley, whipped up popular support with
statements like 'The Kaiser and his hellish hordes are possessed by the
soul of Satan.' The war became a battle for civilization against
barbarism – a battle of heaven against hell.

There was no shortage of learned clergymen who would exploit the
damning evidence of German barbarism as religious justification for the
war. 'Can I forgive the unforgiveable?' asked the Reverend Prenderbery
Burn,

To the question thus expressed, a Christian can answer 'No' with a
clear conscience. Divine Love is revealed as wrath against all unrighteous-
ness. Our Lord Jesus Christ showed at times the most terrible wrath
which can be imagined against foul injury to the weak and helpless,
against that lie in the soul which betrays a man into calling evil good and

good evil. What the Bible calls the Wrath of the Lamb is the righteous anger of the meek and gentle flaming into fury for the sake of others.[37]

Delusion abounded once God had been enlisted in support of the cause of righteousness and the cause of the weak. The war had become a Holy War – a crusade – with Britain in the role of the White Knight in shining armour. The Church's support for the war produced some staggering logic. In the *Optimist* one clergyman exalted the unity of the nation as 'the work of self sacrifice, of altruism, of that mystic presence we know to be the Holy Ghost. August 4th 1914 was the most sacred hour in the history of Great Britain and Ireland . . . on that day the whole nation renounced its past, was born again, *died* to self and rose again for others.'[38] The Bishop of London saw the war as 'the greatest fight ever made for the Christian Religion . . . a choice between the nailed hand and the mailed fist . . . the day of God', and the Reverend F. B. Meyer, a Free Church pastor, exhorted his ministers to fight in the ranks because 'This is a holy war in which we fight with heavenly Allies beside us.' Sentiments like these pervaded writings on the war.

Germany became the focus of a poisonous hatred which consumed the civilian population fed by such propaganda. The Kaiser became a monster and a devil dedicated to the destruction of European civilization, worshipping 'a deity more akin to Odin than to Christ'. The German people were seen as efficient machines and thus as the antithesis to Christianity and the spiritual life of Europe. Propaganda reduced the German nation to the level of monsters and savages by describing their 'frightfulness' in warfare, and stressing their worship of militarism. It denigrated German *Kultur* by portraying it as merely the fount of inspiration for militarism. The belief, expressed by Wickham Steed, that the war was 'a struggle between two incompatible concepts of civilization' did indeed cloud the mind and emotions of the population throughout the war.

Propaganda worked, not in the interests of an evaluation of the war, but to persuade the population, by any means, to continue fighting. It was given a licence to lie to achieve the end product of encouraging bellicosity and a hate-inspired lust for revenge. It was afterwards that the full impact of propaganda's simplifications were to be felt, when disillusion was the prevailing mood, and the notions of glory and sacrifice for the cause of right against the Evil Hun had been obliterated by knowledge of the real facts of war.

Chapter Six

Aliens and Spies

We are so sick of the Germans, of their treachery, their sneaking, their spying, their lying, their brutality, their arrogance, their loutish conceit, their cold blooded dastardly cruelty, their murderous bitter hatred, that we never want to see or hear a German again, nor to touch anything made by Germans . . . To every decent Briton, a German is an unclean danger-ous and bloody monster. Such is the fact. And the people are right to demand that every Hun should be put behind wire or bars . . . It is not only that the Germans are enemies and spies. We loathe them. We feel they pollute the air. We see blood on their hands . . . We demand that the wretched creatures be removed. The thought that there are 20,000 of them walking in our streets was enough to make all London sick.

Weekly Dispatch, 16 May 1915.

Robert Blatchford wrote that in 1915, just after the sinking of the *Lusitania*. It was part of a propaganda campaign against enemy aliens which bracketed them with Germany as the chief threat to the war effort.

The war was represented by official propaganda as a moral crusade against all manifestations of the Evil Hun. Enemy aliens – Austrians, Germans and Hungarians living in Britain – were portrayed, mainly through unofficial propaganda, as representatives of the enemy. They became an accessible target of revenge.

Anti-alien feeling was in part a spontaneous reaction to the outbreak of war. It was an aspect of the hostility and suspicion of all things German and everything connected with the enemy which accompanied jingoism. What propaganda did was to exploit these instinctive and essentially racialist emotions and legitimize them in the name of a broad patriotism.

The precise aim of propaganda was to denigrate the minority living in this country, and to get rid of their uncomfortable presence. The theme was that the 'enemy in our midst' was a contamination – 'The German Cancer', as Mr Hughes, Prime Minister of Australia, chose to put it, which must be 'extirpated, root branch and seed', if the Empire was to survive and win the war. The campaign, which was pursued mainly by unofficial groups and in the press, exaggerated out of all proportion the real dangers from enemy aliens. It was a campaign rooted in war hysteria, which fed on the fears and fantasies bred by war. It contributed directly to the most appalling hardship for enemy aliens and people with German connections, most of whom were entirely innocent and harmless.

Popular outbursts against enemy aliens occurred during three separate periods of the war: in October 1914, when the rapid German advance across Belgium and France was causing alarm, when the first news of British casualties came through, and when fear of spies was at its height; in 1915 as a direct response to the sinking of the *Lusitania*, and the findings of the Bryce Report on German atrocities in Belgium; and in July 1918, when Britain was reeling from the successful German offensive on the western front. During the periods in between, prominent individuals constantly drew attention to the presence of 'the enemy in our midst' but they failed to rouse widespread popular support.

The nature and organization of the campaign changed as the war progressed. In 1914, it was mainly a newspaper agitation, led by the Northcliffe press, which took the line that in the words of Robert Blatchford, a leading campaigner on the subject, 'Every German, young or old, is a *potential* spy.' Their propaganda aimed to get popular support for the campaign to persuade the government to take more rigorous measures against enemy aliens, specifically, to lock them all up. 'The only safe plan,' wrote Blatchford, 'is to arrest and deport every German. No excuse should be accepted . . . While Britain and Germany are at war, the only safe place for all Germans is a concentration camp.'[1] A number of influential people, principally Admiral Lord Charles Beresford, spoke in and out of parliament in support.

In 1915, the alien agitation was a direct response to the sinking of the *Lusitania*. Indignant anti-Germanism was channelled into a popular movement embracing titled ladies, businessmen in Chambers of Commerce, and working men in Smithfield market, who amplified the call to make a 'Clean Sweep' and 'Intern Them All'. By 1918, the campaign had broadened its base; it was led and coordinated by the National Party and the British Empire Union, with influence in parliament, among local councils and in the press. They organized demonstrations and petitions protesting against the presence of the 'enemy in our midst', and advocated the elimination of all German influence in business, finance and government, a boycott of German trade after the war and an overall policy of 'Britain for the British' – a cry of patriotism with roots in Chamberlain's pre-war movement for Protection.

In 1914, propaganda played on emotions already aroused by war itself. There was widespread contempt for anything German. German music was banned at promenade concerts. German brass bands, which had been a regular feature of pre-war life, disappeared. Dachshunds were stoned in the streets. *The Times* journalist, Michael MacDonagh, described the atmosphere in London during August 1914:

That jade Rumour has begun to flap her wings. London is said to be full of German spies. Popular resentment against German tradesmen, principally bakers, provision dealers, watch-makers, waiters and barbers, has developed in some instances into wrecking their shops. It is said that German purveyors of food are putting slow poison in their commodities. As for barbers, it is said you run the risk of having your throat cut by them instead of your hair.
In reality all I could discover as I walked about town is that in the windows of German provision shops, such *delicatessen* as *Sauerkraut* and liver-sausage are now labelled 'Good English Viands' and that Union Jacks are being flown over the doors . . . But these precautions did not save some of the shops in the East End from being plundered.[2]

Propaganda identified enemy aliens as traitors and spies. In 1914, the population was jittery. Before the war, spy stories had prepared the civilian imagination with a scenario for invasion which involved betrayal by spies, specifically by an army of expatriate Germans disguised as waiters and provision dealers. These figures from spy fantasies took on a more real and menacing appearance under the stress of war, when, particularly in 1914, invasion constantly seemed possible.

Fears were intensified when the absence of conspicuous British naval and military victories in the first few months of the war was attributed to the activities of spies. Spy mania engulfed the nation. Michael Mac-Donagh recorded his impression that

a large section of the population continue to suffer from the first bewilder-ing shock of being at war. Their nerves are still jangling and they are subject to hallucinations. They seem to be enveloped in a mysterious darkness, haunted by goblins in the form of desperate German spies, and they can find no light or comfort afforded them by the Press or Govern-ment. What is it but a bad attack of hysteria – coupled with a decline of humour and a rise in the disposition to believe in impossibilities under war stress?[3]

The press contributed to the atmosphere of fear, in part inadvertently, and in part deliberately. With so little information from the front the newspapers naturally concentrated on home news. They failed to check rumours, and gave great prominence to, and sometimes sensationalized, reports of arrests of people with 'foreign appearance', though many of the victims were released. The impression was given, as 'An English-woman' in the *Daily Mirror* wrote, of 'hundreds of Germans and Austrians arrested each day for good cause, many of them in the act of spying . . . What proof have we,' she went on, 'that the hundreds still left are not uncaught spies or ready to sell any information they can get?'[4]

In October 1914 the Northcliffe press contributed deliberately to the fear, by launching an attack on the government to demand stronger measures against enemy aliens, specifically internment. By the second week of October 1914 the *Daily Mail* was running almost daily editorials complaining of 'the ludicrous freedom permitted to enemy aliens resident among us' and demanding 'The most stringent precautions . . . to render them incapable of doing us harm.'[5]

An editorial claimed:

The German spy network is so wide, so extraordinarily efficient, so immensely dangerous that it cannot be too severely repressed. Bitter examples in Belgium and France have already shown the peril of tolerat-ing too easily and too generously German guests. Life and death are the stakes for which the nation is playing against the most determined, merciless and unscrupulous of assailants. The presence in our midst of 40,000 Germans and Austrians, with probably at least as many of the same nationalities who have been recently naturalized must be a source of constant anxiety to the public.[6]

The Liberal government, with Reginald McKenna as Home Secretary, had taken steps to control enemy aliens, through the Aliens Restriction Act, passed on 5 August 1914, which gave them powers to prevent the entry and embarkation of enemy aliens and to remove them from 'prohibited' areas, mainly coastal districts and areas of military opera-tions. All enemy aliens had to register with the local police and notify them of changes of address. Later Orders of Council prohibited the ownership of carrier pigeons and wireless sets and prevented the dispatch of letters abroad. Under DORA regulations, espionage was made a military offence tried by court martial with a penalty of death.

On the outbreak of war, arrests were made of twenty known spies, and up to 200 suspects who had been under close observation by the Secret

THE TIP.

Figure 15

Service were rounded up. On 8 September 1914 McKenna made known these facts for the first time and expressed his confidence that the German spy network had been broken up and no new one had been established. By that time, rumours were flourishing freely, and fears were so heightened that few were prepared to believe him.

Examination of the facts shows that throughout the war there was a gap between popular unfounded assertions and the true situation. By 1917, twelve spies had been executed, six had had their death sentence commuted to penal servitude, and six more had been sentenced to penal servitude. A grand total of twenty-four. In addition, 201 people had been arrested for communicating information to the enemy (the majority, according to Sir George Cawe, Home Secretary in 1917, not of enemy origin[7]), and 169 enemy aliens had been recommended for deportation.[8]

The *Daily Mail* was not the least bit reassured by any facts given by the government. Being convinced that spies were betraying the country, that paper started a campaign to seek out the dangerous elements itself, and called on the public to assist.

The *Daily Mail* chose to find 'The Hidden Hand' of betrayal concealed beneath the napkins of German hotel managers and waiters. They called for a boycott of all hotels employing German staff. 'These alien staff,' revealed the editorial of 16 October, 'are usually to be found at the centres where naval intelligence abounds.' Readers were invited to submit the names of establishments employing German and Austrian staff 'whether naturalized or not'. Hotels responded immediately, and most major London ones proclaimed their innocence. A 'White List' of hotels cleared of alien staff built up daily. The Trocadero wrote in announcing that by 19 October all 500 German and Austrian employees would have left. Clearly the campaign was having an effect. It prompted a host of letters alleging ghastly treatment of English staff by German managers.

The *Daily Mail* then pounced on all German waiters. In a small black box the public was called upon to: 'REFUSE TO BE SERVED BY AN AUSTRIAN OR GERMAN WAITER. IF YOUR WAITER SAYS HE IS SWISS, ASK TO SEE HIS PASSPORT.' and in another box the paper proclaimed: 'THE NATURALIZATION FORM IS JUST A SCRAP OF PAPER. ONCE A GERMAN ALWAYS A GERMAN.'

Jubilantly, the editorial of 19 October concluded that 'The nation is deadly serious. It has realized that the Germans and Austrians in our midst constitute a national peril which must be dispelled without any more waiting and seeing.'

This campaign produced an immediate increase in rumours and incidents concerning spies. In Aberystwyth, a demonstration to protest against the presence of Germans turned into a mob hunt to clear the town of Germans, and ended with a congratulatory telegram from 'a prominent London businessman' being read out to the crowd. 'Bravo Aberystwyth,' it said. 'But was there no street lamp and a hempen rope available? Most useful for murderers.'[9] Similar incidents occurred in other parts of the country.

On 18 October, riots broke out in Deptford, ostensibly, according to the *Daily News*, after the arrival of a number of Belgian refugees. For three nights mobs, estimated at 5,000 people, roamed the streets attacking and looting German shops and restaurants. Youths gathered to sing patriotic songs. Fires broke out in various parts of the town. 200 policemen and 350 men of the Army Service Corps were brought in to control the crowd and twenty arrests were made.[10]

The *Daily Mail* denied any responsibility for the outbursts. 'Mob Law,' stated the editorial, 'always takes charge when the government lags behind public opinion. The people have taken the law into their own hands. They are irritated beyond measure with the apathy of officialdom in dealing with the German and Austrian subjects in our midst.'[11]

The Liberal *Daily News* blamed press propaganda. A stinging editorial, headed 'The Pogrom Mongers', lashed out at

that section of the press which for days past has been assiduously inciting against unfortunate aliens in this country every cruel passion which insane suspicion can arouse and mean vindictiveness cherish into flame . . . The result of that campaign is now plain, and it is scarcely satisfactory that only the misguided dupes should have to pay for the unscrupulousness of its instigators.[12]

There were others, some of them influential people, ready to echo the *Daily Mail*'s assertions. Admiral Lord Charles Beresford, a Conservative and a former adversary of Admiral Fisher at the Admiralty, was, in 1914, one of the chief advocates of 'Intern Them All' policies. In a speech at Aberdeen on 2 October 1914 he claimed that three cruisers, the *Aboukir*, the *Hogue* and the *Cressey* had been 'lost by information given from this country to the German Admiralty', and asserted 'all enemy aliens should be locked up . . . our people in the Army and Navy should not be stabbed in the back by assassins in the shape of spies'.[13]

The Director of Public Prosecutions picked up his comments and requested access to the information on which he based his statement. Lord Charles was 'satisfied that it was correct', and offered no further facts, only the warning: 'I intend to do all in my power to wake up the people of this country to the danger which threatens from all alien enemy spies.'[14]

He advocated the formation of Vigilante Committees, and called for public meetings to be held in every town to protest against the tolerant treatment being afforded to enemy aliens.[15] 'Public men,' he wrote, 'would be traitors if they did not call attention to facts liable to cause disaster.'

John Bull, always willing to take up the cause of vulgar chauvinism, ran a campaign against individual 'Germhuns'. 'Foreign Foe in Tramway Office' was a man of German origin who had lived in Britain for thirty years, and whose only fault was that he was in any office at all. Readers were warned against 'Germhuns' who worked for the water boards (they could flood London) and in electricity offices (they could sabotage the supply).

The *Daily Mail* called not only for a boycott of waiters but also a boycott of German goods. British companies exploited the xenophobic atmosphere for the benefit of their own profits. The 'C-B' Corset Company announced an 'Invincible Assault on all Corset Trade which is not British'.[16] Wolsey Ltd advertised their patriotic corsets:

The woman who buys British goods now in preference to German goods is the woman who is going to do great things for the trade of this country . . . A certain amount of personal inconvenience may be the price we shall have to pay for this patriotism but what is that compared with what our soldiers and sailors are undergoing to protect British Woman's Health and Home?[17]

Bovril declared that it was 'BRITISH TO THE BACKBONE' and published a list of its impeccable all-British directorate.

Companies took to libelling their rivals publicly by exposing any German connections. In *John Bull*, Lipton's Ltd, makers of tea, accused J. Lyons and Co. of harbouring German directors, strongly implying that anyone buying their tea was helping the enemy. J. Lyons and Co. protested that the company was an 'ALL BRITISH COMPANY WITH ALL BRITISH DIRECTORS, HAS 1,400 ALL BRITISH SHAREHOLDERS AND 160,000 ALL BRITISH SHOPKEEPERS SELLING LYONS TEA.'[18] De La Rue warned against their rival, Watermans: 'Be it known that the Waterman "Ideal" Fountain Pen is sold in this country through the Austrian controlled firm of pencil makers, L. and C. Hardmuth Ltd. EVERY WATERMAN PEN SOLD, THEREFORE, IN THIS COUNTRY MEANS PROFIT TO THE KING'S ENEMIES.'[19] Watermans took out a full page advertisement to deny the accusation.

Others joined in. *John Bull* led a farcical demand for 'patriotic pickles' when it discovered that British soldiers were being served pickled beans on plates blatantly marked 'Made in Germany'. The *Daily Express*, which played a leading part in anti-alien propaganda, publishing many of the advertisements, and whose editor had the German-sounding name 'Blumenfield', took the trouble to proclaim its patriotic purity:

The Chairman and Editor of the *Daily Express* is not and never has been a German.
The paper on which the *Daily Express* is printed is not and never has been made in Germany.
There is not one German on the staff of the *Daily Express*.

Inevitably this contributed to the mounting paranoia about the presence of Germans in Britain. Rumours and scares reached a height of absurdity. There were scares about wireless spies and carrier pigeons, which, according to the *Daily Mail* (6 November 1914), were sent off in droves from neutral shipping. Ludicrous stories circulated that concrete structures were being used as gun platforms, after rumours came from Belgium that German factory owners had secretly prepared gun platforms to help the German bombardment of Maubeuge. One correspondent wrote to the *Daily Mail*: 'Is it too much to ask that our kid gloved government will ascertain how many German owned factories have been built in this country which incidentally command Woolwich, Dover, Rosyth? A timely inspection might reveal many concrete structures.'[20] *The Times* directed attention to various factories which commanded views of London, including one in Brixham which was reported to have concrete floors six feet thick, though on inspection they were found to be only six inches thick. Reports that messages to spies in Belgium were scratched on the back of enamelled advertisements prompted voluntary screwdriving parties to examine all such advertisements in London.

The volume of rumours circulating was immense. It was extremely difficult to trace the sources, but in at least one case, which was checked, the source was someone who had a very close connection with the campaign to intern all aliens. Lord Leith of Fyvie, who was later to become president of the British Empire Union, the organization most closely concerned with the boycott of German goods, and the 'Britain for the British' campaign, wrote to the Home Secretary calling attention to the alarming fact that 'spies and alien enemies had been arrested along our south shores making communication with steamers'. He claimed two spies in khaki uniform had been seen getting on to a boat, and that it was only because of the good look-out kept on board the mail steamers at Folkestone that these men had been stopped. Viscount Allendale challenged Lord Leith in the House of Commons with the facts. The Home Office had made inquiries of the Folkestone police, who knew nothing about the arrests. Lord Leith later admitted that he personally had not seen the incidents, but that the captain of the steamer *Onward* had. Further inquiries revealed that one man had been stopped getting on a boat. Far from being an enemy alien spy, he was an eager young man trying to get to the front quickly.[21]

Michael MacDonagh described the range of rumours which circulated during October 1914:

The wildest stories are being circulated . . . of outrages committed by Germans in our midst. Attempts have been made to destroy the permanent ways of railways and wreck trains! Signalmen in their boxes, and armed sentries at bridges, have been overpowered by bands of Germans who arrived speedily on the scene and, their foul work done, as speedily vanished! . . . Carrier pigeons have been found in German houses! More damnable still, bombs have been discovered in the trunks of German governesses in English country families! The fact that these things are not recorded in the newspapers does not prove them untrue – at least not to those subject to spy mania. What about the Press Censorship? The Government deny that there is any foundation whatever for the rumours; but then the Government – these people argue – are not going to admit what everyone knows them to be – footlers, blind as bats to what is going on around them. Why, they have even failed to see that tennis courts in country houses occupied by Germans were really gun platforms.[22]

Encouraged by the *Daily Mail*, which equated patriotic duty with catching spies, citizens developed the habit of snooping. People were jittery, especially in coastal districts where there was a possibility of signalling to the enemy. The slightest unconventionality or irregularity of behaviour was liable to arouse suspicion. For instance, in the West Country, a woman who drove home from Christian Science meetings after dark was visited by the police after neighbours had seen the lights of her car. An artist in the same area aroused suspicion because he wore a soft brimmed hat and his wife wore 'a cloak of an unusual shape.'[23]

Many who were critical of government methods determined to take the matter into their own hands, a course of action which embarrassed some, made others acutely uncomfortable, and aroused the ridicule of those like Major General Sir Charles Callwell, who wrote:

During many months of acute national emergency, while the war was settling into its groove, there was no more zealous, no more persevering and no more ineffectual subject of the King than the Self Appointed Spy Catcher. You never know what ferocity means until you have been approached by a titled lady who has persuaded herself that she is on the track of a German spy. We Britons are given to boasting of our grit in adversity and of our inability to realize when we are beaten. In no class of the community were these national traits more conspicuous in the early days than in the ranks of the amateur spy-catching fraternity and sisterhood – for the amateur spy catcher never caught a spy. Only after months of disappointment and failure did these self appointed protectors of their country begin to abandon a task which they had taken up with enthusiastic fervour, and which they prosecuted with unfaltering resolution.[24]

Under increasing pressure from the press and a panic-stricken civilian population even staunch Liberals began to criticize McKenna's handling of the problem, though most Liberals believed that it was the product of newspaper agitation. Sir John Simon, in reply to a letter from the Liberal writer, L. T. Hobhouse, asking for something to be done to prevent further outbreaks against Germans, counselled an appeal to reasonableness, but felt bound to point out that 'There are a number of unidentified persons in this country, who have been making treacherous communications and who were not known to us at the beginning of the war.'[25] With the Germans at Ostend, he argued, the dangers of invasion were increased, and caution was necessary.

Lloyd George, who was to handle the problem differently in 1918, criticized McKenna's actions in his memoirs:

'His policy towards residents of enemy extraction in this country was thought to be too protective, too indifferent to the dangers which might arise from espionage . . . McKenna's rigid and fretful answers, though always technically complete, were provocative.'[26]

On 17 October 1914 a Cabinet report dealing with enemy aliens was circulated as a matter of urgency. On 22 October the Home Office ordered the arrest of all unnaturalized male Germans, Austrians and Hungarians of military age: seventeen to forty-five.

Figure 16 *Hans in Hand*

P. C. Bull: 'You made me shove you – I didn't want to do it!'
For the wholesale arrests of alien enemies in our midst the Germans have
only their own all-pervading spy system to thank

The press was filled with figures of arrests all over the country, while the *Daily Mail* kept a close count on those aliens still free. Internees were sent to Olympia and from there to internment camps throughout the country and on the Isle of Man. By 28 October arrests had to be suspended for lack of accommodation. An increasing number of aliens were applying to leave the country.

The victims were of no account during this whirlwind of intolerant patriotism. Thousands of harmless aliens were thrown out of work and made destitute for the rest of the war. Sylvia Pankhurst records that not 1 per cent of them could get work. They were constantly ostracized. Groups such as the East London Suffrage Federation and the Quaker Emergency Committee for the Relief of Germans, Austrians and Hungarians in Distress, which was formed to help the British-born wives of interned aliens, were branded in the press as 'Hun Coddlers' and traitors. One newspaper comment (in the *Evening News*) epitomized the hatred they provoked: 'The efforts of the Emergency Committee to

soften the heart of the German tiger by offering a lump of sugar to its
cubs in this country are not only farcical but indecent. The heart of
Germany can only be softened by high explosives.'[27]

The victims were not only the poor Germans. Having successfully
ostracized waiters and provision dealers, attention was soon directed
towards rich, famous and influential people who had German origins or
German connections. The anti-alien agitation became a witch hunt.

Government measures did not satisfy the die-hards. Because the
government refused to take extreme measures, sections of the press concluded that the government were actually protecting spies. Northcliffe,
whose views informed the editorial line of the *Daily Mail*, wrote to Bonar
Law in November 1914: 'It is beyond question that, for some reason, the
government are protecting spies – and spies in high places.'[28] It was a
theme which was to preoccupy the scaremongering press and the spy-
catching busybodies till the end of 1914 and early 1915, and was to be
revived again in 1918.

What the campaigners were looking for was a scapegoat. They searched
first amongst Liberals, at a time when the Liberal government was coming
under increasing attack, especially from the die-hard patriots, not only
for their handling of the enemy alien problem but for their whole conduct of the war. Fantastic accusations were levelled against Members of
Parliament, Cabinet Ministers and prominent Liberal supporters –
founded on the flimsiest evidence and calculated to provoke the cheapest
malice. Anyone with suspected German connections was the target of
scurrilous gossip.

The Asquiths were accused of keeping German maids and governesses.
Lewis Harcourt, the Colonial Secretary, was branded as a traitor because
he kept a German chauffeur, though he protested he was naturalized.
John Bull, in an article headed 'Pro German Sympathy in High Places',
revealed that Henry Webb MP kept a butler with a German-sounding
name and a German housekeeper. Three prominent Liberals – Sir
Alfred Mond, Sir John Brunner and Sir Edgar Speyer were accused of
pro-German sympathies because of their pre-war financial connections
with Germany. Sir Edgar Speyer eventually returned to New York to
escape the whispering campaign.[29] *John Bull* exploded into paragraphs
of rage that Lord Haldane had a dog named 'Kaiser'. A reader sent a
letter to the *National Review* claiming that Haldane had a 'full-blooded
German chauffeur who regularly drove him to Olympia where he hob-
nobbed with the German prisoners and brought them cigarettes'. Even the

right-wing *National Review* thought this too ridiculous to print, but a
letter in the Unionist *Morning Post* (14 May 1915) said exactly the same
thing.[30] Not surprisingly under such pressure, many people changed
their names – 'raided our surnames' as the *Daily Mail* put it. Ford
Maddox Hueffer changed Hueffer to Ford. The Royal Family, who had
very well-known German connections, substituted Windsor for Saxe
Coburg in 1917.

Later in the war D. H. Lawrence was exiled from Cornwall for alleged
espionage, and he described how it felt. He had frequently made his
hatred of the war known, but it was the presence of his aristocratic
German wife, Frieda, a von Richthofen whose cousin Manfred was a
famous airman and whose father was an officer in the Prussian army,
which aroused the suspicion of neighbours and then the police. They
were living in a remote cottage overlooking the Atlantic shipping routes.
No evidence was found to implicate them in espionage, though Lawrence
perversely took to singing German folk songs when he discovered he was
under suspicion. On a visit to London they were trailed by detectives
while their house in Cornwall was searched.

The police eventually implicated them in contravention of lighting
regulations when the housekeeper in a house where they were dining
passed an uncurtained window carrying a candle on her way to bed.
Lawrence was so outraged at the expulsion order that he made a bonfire
of all his old manuscripts. On the train to London he sat 'feeling that he
had been killed; perfectly still and pale, in a kind of after death'. In *The
Lost Girl* he expressed his disillusion with England by describing it seen
from a boat sailing from Dover: 'England beyond the water, rising with
ash grey, corpse grey cliffs and streaks of snow on the downs above.
England, like a long, ash grey coffin, slowly submerging'; and in
Kangaroo: 'No man who has really consciously lived through this [war]
can believe again absolutely in democracy . . . During the crucial years of
the war, the people chose, and chose Bottomleyism. Bottom enough.'
He never quite recovered from the shock of the expulsion, nor the insanity which provoked it. At the memory of it five years later, he
'trembled helplessly under the shock'.[31]

In 1914 attention centred on men in powerful public positions,
especially on two concerned with the naval and military operations of the
war, namely Prince Louis of Battenburg, the First Sea Lord, and Lord
Haldane, the Lord Chancellor and Minister for War until 1912. The
attack which mounted against both these men, mainly in the press, was

started because they both had German affiliations. They were made scapegoats to satisfy the insatiable appetite of the spy catchers.

Prince Louis, like most of the royal circle, had strong family connections with the enemy. His father, Prince Alexander of Hesse, was a high-ranking figure in the Austrian army. Prince Louis became a naturalized Briton at the age of fourteen and pursued an impeccable career in the British navy. In 1912 he was appointed First Sea Lord at the Admiralty.

His vulnerability because of his background was compounded by the growing public feeling that the navy was not playing its expected role in the war. As major operations centred on the army, the expectations of splendid naval victories faded, and the navy appeared to be almost inactive. News which did reach the public was by no means reassuring, and did little to raise public confidence. At the very beginning of the war two important German battleships – the *Goeben* and the *Breslau* – had managed to elude the British and had taken refuge in Constantinople, from where they could easily inflict further damage. The navy also failed to catch the *Emden* which was having conspicuous success attacking British vessels. The *Audacious* was sunk by a mine in October 1914, though this fact was not officially disclosed at the time. Losses at sea increased. Someone was to blame.

There was growing concern that a man with his connections should be occupying such a high position, expressed yet again by Admiral Lord Charles Beresford in private, and in public in the *Globe* newspaper, which launched an outright campaign for his dismissal. Horatio Bottomley, never known to mince his words, attacked him with characteristic vitriol in *John Bull* on 24 October 1914: 'Blood is said to be thicker than water; and we doubt whether all the water in the North Sea would obliterate the ties between the Battenburgs and the Hohenzollerns when it comes to a life and death struggle between Germany and ourselves.'

Prince Louis could not fail to be aware of the accusations, and was showing signs of being under considerable stress. On 28 October 1914 he handed in his resignation to Churchill, having been 'driven to the painful conclusion that at this juncture my birth and parentage have the effect of impairing in some respects my usefulness on the Board of Admiralty'.

Churchill commented on Prince Louis' position in *The World Crisis*: 'He was placed in an invidious position of having to take great responsibilities and risks day by day without the support in public confidence to which he was absolutely entitled, and with the certainty that accidents might occur from time to time.' Churchill's own conduct at the Admiralty was under criticism at the time. Public confidence in the navy was ebbing. The whispering campaign against Prince Louis provided Churchill with the opportunity to inject new blood into the Admiralty. He replaced him with Admiral Lord Fisher, who commanded not only the respect of the public, but also the Conservative Opposition.[32] Churchill's letter to Prince Louis overflowed with appreciation of his services and of the reasons for his decision; 'This is no ordinary war but a struggle between races of the most terrible kind. It effaces the old landmarks and frontiers of civilization.'[33] It prompted criticism from *The Times*: 'Honest men will prefer the brevity of the retiring Admiral to the rhetorical document which accepts his decision.' *The Times* regretted his resignation as 'unquestionably the result of a campaign of suggestion', and continued, 'Gossip of this kind is, we suppose, the inevitable concomitant of democratic government. It exhibits none the less the most contemptible side, and honest men will not care to remember its results.'[34]

The campaign against Lord Haldane, the next expiatory victim, was even more vicious. On the outbreak of war, *The Times* opposed the appointment of Lord Haldane as Secretary for War, because:

Lord Haldane has been long and honourably known for his predilection for Germany. He was partially educated in that country, he has frequently spent his leisure time there, his mind is coloured by his unremitting study of German literature and philosophy, he cherishes many close German friendships . . . He has constantly been strenuous in his efforts to promote Anglo-German friendship and in pursuing this course he has unwittingly contributed to cloud British perception of the arrogant and dominating aims of German national ambition . . . We in England know that Lord Haldane laboured with the best of motives, but France has watched his well meant works with a keener understanding of German intentions . . . To France, Lord Haldane had seemed the friend of Germany and she would regard his appointment to the War Office with dismay.[35]

Masquerading behind the mask of French opinion this attack contained the seeds of deepening malice against the man who had, in the words of Lord Esher, 'more than any living Englishman prepared for this appalling war',[36] and to whom General Haig wrote on 4 August 1914, 'No one knows the details of the problems of organization as you do! . . . I do hope you will set to work at once to complete the organization you started in 1906.'[37]

Public attacks on Lord Haldane were led by the Tory press with contributions from the *National Review*, edited by Leo Maxse, the *Morning Post*, the *Daily Express* and Northcliffe's papers, which were now conducting an increasingly strident campaign against the Asquith administration's entire handling of the war. Maxse expressed his attitude towards Lord Haldane in a letter to R. D. Blumenfield, editor of the *Daily Express*:

> In the general moral cowardice of the age in which we live, any news-paper which would devote itself in season and out of season to the exposure and expulsion of this most dangerous charlatan would not only perform a conspicuous service but would gain undying kudos which even the business end of the newspaper would ultimately appreciate.[38]

In early 1915, the exposure began in earnest.

Daily Express columnist Arnold White, obsessed since before the war with the fingerprints of 'The Hidden Hand' in government departments, made out 'The Case Against Lord Haldane' in four separate articles, between December 1914 and January 1915, alleging that he had 'deceived the public about the Army, about Germany and about spies'. That newspaper summed up its aversion to Lord Haldane in a little cameo of malice:

> No-one accuses Lord Haldane of having acted in any sense traitorously
> . . . [But] if Lord Haldane had not had the wool pulled over his ears by the astute Kaiser, he would probably have listened to Lord Roberts
> AND
> Then we would have had a million men under arms on 4 August 1914
> AND
> THERE WOULD NOT HAVE BEEN A WAR![39]

Inevitably Haldane was identified with a policy of leniency towards enemy aliens. By attempting, in common with many Liberal colleagues, to take a balanced view, he only provoked further attack. By 1915 he had replaced McKenna as the target for criticism and innuendo about government apathy. Lord Crawford was among many who were con-vinced that it was in part 'Haldane's casuistry' which prevented the Cabinet from taking stronger action against enemy aliens.

In the market place of public rumour, press allegations acquired new dimensions of mendacity. As Haldane recorded:

Every kind of ridiculous legend about me was circulated. I had a German wife; I was an illegitimate brother of the Kaiser; I had been in secret correspondence with the German government; I had been aware that they intended war and withheld this from my colleagues; I had delayed the dispatch and mobilization of the Expeditionary Force . . .[40]

He was threatened in the street and made the object of catcalls at public meetings. In response to an appeal from the *Daily Express*, 2,600 letters protesting against his supposed 'disloyalty to the interests of the nation' were sent to him at the House of Lords. Despite these persistent demands for his resignation in the hate-mongering press, Haldane did not resign. But the objective was achieved when in May 1915 the Liberals were forced to form a coalition with the Conservatives. Bonar Law made it a condition of service that neither Haldane nor Churchill should remain in office. Asquith complied reluctantly, despite muted protest from some Liberal colleagues. Haldane was consigned to the political wilderness for the rest of the war.

Since October 1914 the main force of the anti-alien agitation had concentrated on attacking public figures. In May 1915 came an opportunity to renew hate propaganda against the enemy, which had savage repercussions for enemy aliens in Britain. On 7 May, the *Lusitania* was sunk, and within a week the Bryce Report on German atrocities in Belgium was published by the Secret War Propaganda Bureau.

The press was united in its hysterical condemnation of this, 'The World's Greatest and Foulest Crime'.[41] The *Daily Mirror* described 'Huns gloating over their Victims', the 'Sea Murderer's Toll of Thirty Little Babies' and 'The Kaiser's War on Children' (9 May). The *Daily Express* commented 'This is not war even as understood by savages or by Attila the Hun whom the wretched homicidal Kaiser seeks to emulate. It is murder that not only brands the German race as noxious vipers, but stains the century that gave them birth with shame.'[42]

Northcliffe's *Weekly Dispatch* renewed the campaign to 'Intern Them All' adding that '[The German race] should be stamped for all time, out of existence'. Under the banner headlines 'The Branded Race' and 'No Compromise with the German Savages', Robert Blatchford called for drastic measures against all representatives of the German race, arguing that

It is not the Kaiser, nor the Kaiser's generals who sank the *Lusitania*: it is the men and women of Germany; the German people. Those gross and loutish savages are mad with the exposure and the failure of their

inglorious war. There is no crime too bad for them . . . Why are any
Germans left outside gaols in Britain?[43]

Horatio Bottomley excelled himself:
'I call for a vendetta – a vendetta against every German in Britain –
whether "naturalized" or not . . . You cannot naturalize an unnatural
abortion, a hellish freak. But you *can* exterminate him.'[44]
Such provocative press statements had an immediate effect on a population which was genuinely shocked by the event. Angry demonstrations
were held throughout the country, and developed into riots in London
and most provincial cities. In Camden Town and Kentish Town over 150
German-owned shops were destroyed and looted. At Smithfield Market
German and Austrian traders were attacked and their shops destroyed.
In the East End mobs stoned Germans, destroyed shops and distributed
the contents in the streets. In Liverpool it was the same story. Crowds
attacked and burnt an estimated 200 shops. Troops had to be brought in
after three nights of rioting. Aliens were interned for their own protection.[45] While the riots were reported as anti-German, the looting was
so widespread that Sylvia Pankhurst was convinced that some of the
disturbances in the poorer areas were hunger riots.[46]
The press on the whole deplored the riots but did not fail to sensa-
tionalize the looting and burning. Liberals were still convinced the press
was to blame. Sir John Simon wrote: 'They are the sort of thing which is
published by Harmsworth and which he and his like have instigated. It
must be a great satisfaction to him to feel that he has sold his country
for ½d.'[47]
The incident had its effect in other ways. The London Stock Exchange
excluded brokers of German birth, naturalized or not, and members –
several hundred from the City 'dressed in their best and top hatted',
formed a procession and marched to the Houses of Parliament 'accompanied by a straggling and cheering crowd, at least 2,000 strong, all
infuriated against the Germans' to demand that all aliens should be
interned forthwith.[48] They were met by Admiral Lord Charles Beresford and Sir Henry Dalziel, who contributed to the atmosphere of panic
by asserting that Germans were posted all over London ready, in the
event of Zeppelin raids, to set fire to the city.
A meeting of businessmen at Tower Hill protested against 'any kith
and kin of German mutilators of prisoners and murderers of men,
women and children being any longer at large in the British Isles'.[49] At

Figure 17 *A Clean Sweep*

Mrs Britannia: 'It has to be done: so I might just as well do it first as last – and so get rid of all the dangerous microbes'

the Mansion House, another meeting called on the government to 'free our country of the menace of the alien enemy in our midst'. Germans were boycotted from clubs and businesses. Members of the Hull Pacific Exchange signed a petition demanding the resignation of all Germans, and the Royal Automobile Club banned all German, Austrian, Hungarian and Turkish members for the duration of the war.

Horatio Bottomley called for more colourful reprisals against Germans. All German property should be confiscated and all Germans locked up. Naturalized Germans should wear a distinctive badge and not be allowed out after dark. Their children should not be allowed to attend schools. And, after the war, 'If by chance you should discover one day in a restaurant you are being served by a German waiter, you will throw the soup in his foul face; if you find yourself sitting at the side of a German clerk, you will spill the inkpot over his foul head.'[50]

The government capitulated on 13 May 1915. Stricter measures authorized the internment of all unnaturalized aliens between the ages of seventeen and fifty-five, with provisions for the repatriation of women and children in suitable cases. All registered enemy aliens still at large were kept under close observation by the police. Asquith stated his reluctance either to treat all aliens as spies, or to initiate a vendetta against them which would be 'disgraceful from a moral point of view and impolitic from the point of view of the country's best interests'. He was very aware of the dangers of reprisals on British citizens abroad. The fact that no measures were taken to 'Intern Them All', nor to clear Germans from 'high places' left many members of all parties 'in so great a rage even against naturalized Germans that they were foaming at the mouth'.[51]

Alien agitation subsided when, a few days later, attention was diverted by the coalition crisis, which gave the Unionists a foothold in government, and the shells scandal, which was the culminating point of Northcliffe's attack on the government's handling of the war.

The outbreak of public anger in 1915 led to a more organized anti-alien campaign in parliament and among groups in the country. The British Empire Union (BEU), formerly the Anti German League, became the leading and most vociferous body in a campaign to boycott German goods and rid Britain of German influence. It was a jingoist, Imperialist organization with Unionist and Protectionist backing. Lord Leith of Fyvie was its president, Lt Col. Manningham Buller was chairman, and its secretaries were H. S. A. Foy and F. E. Culling Carr. There were a number of MPs among its active members, notably William Joynson Hicks, a Conservative, and Ronald McNeil, and it had the active support of Admiral Lord Charles Beresford, Dr T. Ellis Powell, the editor of the *Financial Times*, and the leader of the Seaman's Union, Havelock Wilson.[52]

The British Empire Union was dedicated to all aspects of hate propaganda against Germany. Its aims were to defend British Industry and British Labour against German competition, and to fight against 'German influence in our social, financial, industrial and political life', which included removing all persons of enemy origin from public office, preventing the employment of German labour, boycotting German goods, and investigating all reports of suspicious movements by Germans or pro-Germans observed by its members. It also advocated the formation of a customs union to protect British trade.

Its slogans concentrated on the themes 'Britain for the British', and 'Destroy German Influence; Prohibit German Labour; Boycott German Goods'; which appeared on numerous propaganda leaflets. In 1918 it was responsible for the film *Once a Hun, Always a Hun*, a series of dramatic episodes with the message that there should be no trading with the Germans after the war.

The Union held regular public meetings and demonstrations to campaign against enemy aliens whom they described as parasites feeding off the life blood of the British Empire.

Typical of its pamphlets are the following:

BRITISH WAGES FOR BRITISH POCKETS
There are still thousands of Germans at large in London alone,
Think of it! Thousands of enemies with their hands in British pockets.
Thousands of Germans taking bread out of British mouths!
BRITONS WAKE UP ! ! !
Do you want as fellow citizens the murderers of Miss Cavell and Captain Fryatt?
KEEP THEM OUT.[53]
and:
REMEMBER!
Every German employed means a British Worker Idle.
Every German article sold means a British article Unsold.[54]

In addition to the British Empire Union, there was a hard core of extremists in parliament, notably Sir Henry Dalziel, Joynson Hicks, Lord Charles Beresford and Lord Leith of Fyvie, president of the BEU, who kept up a running stream of questions about the security risk of uninterned aliens. In August 1917 the National Party was formed by a group of Unionist MPs disillusioned with the party system. The founder was Brigadier General Henry Page Croft, a leading light in the Tariff Reform League. These groups were to form the hard core of the anti-alien agitation in 1918.

Popular support for anti-alien agitation subsided, however. Kitchener's death in July 1916 on his way to Russia was attributed to the activities of spies and riots broke out in Islington. But spy mania, as Michael Mac-Donagh related, became

limited in its range, but it is more than ever a form of mental derangement. It is extraordinary the number of fussy and interfering busybodies – 'nosey parkers' – that are at large . . . while their impudence in poking their noses into other people's business is a nuisance to many it is a source of great amusement to most.[55]

In June 1918 the anti-alien agitation escalated once again into a public issue – at a time when the successful German offensive on the western front was causing considerable anxiety about the outcome of the war.

Again, the Northcliffe press furthered a propaganda campaign to 'Intern Them All', and to 'make a clean sweep' of people of enemy origin from public office and government departments, to close German businesses and banks, to eradicate all signs of German influence and to boycott German goods. This time it was echoed in an organized campaign in parliament and in the country.

The spark which galvanized and focused public opinion was an event revealing the extraordinary gullibility of the public in wartime. The central figure was Pemberton Billing, MP, a brash young ex-Squadron Commander in the Royal Naval Air Force, who had made a name for himself advocating a stronger air policy and reprisals against the Germans with the slogan, 'Bomb the Hun Homeland'. Clementine Churchill, wife of Winston, thought he was 'rather a flashy young man' who 'is just out to make people's flesh creep'.[56] He was a disciple of Horatio Bottomley, and ran his own paper, the *Vigilante*, formerly the *Imperialist* with sensational news and gossip on similar lines to *John Bull*.

Like Bottomley, he also had a flair for self-advertisement. The alien question provided an opportunity to further his public image. In June 1918, he was sued by the dancer, Maud Allen, whom he accused in an article in the *Vigilante* of sexual perversion. His evidence was a dance she performed in Oscar Wilde's banned play, *Salome*.

The six-day trial attracted enormous press publicity, chiefly because of the sensational revelation of the existence of a German 'Black Book'. It allegedly contained the names of 47,000 English men and women with records of their moral weaknesses and sexual vices. Compiled by German agents in Britain, it was to be used to get information by blackmail. The names were said to include the judge at the trial, Justice Darling, the Asquiths, Lord Haldane, and a number of people distinguished in politics, literature, finance and the diplomatic service, and apparently anyone else who lacked extremist views.

Pemberton Billing was acquitted amid cheers from the supporters in the gallery and from a crowd of a thousand people who greeted him outside the court.

He pursued his campaign in the House of Commons, where, on one occasion, he was frogmarched out by six men for persistently interrupting with a question about 'the number of damned aliens roaming about the country'. At the Finsbury by-election, he sponsored an 'Intern Them All' candidate, Captain Spencer, whose campaign was remarkable for the number of angry incidents in it and the degree of character assassination carried out against the opposing and ultimately successful candidate.

Pemberton Billing's preoccupation with German head-hunting in high places resulted only in the 'unmasking' of Sir Albert Stanley, President of the Board of Trade, whose real name, declared Pemberton Billing, was Nuttmeyer. Sir Albert explained that his family had lived for centuries in Derbyshire, that he had been born there, and that his father had originally had the Scandinavian name of Knatriess, which he had changed on emigrating to Canada.[57] The *Daily Chronicle*, meanwhile, took great delight in reminding its readers that Pemberton Billing had a part-Prussian wife.

The trial was the cue for renewed agitation in the press, which could hardly be expected to soft-pedal a story of such sensational value as sexual perversion and blackmail in high places. It brought out all the old spy catchers from under their stones.

The Northcliffe press picked up the scent of enemy aliens with renewed bloodthirstiness. On 5 June, the day after the trial ended, Northcliffe's *Daily Mail* launched an attack against the Home Office for refusing to remove aliens from coastal and prohibited areas. The public, it said, was exasperated at the government's failure to 'quench the burning riot of enemy activity in this country'.[58] For two weeks the *Daily Mail* ran almost daily editorials on the subject of aliens taking over businesses and continuing to run banks; while demanding a boycott of German goods and the return of 'Britain for the British'. By 19 June there were signs of public response. Dorking Chamber of Commerce passed a resolution demanding that the government 'Intern Them All' which was followed by other resolutions from six other local councils and from the British Empire Union to the same effect.

Northcliffe was relentless and quite unscrupulous in his campaign. He was, in 1918, Director of Propaganda to Enemy Countries in Beaverbrook's Ministry of Information. His obsession was with people of German origin in public office. He was 'a prey to rampant suspicion of all aliens'. He was 'ready to listen to anyone who professed to have news of enemy activity in London or elsewhere on the home front', and

Figure 18 *Swat those Hun Flies!*

constantly, on the flimsiest evidence, reported names of enemy aliens to Sir Basil Thomson, Head of Scotland Yard.[59] He wrote to H. G. Wells: 'I would intern every one of them who had been naturalized within five years of the outbreak of the war . . . The freedom of a good many of the Germans in England is due to snobbery and worse in *very high places*'.[60]

His views were communicated in instructions to his newspapers. The *Daily Mail* was the forum for his obsession. On 8 July he urged his editor to persevere with the alien campaign 'without being strident'. To *The Times* he sent a communiqué on 11 July: 'Some people are trying to make me modify my actions on enemy aliens . . . I find that the public think the government will not move because of Lord Milner. A statement as to Lord Milner's ancestry might be worthwhile.'[61] Milner was Secretary for War. Northcliffe believed he was the architect of plans for a negotiated peace, and connected this with the fact that he was born in Germany of English descent.

By the beginning of July, the campaign was taking off. Local councils throughout the country were passing resolutions demanding a clean sweep and 'Intern Them All'. Local vigilante committees were set up in places like Ealing (where Herbert Nield of the BEU was the local Member of Parliament), to provide reliable information on known enemy aliens in the district. *The Times* reported that 105 aliens had been discovered in Hendon, which was 'thought to be an unnecessarily high proportion of them among its inhabitants'.[62] On 13 July, Northcliffe called for a leading article giving the names of all public bodies which had come out against aliens. 'I have read of at least 100. This will be a reply to the Home Office contention that the agitation is the product of my wicked newspapers. We must watch this thing day by day.'[63] Two days later the *Daily Mail* published the names of sixty-four borough and local councils and other institutions which had passed resolutions. They ranged from the London Chamber of Commerce, Manchester Royal Exchange, and the Baltic Exchange, to Newcastle (Staffs) Trades Council, Harrow Trades Association, the Enemy Influence Committee and the National Party.

The government under Lloyd George was in a far more placatory mood than it had been under Asquith. It consisted predominantly of Conservatives. Lloyd George was at pains to avoid the mistakes made by Asquith and McKenna, which he described in his memoirs. McKenna, he thought, had been provocative on the issue and . . .

... The nation was uneasy. Its sons were falling and information was undoubtedly getting through from the shores of Britain which helped the enemy in the slaughter. Subsequent events proved that intelligence of great value to the enemy percolated through the agency of persons living unmolested in England under McKenna's regime.[64]

Though the press made enemy aliens the scapegoats, at least two sources provide a contrary view. Sir George Cave, Home Secretary, stated in the House of Commons that people communicating information to the enemy, far from being enemy aliens who were under close observation, were mainly neutrals living in this country.[65] Lord Hankey, Secretary to the Cabinet, provided a further insight:

The real danger of leakage of important information, however, was never checked in Britain or any other country, namely society gossip. Of course there was no deliberate malice in it, much less treachery, but among some people, the appetite for news was insatiable, and they persistently tried to pump Cabinet Ministers and others 'in the know' ... Among the people who frequented society were a certain number of international financiers, business men, etc., men far above suspicion of deliberate espionage, but who were accustomed to talk freely ... These latter passed freely into neutral, allied and enemy countries. Without any intention of revealing secrets they would tell in one country the gossip they had heard in another. This was a prolific source of leakage. It was also, let it be admitted, a useful source of intelligence to us.[66]

Lloyd George, however, appreciated the power of press propaganda and he could see indications of a more popular and organized campaign. Although in private he expressed contempt for the extremists, his public utterances indicated some measure of sympathy with their demands. He said, on 11 July:

The press can call up no spirits from the vasty deep unless the spirits are there. And they are there. The Germans have roused them ... The outcry of the press is a sign of a general feeling in this country. The risks are too great for the enemy aliens not to be searched out ruthlessly even to the point of individual hardship. The only limit to be placed upon it is that we should not enter into competition with Germany in its inhumanity, injustice and unfairness. Do not let us commit the folly of over-trustfulness to the extent of endangering the country.[67]

The parliamentary agitation was having its effect. On one day, 24 June 1918, questions on aliens were asked by six MPs: Major Newman, Sir Arthur Fell, Joynson Hicks, Sir Richard Cooper, Sir Stuart Coats and Ronald McNeill. Some of them were members of the Unionist Enemy

PATRIOTISM IS NOT ENOUGH

HERBERT COLE -1915-

The Daily Herald

No. 53. [REGISTERED AT THE G.P.O. AS A NEWSPAPER.] TUESDAY, AUGUST 18, 1914. ONE HALFPENNY

THE INTERNATIONAL ARMAMENT ASSOCIATION GUN MAKERS TO THE CROWNED HEADS OF EUROPE

CURRENT PHRASES
"The Fortunes of War."

31

31 & 32. War is . . . 'the organised murder of tens of thousands of workers of other lands who go to kill and be killed at the command of rulers to whom the people are as pawns.'
I.L.P. Manifesto

The Daily Herald

No. 75. [REGISTERED AT THE G.P.O. AS A NEWSPAPER.] THURSDAY, AUGUST 13, 1914. ONE HALFPENNY

"NO SCARCITY OF FOOD"
[Autocracy all over Europe has its fill, while wealth-producers go hungry.]

The caption reads, 'Autocracy all over Europe has its fill, while wealth-producers go hungry'

MILITARISM—"*ITS PLACE IN THE SUN*"

33 & 34. 'Europe is rattling back to barbarism. In Christian Europe, thousands of men are preparing to murder each other, to wreck whole cities, to spread pestilence and famine, turning earth to red hell. They are like fiends, not because they have a grievance against each other, but because their rulers are liars and cheats'
W. C. Anderson, 6 August 1914

The caption reads,
'WAR – PROFITEER: "Ah, if these ruffians pause to object to me picking their pockets at such a moment as this the country will know them for the unpatriotic shirkers they are!"'

35. The British Empire Union wanted to rid Britain of all German influence after the war

36. Election, 1918. The call for vengeance

37. Before the war had ended, patriotic propagandists warned of the dangers of a German peace

35

37

Influence Committee which worked with the British Empire Union in early 1918 unofficially investigating the cases of 2,000 enemy aliens.[68]

In early July Lloyd George appointed an Alien Committee, which consisted of five MPs, some of whom were known for their extremist views. The members were Joynson Hicks, Sir Henry Dalziel, Sir Richard Cooper, Mr Kennedy Jones and Mr Bowerman. The *Daily Chronicle* expressed relief at the exclusion of the manic Pemberton Billing. The recommendations of the Committee reflected its bias. They called for the internment of all alien women, a review of naturalization certificates issued since January 1914 by an Advisory Committee, the removal of all people of German origin from any government department or public office, and the removal of all aliens from prohibited areas. The committee also called on the Board of Trade to wind up enemy businesses and close banks.

Most of the proposals, with the notable exception of clearing aliens from public office, were accepted by Sir George Cave, the Home Secretary, who was careful not to endorse 'Intern Them All' views, especially when people of German origin had sons fighting abroad. Very few spies, he said, had been caught, and most of them were not even of enemy origin. No serious charge of disloyalty was brought against any naturalized German.

The extremists were not satisfied. The 'Whitehall Wire-pullers' and 'Friends of Fritz' had escaped scot free. Northcliffe was convinced 'on excellent authority' that certain Home Office officials were 'determined to protect their friends'.[69] The *Daily Mail* editorial on the proposals noted 'a sinister absence of protest from the Parliamentary friends of the Hun, who are evidently of the opinion that nothing much will be done'. It concluded that Lloyd George had 'made some concessions to the wire-pullers'.

Sir Henry Dalziel, Joynson Hicks and General Page Croft, all in the forefront of the parliamentary agitation, echoed the accusations against 'someone at the Home Office who was powerful enough to prevent action being taken'.[70] Other members of the Committee continued the campaign inside and outside parliament. Mr Kennedy Jones was the leading light in the Aliens Investigation Committee, formed on 25 August and chaired by Justice Sankey to look into cases of 6,000 Germans and 18,000 other enemy aliens who were still at large. Having managed to net only 300 out of an alleged 24,000 possible cases for investigation, they were duly chastised by the *Daily Mail* for leniency. Sir Henry Dalziel and Sir

Figure 19

Richard Cooper formed an Alien Watch Committee, chaired by Sir
Edward Carson, to look into the employment of people of enemy origin
in government departments but came up with very little material.

In the House of Lords, debate centred on the attempt to strengthen
the Denaturalization Bill which would revoke naturalization certificates
issued after January 1914. An attempt to prevent people of German
origin sitting on the Privy Council, which would have immediately
affected at least three of their Lordships, was defeated, as was the
demand to increase from five years to ten the period after the war during
which aliens could not be naturalized.

Outside parliament, the clamour for complete internment was organized
by the British Empire Union and General Page Croft's National Party,
and was supported by the right-wing Merchant Seaman's League, led by
Havelock Wilson. On 13 July 1918 a large demonstration in Trafalgar
Square, organized by Mrs Dacre Fox of the National Party, passed a
resolution 'to turn out the accursed, insidious and dangerous enemy
alien'. *The Times* reported the event:

There can be no more proof of the earnestness with which the general
public regard the danger of allowing Germans to be at large in our midst
than the demonstration in Trafalgar Square on Saturday afternoon. It
was the biggest crowd seen in the square since the outbreak of war. In
spirit and temper it was also the most determined. On each side of the
plinth of the Nelson Column were two large placards inscribed: 'A Clean
Sweep' and 'Intern Them All'. These mottos well expressed the sentiment of the great throng that filled the square.[71]

A British Empire Union meeting in Hyde Park on 20 July was followed
by a National Party mass meeting at the Free Trade Hall in Manchester
on 24 July, addressed by Brigadier General Page Croft and Havelock
Wilson, and a mass rally at the Albert Hall on 30 July to demand the
'instant destruction of the organized German spy system in government
departments' and the end of the 'elaborate and influential Hun
treachery'. On 1 August, Newcastle and Hammersmith Councils demanded total internment and Liverpool debated the subject. Mrs Dacre
Fox sent a letter to all the Mayors in the country asking them to call
meetings and set up local Committees of Public Safety. The British
Empire Union held weekly rallies in London, which culminated, on
24 August, with a huge demonstration in Hyde Park to present a petition
organized by the National Party. It was addressed by speakers from five
separate platforms.

Michael MacDonagh reported the event:

A monster petition to the Government forthwith to intern every alien without distinction of any kind, and take drastic steps to eradicate German influence in Government circles was adopted at a meeting in Hyde Park this afternoon.
The petition had 1,250,000 signatures. It was over two miles in length. Rolled up like a drum, it was carried from Hyde Park to Downing Street in a lorry decorated with the Union Jack, the Stars and Stripes, the French Tricolour and the flags of the other Allied nations. It was escorted by a procession with bands and banners almost as long as itself and of so diversified a composition as to be possible only in London in wartime. In the marching ranks were thousands of discharged soldiers and sailors, and groups of Dominion soldiers in furlough. There were representatives of the British Empire Union, members of Trade Unions with their big allegorical banners, deputations from the Committees of Public Safety which have been formed in cities and towns throughout the country for the special purpose of hunting down German spies. At the end was a long array of the general public; men and women, which included many representative City men of the Baltic and Stock Exchange – an impressive array of silk hats and frock coats. The route lay through Oxford Street, Regent Street and Cockspur Street to Trafalgar Square, where the procession waited until the return of the deputation who went with the petition to Downing Street. Lloyd George was out of town. One of his secretaries conveyed to the deputation the Prime Minister's regrets that he was unable to receive them personally, and assured them that he would give the petition serious consideration on his return. This message was received by the meeting in Trafalgar Square with 'regret and dismay' as expressed in a resolution that was passed on the motion of Brigadier General Page Croft. 'It clearly indicates,' said the resolution, 'that His Majesty's Government do not appreciate the deep national feeling in regard to the great peril of the enemy aliens at large . . .'[72]

The government, to its credit, procrastinated. There was very little they could do, or wanted to do, beyond the measures already taken and the activities of the various committees. The facts showed that though information had been leaking to the enemy, the sources were invariably not enemy aliens. By the end of August, reports were coming through of Allied breakthrough on the western front. Attention was diverted from enemy aliens to victory.
The propaganda campaign against enemy aliens achieved very little in terms of its declared aim – to safeguard the security of the country. The propagandists were people gripped by war hysteria themselves, who found a convenient scapegoat for the failures of the war in enemy aliens.

The alien question was used as a vehicle for other obsessions – in North-cliffe's case to attack the government, in the case of the British Empire Union and the National Party, to eliminate German business competition and push for Protectionism, and in the case of others, like Pemberton Billing, for self publicity. Propaganda succeeded in building up a fantasy about the enemy within the gates by focusing and then exaggerating fears in the population. In so doing it legitimized the expression of vindictive-ness and hatred against a minority whose actual activities had, in fact, never warranted such abuse. The war against the enemy on the home front was a triumph for hate propaganda.

Chapter Seven

Propaganda for Peace

Out of the darkness and the depth we hail our working class comrades of every land. Across the roar of the guns, we send sympathy and greetings to the German socialists. They have laboured unceasingly to promote good relations with Britain, as we have with Germany. They are no enemies of ours but faithful friends.

In forcing this appalling crime upon the nations, it is the rulers and the diplomats, the militants who have sealed their doom. In blood and bitterness, the greater Democracy will be born. With steadfast faith we greet the future. Our cause is holy and imperishable, and the labour of our hands has not been in vain.

Independent Labour Party manifesto, August 1914.

The voice of dissent in the First World War was isolated, and only a small minority of people in all countries remained aloof from the war hysteria which engulfed Europe. In Britain, they were neither pro-Germans nor traitors, as they were dubbed in the patriotic press, but men and women who, from religious or political convictions, believed that the people had been deceived about the causes and aims of the war, or who believed that war was morally evil. Their main aim was to work for an early negotiated peace.

They were opposed by the great majority of public opinion, which was being whipped up into a frenzy of hatred of the enemy, and was girding up its loins for a fight to the finish. The whole of the press, apart from a few socialist weeklies, was against them. They had virtually no support in parliament. But, though their voice was small, they were feared because they were thought potentially subversive. They became the object of loathing, contempt and ridicule because they threatened the unity of opinion essential to the success of the war. The patriotic press, for instance, advocated that they be 'nipped in the bud' and, if possible, extracted from public life to prevent their propaganda contaminating the general will to fight.

The government took a different view. While the tide of public opinion ran in its favour, the government considered the propaganda of dissent harmless. Legally they found it very difficult to prosecute anti-war literature. The tradition of free speech ran deep in the veins of Liberal consciousness. They relied on the patriotic press to counteract pacifist propaganda while the euphoria lasted. But by 1916 there was an atmosphere of war-weariness, growing industrial unrest, and increasing criticism of the government's conduct of the war. The government took action to counteract dissident and pacifist propaganda only when it appeared it was influencing industrial workers to strike, and when its central theme, the call for a negotiated peace, began to find its echo in a population which had suffered too long under the strain of war.

There were a number of strands of opinion in anti-war and pro-peace propaganda. A few radical Liberals, disillusioned with the secret diplomacy of pre-war foreign policy, formed the Union of Democratic Control (UDC), which formulated a democratic basis for foreign policy after the war. Their attention increasingly turned to criticism of the government's handling of the war and a call for an early negotiated peace. Another group were the socialists and anti-militarists of the Independent Labour Party (ILP), who opposed all war and particularly this war, which violated all the basic socialist beliefs in internationalism, the sacredness of human life and progress. Then there were the pacifists of the ILP and the Labour Party who joined religious anti-war groups like the Quakers, in the formation of the No Conscription Fellowship. A further strand of dissenting opinion was represented by the socialists and revolutionaries of the British Socialist Party and the Socialist Labour Party, concentrated on the Clyde, who saw in the war the opportunity to bring about a crisis in the class struggle, and who, rather than working for an early end to the war, worked through the exploitation of industrial shop floor grievances to bring about a new awareness of the class struggle in preparation for the downfall of capitalism.

With the exception of the Clyde workers, the propaganda of these groups made no real impact until 1916, when the conscription debate split both the Liberal Party and the country. After 1916, industrial unrest aggravated by war-weariness led to a situation where the call for an early peace began to have considerable impact on the civilian population.

During the first two years of war, the propaganda methods of these groups were the product of their isolation. They persistently put the case against the war and worked away slowly at influencing people who, they thought, would gradually become more receptive the longer the war went on. Phillip Snowden of the ILP thought 'the temper of the people was such that, at that time, an appeal [for peace negotiations] would have little effect on the mass mind. It needed a longer experience of the horror and suffering inflicted by the war to bring them into a frame of mind that such appeals would receive consideration.'[1] Ramsay MacDonald agreed: 'We have to peg away quietly at it . . . I think there are a great many people ready to receive a *little* light . . .'[2]

Their channels of propaganda were limited. One was parliamentary agitation – by radical Liberal MPs in the UDC, and by the Labour Party members of the ILP, who put pressure through personal influence and in the House of Commons. Generally this met with a wall of solid patriotism. As late as 1917, Liberal MP Arthur Ponsonby admitted to E. D. Morel, founder of the UDC, that 'our little gang' in parliament had been ineffective.[3]

Their influence depended on a broadly based organization. They directed their propaganda at individuals, especially intellectuals, but more important, they aimed at getting the support and affiliation of Labour organizations, trades union branches, cooperative societies, local Labour Parties, women's sections of the Labour Party and other large groups. By October 1915, forty-eight out of 107 of the UDC's affiliated bodies came from the Labour Movement.[4] In June 1918, 174 Labour bodies with a membership of more than half a million were affiliated.[5] The Independent Labour Party already had well-established connections with trades councils, local Labour Parties and the trades unions, which they used to propagate their anti-war position.

Although there were a number of small circulation socialist newspapers, like *Labour Leader*, the *Daily Herald*, *Forward* and the *Bradford Pioneer*, along with some created during the war – the *UDC*, the *Tribunal* and the *Worker* – there was no national newspaper. Press propaganda was supplemented by pamphlets, leaflets and other literature distributed through local organizations and at meetings. Public meetings – from street corner soap boxes to large rallies, were another forum for the views of the anti-war groups, though they were frequently disrupted by patriotic elements.

Though there was contact and cross-fertilization between these different groups, the precise nature of their opposition to war differed. The Liberals of the UDC concentrated on foreign policy, arguing that the war was the outcome of mistaken foreign policies, and could have been prevented. Initially they called for post-war parliamentary control of foreign policy and the abolition of secret diplomacy 'aimed at creating alliances for the purpose of maintaining the balance of power'. By 1915 they were arguing that, however the war had been started, it should be ended by negotiation at the earliest opportunity. By 1917 they had formulated specific peace proposals based on open diplomacy, democratic control, no annexations or indemnities and the establishment of an International Council or League of Nations to keep the peace.

The co-founders of the UDC were Arthur Ponsonby, founder of the pre-war Liberal Foreign Affairs Group, C. P. Trevelyan, who resigned as Parliamentary Secretary to the Board of Trade on the outbreak of war, E. D. Morel, founder of the Congo Reform Association, Norman Angell, founder of the Neutrality League, and Ramsay MacDonald of the Independent Labour Party. Outside parliament it was actively supported by intellectuals including J. A. Hobson, C. Lowes Dickinson, Bertrand Russell and C. R. Buxton. They lost the support of a wider group of Liberals, including Philip Morrell, Arnold Rowntree and the editor of the *Manchester Guardian*, C. P. Scott, chiefly because they criticized current government policies, and also because their analysis of the causes of the war led E. D. Morel, particularly, into the unpatriotic position of justifying Germany's case as a reaction to encirclement, at the same time repudiating the government's justification of the war in defence of 'Little Belgium'. (E. D. Morel, *Truth and the War*, and *How the War Began*.)

The Independent Labour Party's anti-war position was broader than that of the UDC. It stemmed from a socialist repudiation of war, which, they argued, was the 'organized murder of tens of thousands of workers of other lands who go to kill and be killed at the command of rulers to whom the people are as pawns'.[6] They were committed to the Resolution of the Socialist International Conference of 1907 that, if war threatened to break out they should aim to prevent it by a general strike of the working class throughout Europe, but if this should fail, 'their duty is to intervene to bring it promptly to an end' and 'use the political and economic crisis created by the war to . . . hasten the fall of capitalist domination'.[7]

When war broke out, the ILP focused not so much on the fall of capitalism as on the attempt to bring about an immediate peace by negotiation. They emphasized the class nature of the war and the violation of internationalist socialist belief which it represented. Their statement exhorted:

Workers of Great Britain, Down With War. You have no quarrel with the workers of Europe. They have no quarrel with you. The quarrel is between the RULING classes of Europe. DON'T MAKE THEIR QUARREL YOURS . . . Stand true in this hour of crisis. The flag of International Solidarity is greater than the flag of Britain, of Germany, of France, of Russia, of Austria. It waves over all . . . your fathers, your brothers, your sons. You have no quarrel. But you will have to suffer.[8]

The only beneficiaries of the war, argued Keir Hardie, were rich vested interests. He repudiated all the government's idealistic justifications for war:

The present war is not being waged in 'freedom's holy cause': it is not meant to safeguard the 'rights of small and weak nations'; it is not meant to put down oppression; it is not meant to elevate the downtrodden and oppressed. If it had been for these objects, every government in Europe would have opposed it to the death. The present war, like most others, has come because many great and powerful interests demanded that it should; because statesmen have . . . deceived the people into false beliefs.[9]

Their anti-war stand isolated the ILP from the Labour Party which supported the prosecution of the war and the recruitment drive. They continued to work within the party despite strenuous attempts by the moderate centre and right-wing to disown them and exclude them from the policy-making bodies of the Labour Party. Only in 1917 did the ILP have any effect in changing the Labour Party view of the war.

Their aims were twofold. The long-term campaign was for a negotiated peace along UDC lines. Few favoured an immediate call to stop the war. There was disagreement as to whether an Allied victory was a necessary prerequisite to peace. Moderates, like MacDonald, thought it was, the extremists argued from the unchanging stalemate at the front that it was not, indeed, that a military victory was impossible. The short-term campaign was the defence of the conditions of workers and soldiers' dependants, who would be 'plunged into unemployment and destitution by the war. Almost no conceivable effort – even if the food supply of the country holds out – will prevent the occurrence of fearful privation amongst them.'[10] The National Administrative Council recommended participation on local Citizens' Committees to safeguard against the threat that the war would be used for sweating labour, and to fight, not for relief or doles, but for work on full wages, or complete maintenance and adequate state pay for soldiers so that their dependants were not left to what Keir Hardie described as 'irritating, fussy, semi-private, degrading charity which they resent so bitterly'.[11] They called for control of the

EQUALITY OF SACRIFICE

AREN'T THEY WORTH DEFENDING?

1918

Figure 20 *Workers' Dreadnought*'s view of the patriotic appeal for sacrifice

purchase, storage and distribution of food, and the fixing of minimum prices for food and other necessities. Meanwhile branches should continue 'educational Socialist propaganda, with its note of fraternity and internationalism [which], though not dealing specifically with the war, may help to prevent panics, wild jubilations, and excitements, and to repress outbursts of loud and boastful jingoism'.[12]

In the East End of London, Sylvia Pankhurst and her East London Federation of Suffragettes, and George Lansbury, ILP member for Bow, were the most active campaigners against the acute misery caused by war, especially through the government's bureaucratic mishandling of dependants' allowances, which caused considerable privation amongst the poor. Sylvia Pankhurst's *Woman's Dreadnought* and Lansbury's *Herald* publicized both the pro-peace case and the plight of women and children which they witnessed at first hand. Unlike Emmeline and Christabel Pankhurst, who vehemently supported the war, the recruitment campaign and anti-Germanism as an opportunity to push forward the rights of women, Sylvia Pankhurst was a pacifist and a socialist. While the Women's Social and Political Union pressurized the government to give women 'the right to serve' in the national emergency, Sylvia Pankhurst was exposing the usually appalling and always low-paid conditions of women workers, setting up clinics, food and milk centres, and surgeries for the starving wives and children of soldiers, while at the same time campaigning for women's suffrage and equal pay. She led deputations to the government, and at one meeting accused Runciman of helping to starve the men into enlisting 'by failing to provide allowances', and summed up the Local Authority administration of relief as providing 'small doles, mainly in kind, postponed as long as possible'.[13] She also vehemently opposed conscription and publicized the conscientious objectors' case. Her *Workers' Dreadnought* was the first to publish Siegfried Sassoon's statement against the war in 1917.

Other former suffragettes and suffragists with ILP and UDC connections were working for peace. Mrs Pethwick Lawrence became Honorary Treasurer of the Women's International League, campaigned for peace in America and took part in an International Congress at the Hague including German and Austrian representatives, which called for immediate peace. She described the war as 'a moral iniquity . . . we see the liberties for which our brothers went out to fight and die steadily undermined at home'.[14] Charlotte Despard, sister of the Commander-in-Chief, Sir John French, and a pacifist and socialist, actively supported the ILP and Sylvia Pankhurst's campaign for relief for soldiers' dependants, and started the Freedom League which campaigned for suffrage through the magazine the *Vote*. Rosa Hobhouse, Ethel Snowden, Catherine Marshall of the No Conscription Fellowship (NCF), Eva Gore Booth, and Helena Swanwick – who was particularly appalled at the backward step taken by women who drifted into relief work which 'cleans up the messes men make' and 'requires only jog trot feminine capacities and has no permanent effect on policy,[15] – and others whose political awareness had been stirred in the suffrage fight, formed organizations dedicated to securing an end to the male butchery which was being unleashed in France.

One other group active in propaganda was the out and out pacifists. They believed that war was murder and violence was evil and could, therefore, morally take no part in its prosecution. The No Conscription Fellowship was formed by Clifford Allen, Fenner Brockway and C. H. Norman on 3 December 1914 to gather together men of similar views, to fight against conscription, and later to assist conscientious objectors. They worked with religious anti-war groups, particularly Quakers, and had the support of intellectuals among the Bloomsbury Group, particularly Bertrand Russell, Labour Party members including Herbert Morrison, and a small number of Liberals, for instance Phillip Morrell, who described conscription as 'one of the most potent instruments of privilege and oppression', which 'leads inevitably to the spirit of militarism',[16] and F. W. Pethwick Lawrence, who wrote: 'Its nefarious object is to deprive the working class of the means to resist their own enslavement.'[17]

Clifford Allen was the guiding light of the NCF. He was a socialist and a lifelong pacifist. In a speech published as a pamphlet, 'Is Germany Right and Britain Wrong?', he blamed the war on mistaken foreign policies and exhorted his audience 'to face the only possible outcome of our socialist faith – I mean the question of non resistance to armed force. Don't let us deceive ourselves. The sacredness of human life is the mainspring of our propaganda. In my opinion there can be no two kinds of murder.'[18]

The NCF manifesto issued in September 1915 was a declaration of pacifist faith:

We yield to no one in our . . . unflagging devotion to those of our fellow countrymen who have felt it their duty to take up arms. Nevertheless we cannot undertake the same form of service . . . Whatever the purpose to be achieved by war, however high the ideals for which the belligerent countries may struggle, for us, 'Thou shalt not kill' means what it says. The destruction of our fellow men – young men like ourselves – appals us; we cannot assist in the cutting off of one generation from life's opportunities . . . we deny the right of any government to make the slaughter of our fellows a bounden duty.[19]

They declared they would 'sacrifice as much in the cause of the world's peace as our fellows are sacrificing in the cause of the nation's war'.

NCF propaganda methods were the most highly organized of any group. Clifford Allen sent guidelines from prison: 'Every step should be taken to make known *now* the *facts* about our resistance and the reasons that have prompted it. There must be much more literature *particularly leaflets* . . . To secure publicity we should constantly supply information

to MPs. Productive agitation=publicity . . .'[20] During 1915 they established a network of branches and federations throughout the country,
organized on suffragette and possibly Sinn Fein lines, where every
leader had a 'shadow' to take over in the likely event of their imprisonment. Women played a major role after the men were imprisoned. The
political department pressurized MPs and was particularly active during
the conscription debates. Opposition in the Liberal Party melted after it
was introduced. The NCF turned to agitation for repeal of the Act.

   The publications department and press office, run by Hubert Peet and
continued by Lydia Smith after his imprisonment, produced over one
million leaflets, plus articles, news items and letters to the press publicizing the pacifist case, exposing the work of Tribunals and the treatment of
conscientious objectors (COs) after sentence, and giving advice on
'Methods of Agitation'. It also produced posters, including one quoting
the judge at the trial of the first eight National Committee members, who
said 'War would be impossible if all men were to have the view that war is
wrong' – which just about summed up the views of the men on the other
side of the dock. In March 1916 the NCF started their journal, the
Tribunal, which was frequently raided.

   The records department kept files on all anti-conscriptionists, kept
track of all conscientious objectors and provided dossiers on the worst
abuses in their treatment. Altogether there were 16,000 COs, of whom
1,500 were absolutists who refused to take any part whatsoever in the
prosecution of the war. Sixty-nine COs died in prison and thirty-nine
went insane.

   The patriotic press reacted with uniform hostility to all anti-war
groups. Through a combination of verbal abuse, ridicule and misrepresentation of their case, the press built up their image as traitors
who were 'helping to stab the army in the back' and who were 'fighting
for Germany as usefully as the soldiers in the German armies in France'.[21]
The press was successful in stirring up hostility to dissenters. Ramsay
MacDonald wrote 'The opposition to us is tremendous. As soon as one
goes out of one's immediate circle, one meets it in a most cruelly
oppressive way. People do believe we are selling our country and that
we are tainted as with leprosy.'[22] The press were also pressurizing the
government to take drastic action against them.

   The government until 1916 refused to take action, despite frequent
complaints to the Home Office about their publications. After an early
unsuccessful attempt to suppress *Labour Leader*, the authorities tended

to leave the presses alone, until a legal framework was established under the Military Service Act which could be applied to anti-conscription pamphlets. Generally the Liberal conviction that free speech should not be completely stifled held sway. But more important, it was extremely difficult to make out a case for prosecution. For instance, a copy of an ILP resolution sent to the Home Office in June 1915 was minuted by Sir Edward Troup, the Under-Secretary: 'I suppose the intention of the resolution is to embarrass the government, but it is not in itself an unreasonable proposal, only an impractical one. I do not think any action against the authors is possible.'[23]

This soft Home Office approach was not entirely shared by the law officers under the Attorney General, Sir Edward Carson, a man who was later to play a leading part in anti-pacifist propaganda. In July 1915, the Department of Public Prosecutions (DPP) under Carson caused some consternation by raiding the Manchester and London offices of the National Labour Press and the headquarters of the ILP. Six to seven hundred pamphlets and copies of *Labour Leader* were seized. It transpired that Sir John Simon, the Home Secretary, had not been consulted about the raid. The pamphlets were returned after magistrates decided there was no case for prosecution. It was admitted in parliament that, though the ILP, UDC and other organizations were being watched by the DPP, no action was at the time possible.

In the absence of decisive government action, the patriotic press pursued its own campaign to discredit anti-war and pro-peace activists. Anyone who repudiated the war, including on one occasion, Lord Northcliffe, was branded a pro-German, if not an agent of the Kaiser.

The first intimation of hostility came when a private UDC circular was leaked to the press. The *Morning Post* described the UDC as a 'Pro German Intrigue' which was 'secretly being prepared in order to flood the country when the proper time comes' with 'books, pamphlets and leaflets directed to the object of a peace satisfactory to Germany', and advocated that it should be 'nipped in the bud'.[24] The *Daily Express* had no doubt that the UDC was being funded by Germany and called for a government enquiry.

When the UDC started public meetings in 1915, the patriotic press counteracted with a technique which was used throughout the war: namely, inciting the public to break up the meetings. Under the headline 'An Appeal to Patriots', it listed forthcoming UDC meetings and asked 'Will you make a point of attending one of them and holding a watching

brief on behalf of your Country and the men who are fighting for her?'
Meetings were broken up by mobs. For instance, at a meeting in King-
ston, crowds assaulted Ponsonby, Langdon Davies and Seymour Cocks
when they attempted to speak. Before a meeting at the Memorial Hall,
Farringdon Street, the *Daily Express* printed pictures of Morel,
Trevelyan, Clifford Allen and Fenner Brockway and asked 'Londoners,
what do you think of them? Is Germany to hear the wail of peace cranks
from the City of the Empire?'[25] The hall was filled with stink bombs and
soldiers seized the platform before the speakers could begin and passed a
resolution 'that peace shall not be made until Prussia is utterly and
completely crushed'.[26] The *Daily Express* jubilantly reported the 'utter
rout of the pro-Germans'. The *Daily Sketch* called for a ban on all
meetings likely to cause a disturbance since, 'to talk of peace now is
treason, to question the justice of our cause is treason, to demand soft
terms from Germany is treason'.[27]

The leaders were the target of special venom. In July 1915, the *Daily
Express* published under the heading, 'A Trio of Peace Prattlers' pictures
of MacDonald, Angell and Morel resembling criminals on 'Wanted'
posters. On 4 April 1915 the same paper lashed out at Morel: 'WHO
IS MR E. D. MOREL? AND WHO PAYS FOR HIS PRO-GERMAN
UNION?' and described the UDC as 'essentially a pro-German organization' and Morel as 'wholeheartedly pro-German'. In April 1916, in the
House of Commons, Will Thorne, a right-wing Labour MP, contributed
to the rumour that 'Morel has for years been a paid agent of the German
government'. Poison pens sent postcards, like one to Morel which read:
'It is to be hoped that you and your dirty colleagues will be shot as
traitors after the war. You deserve it.'[28] In Trevelyan's constituency, a
district council was reported to have passed a resolution that 'Mr
Trevelyan be taken out and shot.'[29] Bertrand Russell was deprived of his
lectureship at Trinity College, Cambridge, Norman Angell was banned
from the Bath Club of London, and MacDonald from his golf club at
Lossiemouth.

The ILP was an equal target. MacDonald and Hardie were identified
as the ringleaders of pacifism. Hardie was rejected even in his own
constituency, Merthyr Tydfil. His first meeting there had to be abandoned
after he was howled down and drowned out by the singing of 'Rule
Britannia' and the National Anthem. He never fully recovered from the
failure of the Labour Movement to withstand the challenge of war. He
died in 1915.

Ramsay MacDonald became the symbol, more than any of his more extreme associates, of pacifist and anti-war sentiment. In fact he was a moderate. He resigned from the leadership of the Labour Party on 7 August 1914, which isolated him from his party and moved him closer towards identification with the ILP and UDC positions. He was circumspect and contradictory in his opinions, and totally unsuited to interpret the world in black and white propagandist terms. Consequently he was vulnerable to misrepresentation. He attracted the hatred of patriots and the hero-worship of pacifists. Neither response was justified.

He was never a pacifist, but he was deeply suspicious of Sir Edward Grey, which led him at times, and particularly the day before war was declared, to put the whole blame for the war on Britain. He supported the call for recruits, and believed that an Allied victory was necessary before peace negotiations could start – a view not shared by the majority of his colleagues. 'History will in due time apportion the praise and the blame,' he wrote to a recruiting rally in his constituency, Leicester, 'but the young men of the country must, for the moment, settle the immediate issue of victory' (September 1914).[30] While supporting the war effort, his hatred of militarism led him to aim at keeping the way open for peace. He spoke for the UDC and the ILP on that subject, though they both repudiated the need for an Allied victory.

MacDonald was the sacrificial victim for the patriotic knives, partly because of his outspokenness against Grey's policies, also perhaps because he appeared to have a foot in both camps – an intolerable stance when the belligerent atmosphere demanded that everyone be on one side or the other. The patriotic press put him on the other, called him 'Germany's Best Friend', accused: 'MacDonald Scoffs at the Army', and generally did their best to whip up hatred against him and, by implication, everyone he represented.

In 1916, the first real confrontation with the government and press happened over conscription. It hardened the government's reaction to dissenters and provoked an intensified and more virulent campaign against them in the press. In opposing the introduction of conscription, the pro-peace and pacifist groups were for the first time in agreement with a large proportion of Liberals and most of the Labour Movement. They intensified their campaign among MPs, in the Labour Party and among trades union organizations, concentrating on conscription. The Military Service Act passed into law nevertheless. They turned to

6

agitation for repeal of the Act and opposition to the Second Military Service Act which would call up married men.

An umbrella organization, the National Council Against Conscription (NCAC), was formed after a deputation to the House of Commons in January 1916 to coordinate the anti-conscription campaign. It consisted of members of the NCF, Clifford Allen, Catherine Marshall, F. W. Pethwick Lawrence; Liberal anti-conscriptionists, like H. W. Massingham, editor of the *Nation*; socialists, among them George Lansbury; and trades unionists, notably Robert Smillie, the miners' leader. They distributed five million leaflets, put pressure on local MPs and aimed to get resolutions passed in all local trades councils, labour organizations and trades unions against conscription, sent letters to the press, parliament, magistrates, ministers, and the Trades Union Council, distributed anti-conscriptionist literature, organized meetings and set up new committees to do the same thing.[31]

In a direct bid to claim the support of the trades unions, they stressed that military conscription was a prerequisite to industrial conscription. *Labour Leader* described conscription as 'Chains of Slavery on Democracy' (6 January 1916) and 'The Sinister Attempt to Militarize the Workshops' (13 January 1916). One NCAC leaflet: 'CONSCRIPTION – Why they want it and why they SAY they want it', stated:

They say they want it to punish the slackers
They want it to punish the strikers
They say they want it to crush Germany
They want it to crush Labour
They say they want it to free Europe
They want it to enslave Europe.[32]

The war, claimed *Labour Leader*, had moved from 'a holy crusade against militarism' to 'an unholy crusade to strengthen militarism'. Bertrand Russell stated his case against conscription:

The motive of those who lead the Conscriptionist campaign is clear: it is to obtain a new weapon against organized labour . . . The appeal of love of country is cynical hypocrisy. From the moment when war broke out, certain enemies of Freedom have seen that it gave a rare opportunity for robbing the wage earners of what little liberty they had achieved and preventing them for many years to come from making any advance on the road to democratic justice. With the enactment of conscription the cruel plot will have succeeded.[33]

The NCF, most of whose members were faced with imminent imprisonment, pleaded: 'Freedom of conscience must not be sacrificed to military necessity, nor British liberty to political expediency. Man's deepest religious and moral convictions must not be swept aside.'[34]

As the anti-conscriptionist campaign gathered momentum, the press retaliated by attacking all anti-war groups. The *Daily Express* was again in the forefront of the attack. Having campaigned for conscription to get out the 'slackers' and the 'shirkers', it now found them out, and in full view in large numbers on the streets. It revived advertisements for their meetings, this time through letters signed 'Anti-German', who wrote: 'No honest man who has ever attended one of these pretended anti-conscription meetings can be under any illusion as to its real object. The so-called anti-conscriptionists are fighting against this country as much as if at this moment they were trying to poison gas the British Army in the trenches.' He called the attention of the authorities and readers to a meeting to be held in Finsbury Park, which was duly swamped by crowds singing the National Anthem.[35] More letters arrived detailing meetings with the recommendation that 'patriots in the vicinity should attend to make a protest', while the same paper advertised anti-pacifist literature, like one pamphlet by a Mr Ernest Thruttle of Sutton, Surrey, entitled 'Punish the Pacifist Traitors', described as 'a warning against Pasty Faces'. 'Pasty face' was the new description for all pro-peace groups, having replaced 'peace crank' as the more abusive term.

Bashing pasty faces became the patriotic sport. The anti-pacifist campaign was supported by sections of the public, including local Conservative parties, and, according to *Labour Leader*, such patriotic bodies as the British National Workers' League – a body set up by right-wing trades unionists specifically to counteract the propaganda of their left-wing and erstwhile comrades. A meeting arranged by Sylvia Pankhurst and George Lansbury in Trafalgar Square in April 1916 was routed by bellicose patriots. 'Anti-German' in the *Daily Express* had exhorted 'every decent man to attend'. The *Daily Express* reported 'The plinth was stormed under a curtain of fire by long-range red and yellow ochre ball artillery, before any speech could be heard.' The procession, under the banner 'Coercion is not Government' and supported by suffragette colours, failed to reach the middle of the square because the hostile crowd barred their way. Sylvia Pankhurst, who attempted to speak, was bombarded with 'a volley of balls of red and yellow ochre in light paper wrappers' and her voice was drowned in the singing of patriotic songs.[36]

Figure 21 *Workers' Dreadnought*'s view of conscription

Meetings held by the ILP in Letchworth (21 January), Newcastle (23 January) and at the Friends Meeting House in Bishopsgate (24 January) were routed by 'soldiers and young men', including colonial soldiers, who took over the platform and passed pro-war resolutions. At Blackburn an ILP meeting was cancelled when the hall was banned to them and all other pro-peace groups.

When the police banned the ILP's Easter meeting in Trafalgar Square, the *Daily Express* was jubilant, and attributed the decision to 'the general public outcry against this disgraceful anti-British campaign' – an outcry for which that paper bore a large share of responsibility.

Appeals to victimize the pacifists fell on fertile ground. After two years of war and stalemate the nation was volatile. Many thousands were grieving for the loss of fathers, brothers and sons in a cause which they were not prepared to believe was futile. Men who advocated a compromise peace and who appeared to challenge the validity of their sacrifice provoked a deep hatred. The press added grist to the mill with its claims that the pacifists were betraying the army at the front. A more extraordinary expression appeared in the 'Letter of a "Little Mother" ', published in the *Morning Post*:

To the man who pathetically calls himself a 'common soldier', may I say that we women, who demand to be heard, will tolerate no such cry as 'Peace! Peace!' where there is no peace. The corn that will wave over land watered by the blood of our brave lads shall testify to the future that their blood was not spilt in vain. We need no marble monuments to remind us. We only need that force of character behind all motives to see this monstrous world tragedy brought to a victorious ending. The blood of the dead and dying, the blood of the 'common soldier' from his 'slight wounds' will not cry to us in vain. They have done their share, and we, as women, will do ours without murmuring and without complaint. Send the Pacifists to us and we shall very soon show them, and show the world, that in our homes at least there shall be no 'sitting at home warm and cosy in winter, cool and "comfy" in the summer'. There is only one temperature for the women of the British race and that is white heat. With those who disgrace their sacred trust of motherhood we have nothing in common. Our ears are not deaf to the cry that is ever ascending from the battlefield from men of flesh and blood whose indomitable courage is borne to us, so to speak, on every blast of the wind. We women pass on the human ammunition of 'only sons' to fill up the gaps, so that when the 'common soldier' looks back before going 'over the top' he may see the women of the British race on his heels, reliable, dependent, uncomplaining.[37]

This spine-chilling affirmation of war received wide acclaim, from the *Morning Post* editorial, which described it as 'expressing with rare eloquence and force the feelings with which the British wives and mothers have faced and are facing the supreme sacrifice', and from soldiers in France, and mothers at home, one of whom wrote 'We women desire to fan the flame which she has so superbly kindled in our hearts.' It was reprinted in pamphlet form. 75,000 copies were sold in less than a week.[38] Robert Graves, at home injured, noted it as an example of the mood. 'England was strange to the returned soldier. He could not understand the war-madness that ran about everywhere looking for a pseudo-military outlet.'[39]

Until 1916, the government's attitude to dissent had been calm. During and after 1916, attitudes hardened. The government was faced with the outright revolt of a minority of conscientious objectors who openly flouted the law and disputed publicly, for moral reasons, its continuation. Lloyd George's view of them, especially those whose convictions were political rather than religious, was that 'I shall only consider the best means of making the path of that class a very hard one.' In the same breath he stated 'I do not think they deserve the slightest consideration.'[40] The revolt which was brewing from another quarter was one which demanded the utmost consideration, and one which was to be the deciding factor in pushing the government into taking steps to counteract the pacifist propaganda of all groups for the rest of the war.

This was the threat represented by the influence of pacifist, anti-war and revolutionary propaganda on the one class of the community which was integral to the prosecution of the war: the industrial workers and especially the munitions engineers.

The centre of activity on the industrial front for the first two years of the war was the Clyde, an area where, before the war, the ILP had one of its strongholds and where the socialist economics classes of the school-teacher and leader of the British Socialist Party (BSP), John MacLean, attracted the largest audiences in Europe. On the outbreak of war the political initiative moved away from the ILP to the British Socialist Party and the Socialist Labour Party, whose centre of power was among the shop stewards in the engineering and shipbuilding works of the Clyde. The stand they took on the war was not pacifist. They were socialists and revolutionaries whose policy was based on that section of the Socialist International resolution which was mainly ignored by other groups, namely, 'with all their energies to use the political and economic crisis created by the war to rouse the populace from its slumbers, and to hasten the fall of capitalist domination'.[41]

The Clyde Workers Committee became the centre of shop steward power. Composed of mostly BSP and ILP members, its power grew because the official union leadership had emasculated its effective industrial power by agreeing, as a patriotic gesture at the outbreak of war, to ban strikes and lockouts and suspend trade customs and liberties for the duration to speed munitions production. Changes in production methods, new machines and the introduction of unskilled labour created new problems which had to be dealt with at shop floor level, thus increasing shop steward power. The confrontation with the leadership, which consolidated the power of the unofficial shop stewards, happened in February 1915 over a pay demand for 2d an hour which had been outstanding since June 1914. When the leadership of the Amalgamated Society of Engineers accepted the employers' offer (of $\frac{3}{4}$d), 10,000 engineers struck in favour of the shop stewards' claim. Led by Willie Gallacher of the BSP and James Messer of the ILP, they formed the Central Withdrawal of Labour Committee, which became the CWC, which itself was the spearhead of the later Shop Stewards and Workers Committee Movement. This strike branded the area as 'Red Clydeside' for the rest of the war.

The CWC agitation focused on opposition to the Munitions of War Acts, which were described as 'a method to furnish the employers with a machine which would shatter to its foundations the whole fabric of trade union liberties and customs'.[42] Their particular attack was on dilution – the introduction of unskilled and female labour into skilled grades – and the 'slave' clauses, especially leaving certificates, which bound workers to their employers by restricting the workers' rights of movement between jobs. The CWC would accept dilution only if all munitions industries were nationalized under state control of management and supply of labour. Apart from being general policy, this was seen as the only way to prevent employers exploiting labour in the name of patriotism and benefiting from the abandonment of trades union rights embodied in the Munitions of War Acts and the Treasury Agreements of March 1915.

The CWC's broad aims were 'to formulate a policy that would adequately protect the interests of workers'[43] and 'to organize the workers upon a class basis and maintain the class struggle until the overthrow of the wages system, the freedom of the workers and the

establishment of industrial democracy have been obtained'.[44] Patriotism
was a commodity which the workers of Glasgow could not afford.
Scrawled over a Kitchener recruiting poster in Glasgow was the verse:

Your King and Country Need You
Ye hardy sons of toil
But will your King and Country need you
When they're sharing out the spoil?

Experience in Glasgow suggested otherwise. The CWC opposed conscription because it was thought, with justice, to be a prelude to industrial
conscription, described by Gallacher in the *Worker* – the CWC broadsheet – as 'the loathsome enemy of freedom', against which he advocated
strike action. Gallacher summed up the revolutionary position of the shop
stewards: 'We are accustomed to hear Irish Nationalists declare that
England's adversity is Ireland's opportunity. I say that the adversity of
the capitalist class is the opportunity of the working class. Let us take
advantage of it.'

The dilution issue boiled over in 1915. By late 1915 it had become the
central issue in the government's handling of munitions production, and
on this the government decided to attack the shop stewards' power.
What convinced them of the need for an offensive was the reaction to a
visit to Glasgow by Lloyd George, Minister of Munitions, and the
Labour Party leader Arthur Henderson, who was looking after labour
problems. Both were touring the industrial centres to explain the need
for dilution. On Christmas Day, 1915, an angry crowd, consisting largely
of CWC shop stewards, virtually howled down the leaders. The ILP
paper *Forward*, which published an account of the fiasco, was immediately suppressed, though the CWC broadsheet, the *Worker*, brought out
its first edition in time to duplicate the report. That propaganda broadsheet lasted for only four editions before being prosecuted for an unsigned
article – 'Should the Workers Arm?'. John Muir, the editor, Tom Bell,
the printer, and John MacLean were arrested for sedition on 1 February
1916.

It was the beginning of the government offensive against the CWC. In
January Asquith declared the government's intention to push through
dilution without further delay. Reports from Glasgow suggested that this
could only be done if the leaders could be got rid of. The Ministry of
Munitions was preparing to deal with opposition to dilution, namely 'to
deport and bring to trial under DORA regulations any person inciting to

strike'.[45] They anticipated a strike if dilution was enforced and a strike if the leaders were arrested. They chose one strike instead of two. This happened when attempts were made to restrict the rights of David Kirkwood, an ILP member and a convenor, to negotiate dilution on the shop floor. He was arrested at Parkhead Forge under DORA, and the engineers struck. Gallacher and Muir were arrested on their return from London. The strike collapsed. Kirkwood, McManus and three others were deported to Edinburgh under police supervision. The core of the CWC – MacLean, Gallacher, Muir and Bell and two others – were arrested and imprisoned for sedition and activities likely to impede the production of munitions.

This broke the CWC temporarily, though it did not end industrial discontent. Their propaganda had spread to other industrial areas, where grievances over the Munitions Acts were also causing unrest. During 1916, Workers Committees of unofficial shop stewards were established in Sheffield – where J. T. Murphy was the most active exponent of principles of workers' control of industry – Barrow, and later Woolwich, as a response to conditions of work, the effects of the Munitions Acts, and the abrogation of official trades union power. In some, but not all areas, developments were influenced by political activists. Discontent was increasingly aggravated by a war-weariness influenced by increases in the cost of living, long working hours, government mismanagement of munitions control leading to accusations of profiteering and inequality of sacrifice, and successive comb-outs for the army. By May 1917, conditions were so bad that grievances erupted in nationwide strikes which almost brought munitions production to a complete standstill.

The atmosphere was not helped by the propaganda campaign, led by Lloyd George, against the evil of drink, which became an attack on the working class in general. The campaigners blamed the failures of munitions production on excessive drinking by the working class. 'Drink is doing more damage in the War than all the German submarines put together,' railed Lloyd George,[46] who failed to notice that it was long-term fatigue, due to excessive hours of working in miserable conditions, that diminished production. Mr Edwin Montague criticised the campaigners: 'It is the habit of mind which treats the working man as a machine with no vested interest in his habits and with no right to humane considerations.'[47] The temperance brigade even attempted the insane step of cutting the rum ration to men going 'over the top' at the front, until rumours that this led to excessive violence against officers stopped them. Spirits were diluted, beer was weakened, and opening times were restricted, actions which only contributed to further unrest on the industrial front.

The press led the chorus of denigration of the workers, especially during the events on the Clyde in 1916, which they treated as another manifestation of the influence of pacifism. Under the heading 'TREASON ON THE CLYDE', the *Daily Express* asserted: 'The Clyde rebels are the allies of the contemptible creatures who plead that their consciences are too tender to allow them to fight for their country and their homes. They are part of the rag tag army that, here in Britain, has enlisted under the blood bedraggled banner of the Kaiser . . .' That paper recommended that the government take over control of the industries vital to the war, that martial law be proclaimed, and that workers who refused to do their duty should be treated exactly as soldiers who mutiny. 'We cannot hope to defeat the enemy in the field,' it concluded, 'if the enemy in our gates is allowed to plot against us.'[48]

The fact was that during 1916 the early euphoria about the war was steadily evaporating as its impact on civilian sensibilities began to erode morale. This was the atmosphere that peace groups had been waiting for. They intensified their calls for an early negotiated peace.

Phillip Snowden was convinced that 'on the surface, the uncompromising "fight to the finish" spirit remained, but beneath it was a growing yearning for peace'.[49] It was not manifested in parliament where a debate on peace by negotiation in February 1916 failed to divide the House. Asquith called their voice 'the twittering of sparrows in a thunderstorm'.[50] But it was to the country, not parliament, that the pro-peace groups turned for their support. The UDC were working on draft peace proposals, published in such pamphlets as C. R. Buxton's 'The Terms of Peace' and H. N. Brailsford's 'A Peace by Satisfaction'.[51] Their propaganda was informed by the conviction which deepened as the year, and especially the battle of the Somme (July to November 1916), dragged on, that a military victory was impossible: 'The Germans could not win the war, but neither could the Allies without fighting literally to the last man and shilling.'[52] They believed that a peace 'with honour and success' was possible before the end of the year, because 'what our people fought for – mainly the independence of Belgium, can be secured now'.[53] The fact that the Allies refused to consider an early peace provided, for them, proof that the government wanted to prolong the war for imperialist and annexationist greed, and that the war had become a war of conquest, which could not be stopped because of territorial ambitions, the worst of which they suspected was the acquisition of Constantinople for Allied Russia, a cause which provoked deep hostility.

The situation was indeed becoming serious, when, in Cabinet, Grey, Lansdowne, McKenna and Runciman revealed that the prospects for the military situation and the shipping, food and financial positions were all reaching a crisis point. In America President Wilson, who styled himself a peace-maker, was making representations to all the belligerent powers on the possibility of peace without victory. Aware of this atmosphere, Lloyd George gave his 'Knock Out Blow' interview. It was given to the President of the United Press of America on 28 September 1916, and was designed as a challenge to the defeatist spirit in Britain, and also to make clear to America that Britain was going to 'fight to the finish, to a knock out blow' and that 'Britain was not going to stop the War because of squealing done by Germans and done for Germans . . . Britain could tolerate no outside interference at this stage . . . the enemy was whimpering and whining. With regard to the duration of the war, there is neither clock nor calendar in the British Army.' He argued that the pitilessness of the fighting which must come before a lasting peace is possible was not comparable to the cruelty that would be involved in stopping the war while there remained the possibility of civilization again being menaced from the same quarter. 'Peace now or at any time before the complete elimination of this menace is unthinkable.'[54]

The UDC reacted to this uncompromising 'Never Endian' spirit with a reaffirmation of their 'unshaken conviction that a lasting settlement cannot be secured by a peace based on the right of conquest and followed by a commercial war, but only by a peace which gives just consideration to the claims of nationality and which lays the foundations of a real European partnership'. Their propaganda then focused on the demand that the government 'announce forthwith clearly, and without possibility of misunderstanding, the objects which they desire to attain and thus initiate negotiations for the termination of bloodshed and the establishment of . . . peace'.[55]

But by the end of 1916 and spring of 1917, the cause of peace took an entirely new turn because of events outside Britain. The first of these was the call for peace which came from an entirely new quarter: the Germans, followed by a peace note from President Wilson. The second was the Russian Revolution in March 1917. Both were exploited in pro-peace propaganda.

The German peace note, issued at the end of December, called for negotiations. It was rejected by the Allies as a sham and a war manoeuvre. The Allied Conference condemned it as 'a device to stiffen public opinion among the Central Powers, mislead the Neutral Countries and justify in advance fresh crimes of submarine warfare, deportations and forced enlistment of alien peoples'.[56]

The President's peace note of 29 December called on the belligerents to outline their peace terms, pointing out that all belligerents, from their published statements, appeared to have the same objects. He urged an exchange on an early peace. This overture was likewise rejected by the Allies who did not believe 'that peace can be durable if it be not based on the success of the Allied cause'.[57] On 22 January 1917, in a speech to Congress, Wilson outlined the possible areas for negotiation and offered his services as mediator.

The President's peace note was the event the pro-peace groups had been waiting for. At last the call for peace was no longer the act of a traitor but the view of a responsible and respectable world leader. Wilson became the standard-bearer for their propaganda. C. P. Trevelyan wrote: 'In President Wilson, the moderate world has at last found its spokesman who is heard above the tumult.'[58] Trevelyan described it as 'a great event', which could add weight to agitation for peace. He wrote 'I do not see how the belligerents can with any semblance of reason avoid now stating their terms. In any case *we* are placed in a most powerful position for agitation if they do.'[59] However, the flight from reason was never more clearly demonstrated than in the Allied reply, which prompted the UDC to conclude that 'The war is being continued on the part of Great Britain and her Allies for the purpose of aggression.'[60] Wilson's views, where they coincided with those of the UDC, were disseminated in pamphlets and speeches. Even when America entered the war in April 1917, they continued to quote him on the subject of negotiated peace, despite Wilson's own bellicose statements about 'no peace with the Hohenzollerns'. When he returned to the fold with his Fourteen Points for Peace speech, in January 1918, he was eagerly embraced as the true apostle of peace.

The cause of peace, with its new-found respectability, now gained adherents amongst the Asquith Liberals (who had recently been ousted from leadership by Lloyd George), and in the Liberal press. 1917 was a year of peace moves – from President Wilson, the Pope, the Germans, from (it was rumoured) the Austrians, and above all, from Russia. By the middle of 1917, the *National Daily News* and *Manchester Guardian* both clearly favoured some sort of compromise peace to save civilization from its impending doom. In parliament the small increase in support was measured in the division lobbies. On 19 July the German Reichstag voted a resolution calling for a negotiated peace based on the *status quo ante bellum*. It was passed by 214 votes to 116, a clear indication to the British peace groups that, as Brailsford wrote,[61] 'We can have peace without conquests tomorrow if that is what we want . . .' It was rejected by Lloyd George, Prime Minister at last, as 'all a sham – sham democracy, sham independence for Belgium, a sham peace'.[62] But at the debate, nineteen MPs voted in favour of the Reichstag Resolution – a reduction, nevertheless, on the thirty-two who had voted in favour of the Russian peace terms in March. The German Chancellor Michaelis's speech was described by the *Nation* as 'the speech for which all Europe was waiting'.

The event which had the most significant impact on propaganda for peace was the Russian Revolution in March 1917, followed in November by the Bolshevik Revolution, the Russian withdrawal from the war and the publication of the Secret Treaties, which revealed the Allied territorial ambitions. The March revolution was welcomed by all those people who had for years viewed Tsarist Russia as a sore on the face of Europe, including the Coalition Liberals whose primary aim at that moment was to keep Russia in the war. It inspired the pro-peace groups with new vigour. Phillip Snowden called on the government in the House of Commons 'to issue a similar declaration on behalf of British democracy and to join the Allies in restating Allied terms in conformity with the Russian Declaration': namely repudiating all proposals for militaristic conquest. Thirty-two MPs voted for the resolution.[63]

The Russian Revolution provided the framework for a new definition of peace terms which was eagerly embraced by the pro-peace groups in Britain. A convention was arranged by Lansbury's Herald League and the newly-formed United Socialist Council, an amalgam of the ILP and the BSP under the chairmanship of Phillip Snowden, at Leeds on 3 June 1917. The slogan was 'to follow Russia in her demand for the repudiation of all materialistic war aims and the establishment of peace without annexations or indemnities'.[64] 1,150 delegates attended from trades councils, local Labour Parties, socialist organizations and women's industrial and political groups, chaired by Robert Smillie, the miners' leader, and attended by leaders of the Labour Party. There was almost unanimous support for the four main resolutions: congratulating Russia on the overthrow of Tsarism; calling on the British government to follow Russia and sue for a democratic peace; demanding the establishment of a charter of liberties establishing full political rights for men and women; and calling for the establishment of councils of workers' and soldiers' delegates, on Russian lines, which would protect the interests of dependants and the conditions of workers. The latter proposal came to very little except where the unofficial shop stewards' committees attempted to set up councils.

As a demonstration of opinion in favour of a negotiated peace, it had some success. The government noted it as a sign of increasing discontent. Its most important achievement was the delegation of a committee to draw up a memorandum on war aims which was to be the basis of Labour's terms for peace. A draft memorandum presented to a special Labour Party Conference in August, advocating the basis for a peace with no annexations, no indemnities and national self-determination[65] was accepted, and became the basis for the Labour Memorandum on War Aims presented on 28 December 1917, which was endorsed by the majority of the Labour Party.

The Conference spawned more vigorous activity on the peace front. The Peace Negotiations Committee, set up by the ILP in autumn 1916, which had local committees all over the country and had sponsored at least two memorials calling for peace, stepped up its campaign in local areas. It got 763,000 signatures for a negotiated peace, though some petitioners were arrested under DORA and warned not to continue.[66] A Women's Peace Crusade was launched in Manchester in July by Mrs Pethwick Lawrence, Mrs Ethel Snowden and Mrs Despard among others; they obtained 1,000 resolutions for a negotiated peace, spoke at meetings and distributed pamphlets throughout the country. Mrs Pethwick Lawrence stood at a by-election in Aberdeen as the peace candidate, but got minimal votes and a great deal of abuse during her campaign, which indicated the lack of popular support. The Women's International League, chaired by Helena Swanwick, also actively campaigned for peace, and passed resolutions in favour of equal pay, family allowances and the vote for women.

There were indications that opinion in the Labour movement was being influenced towards some form of compromise peace which helped to push the government towards countering propaganda. In May the new Petrograd Soviet called for a Socialist and Labour Conference, including Germans, to be held in Stockholm to formulate possible terms for peace. After a visit to Petrograd by Arthur Henderson, an emergency Labour Party Conference endorsed British participation by 1,846,000 for to 550,000 against.

It provoked strong reactions, not only from Conservatives – among whom Lord Hugh Cecil claimed 'I would as soon send a child of three up in control of an aeroplane as agree to the Labour Party sending delegates to Stockholm',[67] but also from the right wing of the trades union movement. Havelock Wilson's National Sailor's and Fireman's Union refused to take MacDonald and Jowett to the meeting at Petrograd, or risk the lives of their seamen for men 'whose sole object . . . is to secure a German peace'.[68]

The government wavered about providing passports for Petrograd, as they were anxious not to offend their ally, Russia. But when it came to granting Henderson a passport for Stockholm, matters came to a head. The Cabinet refused his passport and left him 'on the mat' while they discussed the decision. Henderson promptly resigned from the Cabinet and from then on worked on Labour's Memorandum on War Aims and the Labour Party's new constitution. The Labour Conference decision was later reversed and the Stockholm Conference eventually never took place.

On the industrial front, the government was faced with an even more serious threat to the prosecution of the war. In May, smouldering unrest about dilution exploded into nationwide strikes in the engineering industry when the government attempted to extend dilution to private companies and replace the trade card system – whereby members of craft unions were exempted from call-up – with a Schedule of Protected Occupations, which would vastly extend their powers to comb out men for the army. The strikes spread rapidly to all industrial centres, led in some areas by workers committees set up on the CWC model with the help of released CWC members.[69] A raid on the coordinating committee which was meeting to agree on demands to the government only precipitated further strike action.[70] Grievances differed. In some areas it was dilution; in others opposition to the Munitions Acts in conjunction with high prices, excessive demands of work and bad housing in crowded munitions centres.[71]

The government was conciliatory, but it was a signal for action. In June, a series of Commissions of Inquiry into Industrial Unrest was set up in eight areas, chaired by G. N. Barnes, Labour's representative in the Cabinet. They reported in July. The extent of the disturbance convinced

Figure 22 *For Services Rendered*

A German Decoration for British Strikers
Patriotic propaganda against strikers

some Cabinet members and others outside that immediate government action was necessary to counteract pacifist propaganda.

The results of the Commissions showed that the most frequent cause of unrest was high food prices, and the failure of wages to keep pace with the cost of living. This was aggravated by bad housing. Lack of confidence in official trades union leadership and in the government were given as causes of unrest in London and the North West. The government's failure to cope with profiteering had led to resentment about 'inequality of sacrifice' and bitterness over the voluntary abandonment of trades union customs. The government took note of the criticisms but did very little to ease the situation.

Those who believed the root cause of industrial unrest was the propaganda activities of the pacifists were undeterred. The *Morning Post*, for instance, claimed the strikers 'have been grossly deceived by agitators who are without scruple and whose purpose is not to right industrial wrongs but to ruin the national cause'.[72]

Individuals began to pressurize the government. Lord Milner was the most prominent among them. His plan was to exploit the split in the Labour movement by supporting and encouraging patriotic men on its right wing. In 1916 he had already announced to Lady Roberts, wife of the founder of the National Service League: 'I am at present trying very hard but quietly to further a purely working class movement which I hope will knock out the "Independent Labour Party" and start a "Workers League" among Trade Unionists which will make Imperial Unity and Citizen Service "planks" on its platform. This is confidential'.[73]

The body most suited to his purpose was the Socialist National Defence League, set up by Victor Fisher, a one-time Fabian and member of the jingoist section of the Social Democratic Federation, in April 1915 to oppose the ILP and their 'pro-German and premature peace propaganda'.[74] *Labour Leader* believed its members were active in breaking up UDC and ILP meetings. By 1916 it had become the British Workers' League.

It had very little publicity until Milner stepped in. Three weeks after his letter to Lady Roberts, the British Workers' League emerged in a blaze of publicity, especially in *The Times*, whose editor Geoffrey Dawson was a staunch supporter of Milner, as a new campaign 'to amalgamate National Service, Imperialism and a form of socialism, built on the rock of nationalism', which would attract workers, intellectuals and Members of Parliament to its banner. It was described by the *Daily*

Express as 'the new Labour Party' and by itself as the true voice of Labour. Victor Fisher was its secretary and the committee consisted of MPs Charles Duncan, John Hodge, James O'Grady, C. B. Stanton, Stephen Walsh, A. Willies and chairman A. M. Thompson. It was actively supported by leading trades unionists including Will Thorne and the aged Hun-hater Havelock Wilson, of the National Sailor's and Fireman's Union. Their campaign opened with meetings in all the major industrial centres of Britain.

The British Workers' League specialized in alarmist propaganda transmitted to the government via Lord Milner, as an argument for full-scale propaganda against pacifists. During the May strikes Fisher wrote to Milner warning of 'the very big strides forward made by the ILP and the UDC', whose object, he claimed, was to 'evolve a general strike that would end participation in the war', and 'sow discontent among the workmen'.[75] According to Fisher, Morel was the ringleader – 'everybody knows he is a German Agent, he very nearly succeeded at the end of last week in bringing about a complete Labour revolt in this country'.[76] On the basis of this evidence, Milner wrote to Lloyd George: 'I fear the time is very near at hand when we shall have to take some steps to stop the "rot" in this country unless we wish to "follow Russia" into impotence and dissolution.'[77] As a first step he wanted 'systematic work by Labour men . . . to counteract the very systematic and active propaganda of the Pacifists, and to prevent their capturing the Trades Councils and other bodies who profess to represent, though they often misrepresent, the working classes'.[78]

The first manifestation of this was when Havelock Wilson's Sailor's and Fireman's Union stopped MacDonald and Jowett going to Petrograd to discuss the Socialist Conference at Stockholm. On 10 May Victor Fisher wrote to the *Morning Post* expressing 'the fervent hope that our government will refuse passports and safe conduct to those disgruntled elements in French and British political life . . .' When the government granted passports, Havelock Wilson's Union promptly passed a resolution to boycott any boats carrying the pacifists to Stockholm or Petrograd, supported on 7 June by meetings of seamen in Newcastle and Cardiff, and on 8 June by a British Workers' League demonstration in Trafalgar Square. On 11 June MacDonald and Jowett were prevented from sailing to Petrograd. The *Morning Post* 'sympathized' with MacDonald for being 'again a martyr in the cause of democratic control' because 'Labour, which he claims to represent, keeps him a prisoner in this country'. The

Figure 23 *The Real Voice of Labour*

Tommy: 'So you're going to Stockholm to talk to Fritz, are you? Well, I'm going back to France to fight him.'

The principle of 'divide and rule'

Liberal press was appalled. The *Daily News* complained of 'misgovernment at the dictation of mob orators, and there can be no greater menace to the Constitution than mob oratory in wartime'. The government was, however, taking steps to counteract pacifism. After the May strikes, the Ministry of Labour was directed to collate information each week on labour questions and make a special study of all publications and propaganda relating to labour, to 'indicate the direction government propaganda might take'.[79] By June the first moves were made towards establishing a comprehensive organization.

The government set up the National War Aims Committee, chaired by F. E. Guest, to 'undertake an active campaign to counteract the pacifist propaganda, which at present had the field to itself'.[80] By meetings, speeches and literature, it aimed to bring home the object and nature of the war to the industrial centres of Britain and 'to assist the country during the ensuing months of strain to resist insidious influences of an unpatriotic character',[81] and to support the government's prosecution of the war. Sir Edward Carson was given overall responsibility for propaganda, including propaganda to neutral countries, on 21 August 1917. The Prime Minister, Bonar Law, Mr Asquith and G. N. Barnes presided over this all-party committee, and leaders and MPs spoke at meetings throughout the country.

The first official agency for propaganda to the home front had an amateurish air about it. The Committee relied on private contributions and the voluntary assistance of existing unofficial organizations like the Central Committee for National Patriotic Organizations, which organized meetings and rallies and distributed War Aims Committee leaflets. In November 1917, after Carson had presented a persuasive case to the House of Commons that 'the amount of subterranean influence of a pestilential character that has been developed . . . goes far beyond anything that has been described in this House',[82] finance was authorized out of Secret Service funds. Although their estimated expenditure for six months was £119,000, the NWAC actually spent £28,000 between August 1917 and March 1918, and this was heavily augmented by voluntary contributions.[83]

They used various methods to counteract pacifism. Firstly, they collected all information about pacifist groups and, with the cooperation of the Home Office and Scotland Yard, counteracted pacifist and pro-peace meetings. Thomas Cox, secretary to the Committee, requested the Home Office on 15 November 1917 to provide 'particulars of any such meetings in order that we may get our local committee machinery going'.[84] Basil Thomson of Scotland Yard recorded an arrangement with Cox 'to let him have early intimation of any pacifist movement which came to our notice and he will try to arrange outdoor and indoor meetings as a counterblast'.[85] This was done with lectures, meetings, large-scale demonstrations and speeches reiterating the moral basis of the war, the case against Germany and the need to continue fighting. Meetings were especially prevalent in industrial centres.

Secondly, their propaganda attempted to discredit the pacifists by linking them with German funds. Carson was convinced they were supported from Germany. 'The only really efficient system of propaganda at present existing in this country,' he said, 'was that organized by the pacifists who had large sums of money at their disposal and were conducting their propaganda with great vigour.'[86] Ignoring G. H. Roberts, the Minister of Labour's explanation that 'the ILP not only contains wealthy members, but is rapidly becoming a numerically powerful organization, and so acquiring large funds from its membership,'[87] Carson authorized Basil Thomson, Assistant Commissioner of Metropolitan Police and Head of the CID, to make an investigation into their funds. Thomson's personal view was that 'there is no German money, their expenditure being covered by subscriptions they receive from cranks', but he succeeded in producing an exhaustive report with enough innuendo to satisfy alarmists but which, nevertheless, repudiated any connection between Germany and pacifists.

Thirdly, the Home Office toyed with the idea of censoring publications advocating peace. This was rejected, partly because of widespread opposition to such extended powers of arbitrary censorship, which, as Lloyd George said, 'would give rise to difficult questions'[88] and also because in most cases the prosecution case could not stand up while the government failed to clarify its war aims. The publicity attached to a prosecution would also no doubt be exploited for propaganda purposes by the pro-peace groups. The only precaution possible was to insist that all such publications be submitted to the Press Bureau. This resulted in pamphlets displaying the words 'Passed by Censor' which sounded uncomfortably like official approval until they were changed to 'Submitted to Censor'.

On 10 November the Home Office carried out raids on five different organizations and seized literature. The *Evening News*, unconcerned by the niceties of legal procedure, advocated drastic measures. 'Though it

Figure 24 *Birds of Ill Omen*

Mr Punch: 'Only got him in the tail, Sir.'
*The man from Whitehall: 'Yes, but I mean to get the next **one** in the neck.'*

is something to destroy the poison here and there, it is everything to stop its manufacture and dissemination by putting the poisoners under lock and key' (10 November). There had been precedents. In August 1917 E. D. Morel was imprisoned for six months for sending a copy of his pamphlet 'Truth and the War' to novelist Romain Rolland in Switzerland, on a charge which was patently a trumped-up attempt to remove him from public life. In May 1918 Bertrand Russell was sentenced to six months for an article in the *Tribunal* advocating acceptance of the German peace offer, which allegedly damaged recruiting. Other prosecutions had been made under DORA for articles which were an incitement to strike, damaged munitions production, might cause disaffection in His Majesty's Forces or which could be used for enemy propaganda.

By the end of 1917 the spirit of disillusion was spreading beyond the pro-peace groups and the munitions engineers. Pressure was building up on the government from other quarters to produce a statement of war aims which could infuse new vigour into the fight. Men like H. G. Wells argued that it was necessary to state the conditions of peace in general terms. 'To these terms, the general mind of the world has come today. Why then does the waste and killing go on?' He accused statesmen of prolonging the war: 'They chaffer like imbeciles while civilization bleeds to death.'[89] Lord Brassey wrote to the *Economist*: 'Surely we must ask ourselves, is it worth while indefinitely to prolong the awful struggle, with its lamentable sacrifice of life and waste of resources not easily to be replaced.'[90] And Josiah Wedgewood in the *Nation*, which, like most of the Liberal press was editorially calling for a statement of war aims, said: 'Before everything else we should make it clear to our men at the front what we are asking them to fight for . . . Dying because you are told to is a poor job; they might at least have a cause.'[91]

The platitudes of 'A War to End War' and 'To Free the World for Democracy' were wearing thin in parliament no less than in the industrial areas of Britain, where, in the words of Lloyd George, 'the desire for peace was spreading amongst men and women who, although they were convinced of the righteousness of the war, felt that the time had come for putting an end to its horrors in the name of humanity if it could be done on any terms that were honourable and safe . . .'[92] Pacifist propaganda was having its effect which, he wrote, 'operating on a natural war-weariness, might develop into a dangerous anti-war sentiment that would undermine the morale of the nation at a time when the event depended on the staying power of the nations'.[93]

Even more serious, after Passchendaele doubts about the possibility of a decisive military victory, and a deteriorating industrial and military situation led some people close to the Cabinet to conclude that, in Lord Riddell's words to Winston Churchill: 'If the war continues for another twelve months, in attempting to annihilate Germany, we may annihilate ourselves.'[94]

Lord Lansdowne gave public expression to these fears in a letter published in the *Daily Telegraph* on 29 November 1917. He was the elder statesman of the Conservative Party and the architect of the Entente Cordiale. His letter was a bombshell to the 'Never Endians'. He advocated that belligerents should at least examine the possibilities of a negotiated peace and present their war aims in the first instance. The letter duplicated his memorandum to the Cabinet which had been sat on a year earlier, stating that

we are slowly but surely killing off the best of the male population of these islands . . . generations will have to come and go before the country recovers from the loss which it has sustained in human beings and from the financial ruin and the destruction of the means of production which are taking place . . . the responsibility of those who needlessly prolong such a War is not less than those who needlessly provoke it . . .

This statement was greeted by coalition Liberals and Unionists alike with horror. The *Morning Post* called it 'a stab in the back' and accused Lansdowne of uniting various people 'who are working for Germany, in one clamorous cry'. *The Times*, which refused to publish the letter, declared: 'The sooner the lid is clapped on him and his letter, the better', and the *Daily Mail* echoed, 'If Lord Lansdowne raises the white flag he is alone in his surrender.'

The pro-peace groups claimed this new gift to their propaganda, as they had espoused President Wilson's peace moves. Ponsonby wrote: 'When Lord Lansdowne published his celebrated letter, the despised creed of pacifism suddenly came to the front as the rational view of an experienced statesman.' *Labour Leader* hailed it as 'what so many people have been dying to hear from a person whose words could carry weight'. The Liberal press, which was gradually withdrawing support from Lloyd George and all his works, welcomed it as they now welcomed all statements favouring a declaration of war aims and a compromise peace. The *Manchester Guardian* called it 'a striking appeal . . . a wise endeavour', and the *Daily News* declared 'The torch is lighted; it will not be put out.'[95] A Lansdowne Movement was started, embracing people of all political complexions, who spoke at meetings and collected signatures for a petition calling for a statement of war aims with a view to a compromise peace.

In the end it was not so much the pressure of propaganda as the deteriorating domestic, industrial and military situation which prompted a government declaration of war aims. Food shortages were acute by autumn 1917. Prices had risen by 102 per cent since 1914. War-weariness, increasing discontent about industrial conditions, and the conviction that profiteering was rampant combined to produce a food situation described by Clynes, Parliamentary Secretary to the Ministry of Food, as 'such that, had details of it been generally known, riots would certainly have occurred'.[96]

When the government began, under the pressure of military requirement, to prepare a new Military Service Bill which would force new comb-outs of men from industry, the situation became explosive. Lloyd George's war aims speech was designed to head off trades union opposition to the new measures. It was delivered to an audience of trades unionists at Caxton Hall on 5 January 1918, and closely resembled the Labour Party's own Memorandum of War Aims which had been approved by conference three days before. It was a propaganda speech for home consumption and, incidentally, aimed also at the people of Germany and Austria.

Britain, said Lloyd George, was not fighting 'a war of aggression against Germany . . . The destruction or disruption of Germany or the German people has never been a war aim for us . . . We were forced into this war in self defence.' The first requirement for peace was the restoration of the independence of Belgium and reparation for 'devastation to its towns and provinces'. The second was the restoration of all occupied states and the application of the principle of self-determination to nationalities under Turkish and Austrian rule and in German colonies; and, he added, with an eye on Austria, 'The break-up of Austria–Hungary is no part of our war aims.' His principles for peace were: 'First, the sanctity of treaties must be re-established. Secondly, a territorial settlement must be secured based on the right of self-determination and the consent of the governed; and, lastly, we must seek by the creation of some international organization to limit the burden of armaments and diminish the probability of war.'

While temporarily appeasing some sections of the peace movement the effects of this speech were short-lived. The UDC and ILP were far more impressed by President Wilson's Fourteen Points for Peace, enunciated three days later, and continued to press for a statement of democratic aims embodying no annexations nor indemnities and a reform of international relations after the war.

The attempt to pacify labour was even more short-lived. On 14 January 1918, Sir Auckland Geddes, Director of National Service, announced the government's intention to get a further 420,000 men from among those in civil life and 'to make available to military service a very large number of young men now employed in essential industries'.[97] It meant going back on most of the exemption guarantees agreed with the trades unions. Although the official leadership had accepted this at a Manpower Conference in January, the rank and file had not. Lloyd George mounted a campaign to persuade them. On 18 January he addressed a reconvened assembly of the Manpower Conference:

If you are not going to [fight] with all your might, it is real murder of gallant fellows who have [been in the trenches] for three years (cries of hear hear) . . . If there are men who say that they will not go into the trenches then the men in the trenches have the right to say 'Neither will we remain here!' . . . We could not turn Hindenburg out of Belgium with trade union resolutions, but we could with trade union guns and trade unionists behind them . . . Democracy must mean that the people of all classes . . . must merge their privileges and their rights in the common stock . . . My own conviction is this, the people must go on or go under.[98]

Lloyd George's propaganda failed to get through to the shop stewards' movement which, in August 1917, had formed a National Administrative Council and whose power had been recognized in December 1917 under the National Shop Stewards' Agreement. They were implacably opposed to the Manpower Bill, and now spoke with a national voice. They recommended national strike action to prevent the operation of the Bill. Their policy now fused social and revolutionary aims with the call to end the war – a policy echoed in all the major countries of Europe, especially Germany which was on the verge of revolution. The shop stewards were supported by a considerable section of the ASE local committees and by other engineering unions.

Resolutions opposing the government poured in from shop stewards' committees and Workers' Committees, district Amalgamated Society of Engineers committees and from trades committees and trades councils. At a conference on 5–6 January 1918, the National Committee called on shop stewards 'to demand that the government shall at once accept the invitation of the Russian government to consider peace terms'.[99] Not all bodies supported strike action but most supported a negotiated peace. The Clyde District Committee of the Federation of Engineering and Shipbuilding Trades passed a resolution 'That if the government do not withdraw their new Manpower Bill before the end of January, we advise our members to down tools, and, further, that we ask the government to call an international conference to discuss the terms of peace.' The Sheffield Trades Council demanded guarantees that the government would not prolong the war longer than was necessary to obtain a peace on Russian lines.[100]

Solidarity, the mouthpiece of the shop stewards, heralded the movement as 'THE GREAT REVOLT: AWAKENING OF THE ENGINEERS: STRIKE MOVEMENT TO STOP THE WAR', and declared:

The uprising of skilled and unskilled labour in this country is but part of the revolutionary movement of the people all over Europe . . . In England the engineers lead the way, and it will not be long before they are followed by the whole body of organized labour. Perhaps it will be necessary to start this Class war in every belligerent country before we shall be able to stop the other war.[101]

It was not long before the anti-war movement in Germany also erupted in strike action.

On the other side, the National War Aims Committee had been actively spreading propaganda in industrial centres to counter the shop stewards' resolutions. Churchill, Minister of Munitions, directed: 'It should be possible to obtain from the great munitions areas a stream of resolutions in favour of vigorous prosecution of the war. Such resolutions should appear in increasing numbers day by day in the newspapers for at least a fortnight.'[102] The *Herald* noted that there had been an influx into factories and workshops of war aims experts:

Every facility had been given by the profiteers for their employees to attend these meetings inside the bosses' fence – and after the orations have proved that peace and treason are twins, a motion pledging those present to continue their support for the war is moved and carried 'unanimously'. The boss usually presides at these meetings.[103]

The Manpower Act was hustled through Parliament and passed in February. Throughout the country and in America, the propaganda campaign moved into top gear to emphasize that 'Whatever happens, and whatever the cost, be it of blood or treasure, whatever mortgages we draw upon the future vitality of our stock and upon our future resources, this quarrel goes through to the death.'[104]

The shop stewards' militancy dwindled after the passing of the Manpower Act and collapsed after the German offensive began in March 1918. When the nation was faced with the immediate military danger, the voices for peace were drowned by the clamour of the 'Never Endians' who launched a new and loud campaign to keep up morale and put vigour into the nation's fighting spirit. The spirit of 1914 revived in a new bloodthirstiness, not only against Germany but against anyone who was in favour of peace. Press and politicians alike reiterated the crimes of Germany, the moral struggle of 'heaven against hell' and the need to prolong the war to the crushing defeat of Germany. Propaganda had gone full circle.

Hate propaganda poured afresh from the national press and politicians. Northcliffe kept close watch on those in the Cabinet who might be wavering on the question of peace. 'Watch Lansdowne – And Others', was the *Daily Mail* headline on 21 June 1918. He wrote to his editor at *The Times*: 'Lloyd George has been with Haldane recently and also with Sidney Webb. If there is any sign of peace wobbling, please deal with the Prime Minister drastically.'[105] When Northcliffe got word that Milner was the architect of plans for a negotiated peace, he ordered an investigation into his origins to link him with pro-German sentiment.

The majority of the Liberal press favoured compromise, and became the mouthpiece for the dissemination of both President Wilson's and the UDC's aims for a negotiated peace and democratic foreign policy. Pacifist propaganda now found a national amplifier. There was a steady stream of editorials arguing in favour of acceptance of German and Austrian peace moves after the August Allied offensive, and recommending terms for a compromise peace to end the war as soon as possible. But during the final months of war, they were overwhelmed by the renewed voice of hatred which boomed for the final overthrow of Germany. 'There is only one way of making the Huns pay for their outrages and destruction,' declaimed Colonel E. Cassell of the One Flag League – newly formed to offset the propaganda of 'defeatists' – 'and that [is] by disarming them and forcing them to labour under the bayonets of the Allies, and even that would not expiate their infamy.'[106]

Chapter Eight

Peace

But when the election came it woefully cheapened Britain. The Prime Minister and his principal colleagues were astonished and to some extent overborne by the passions they encountered in the constituencies. The brave people whom nothing had daunted had suffered too much. Their unpent feelings were lashed by the popular press into fury. The crippled and mutilated soldiers darkened the streets. The returned prisoners told the hard tale of bonds and privation. Every cottage had its empty chair. Hatred of the beaten foe, thirst for his just punishment, rushed up from the heart of deeply injured millions. Those that had done the least in the conflict were, as might be expected, the foremost in detailing the penalties of the vanquished.

W. S. Churchill, *Aftermath*, pp. 41–2.

Lloyd George need not have descended so low in his electoral appeals in order to get his majority . . . It was due to a great wave of emotion thrown up by the war and was at bottom an expression of pure anti-Germanism inflamed by Lloyd George's appeals.

diary of C. P. Scott,
29 December 1918.

Peace brought the harvest of four and a half years of anti-German propaganda. The currency of wartime propaganda was hatred against the enemy. It had been used to exhort men to recruit, to counteract pacifism, to keep up morale, to justify the war. The images created by propaganda had stamped Germany as a nation of barbarians and savages, and the Kaiser as the Devil Incarnate. Germany was branded with the sole guilt for the war. The legacy of propaganda of hate could not easily be erased when the matter of peace with the beaten foe was anticipated in the Councils of Europe.

Anti-Germanism was the feeling which dominated the election following the peace. Two days after the Armistice, the general election was announced for 14 December 1918. For the first time for eight years the nation was to have its democratic say in the choice of government. During that time the electorate had expanded from eight million to twenty million with the passing of the 1918 Reform Act. An election was essential, the government decided, because it needed a new mandate to carry out the task of reconstruction and to represent the nation at the Peace Conference.

Lloyd George and Bonar Law announced their intention to stand as a Coalition government – to reflect the continuation of the wartime unity into peacetime. 'Opposition,' said Lloyd George, 'is organized fault-finding', which he considered inappropriate to the great tasks which lay ahead in the building of peace, and the establishment of 'a world fit for heroes to live in'. Official Coalition candidates were issued with a 'coupon' which ensured that Unionists did not stand against Liberals in selected seats. 364 Conservatives and only 159 Liberals, the majority of them Lloyd George supporters, got the coupon. The electoral truce looked like continuing into peacetime until the Labour Party voted to resign from the Coalition and stand as an independent party, thus making themselves the chief opposition. 159 Liberals, mainly Lloyd George supporters, and 364 Unionists got the Coalition ticket. Left out in the cold were the great majority of Asquith's Liberal supporters, who had formed the main Opposition in parliament since the accession of Lloyd George in 1916.

Lloyd George's election campaign started off on a platform of reconstruction and social reform at home, and justice and reform of international relations abroad, including the establishment of a League of Nations. The watchword of the government, said Lloyd George, was to be 'progress, wise progress'. Speaking to 150 of his Liberal supporters at 10 Downing Street on 12 November, he sketched out a policy of almost unimpeachable Liberalism. Warning against 'the example which was set in 1815, when advantage was taken of victory to deny reform', he outlined his programme for improvements in health and housing, 'to bring light and beauty into the lives of the people', and improvements in working conditions, including the introduction of a minimum wage and shorter working hours. He included reforms 'in the acquisition and purchase of land to ensure reasonable access' and envisaged the provision of land for soldiers and sailors. The war had exposed the urgent need for improvements in agriculture and transportation, which were essential to increased production. Above all, he said, National Unity was essential to carry out these reforms and to harness the revolutionary spirit which was in the air. 'Revolution I am not afraid of. Bolshevism I am not afraid of. It is reaction I am afraid of. Reaction and disunion.'

The first half of his campaign was dominated by a note of idealism relating almost exclusively to domestic issues and reconstruction. 'Homes fit for heroes to live in', was the slogan for his Wolverhampton speech on 23 November. At the Central Hall, Westminster, he declared his intention 'so to build that when we are forgotten dust ages to come will look at what was done during the last four and a half years, and what will be done in the next four and a half years and say of the men and women of this generation "They builded well" (cheers)'.[1]

His main comment on the nature and conditions of peace was made to his Liberal supporters on 12 November. To them he posed the question: 'Are we to lapse back into the old national rivalries and animosities and competitive armaments, or are we to initiate the reign on earth of the Prince of Peace?' The conditions of peace, he said, must lead to a settlement which will be fundamentally just. He used the settlement by Germany on France in 1871 as an example of a peace which 'outraged all the principles of justice and fair play. Let us be warned by that example.' In view of what happened later, the nature of his warning was most significant:

We must not allow any sense of revenge, any spirit of greed, any grasping desire, to over-ride the fundamental principles of righteousness. Vigorous attempts will be made to hector and bully the government in the endeavour to make them depart from the strict principles of right, and to satisfy some base, sordid, squalid ideas of vengeance and of avarice. We must relentlessly set our faces against that. The mandate at the forthcoming election will mean that the British delegation to the Peace Congress will be in favour of a just peace.[2]

What happened during that historic election was that Lloyd George's vision of a just peace became clouded under pressure from all sides to demand a peace of vengeance. The pressure came mainly through the propaganda activities of the patriotic press, especially the Northcliffe press, and through pressure groups associated with Tory views.

However, the emotions roused by war itself were complex. The desire for revenge against the enemy was strong in a population which had suffered such heavy loss during four and a half years of war. Press propaganda channelled and amplified these emotions into an upsurge of anti-Germanism, which focused on the demand for revenge. In effect, they created new election issues, which were eventually taken up by most of the official candidates, including Coalition Liberals who, though they had formulated the terms of a Liberal election manifesto, were heavily outnumbered by Conservative candidates who generally favoured a stern peace. By the end of the campaign social reform and a 'Just Peace' had been replaced as election issues with the demand to 'Hang the Kaiser' and 'Make Germany Pay'.

The seeds of that deterioration had been sown by propaganda during the whole of the war, and took root in the latter stages of the struggle when victory was just around the corner. There was, in 1918, an intensification of anti-German propaganda, prompted by the fact that the outcome at the time was touch and go. War-weariness had set in badly. The German offensive in March put the whole question of Allied victory in grave doubt. Throughout 1918 the propaganda efforts of politicians, the patriotic press, voluntary patriotic organizations, and the government's agencies – The National War Aims Committee and the Ministry of Information – had been directed towards keeping up morale, strengthening the nation's will to fight the war to the bitter end, and warding off all talk of a premature peace. The methods were simple. In calling for renewed sacrifice their propaganda took on an apocalyptic tone.

New and fantastic justifications for the war were fabricated to prove the necessity of a final crushing victory. The conflict was freely described as a battle of 'heaven against hell', a 'Holy War – a War of Right against Wrong',[3] of the forces of God against the forces of the Devil. Allied victory was portrayed as a species of divine salvation – and an opportunity 'to vindicate the laws of right and wrong by exacting full and adequate punishment for this defilement of human nature'.[4] 'The War is now a crusade,' wrote Lord Hugh Cecil; the Allies were no longer fighting to save Belgium and France, but to save civilization. 'We fight to overthrow a principle, to stamp out a moral disease, to extirpate an abomination . . . The War is no longer one between two groups of nations. It is the civilized world fighting to chastise rebels against fundamental laws . . . The War must be fought till it ends in the submission of Germany.'[5]

The resolution to fight to the end defined a particular attitude which the patriotic press put forward even when victory was in sight. Blinkered by the habits of the previous two years in counteracting pacifism, when peace negotiations were afoot, they occupied their columns with sniffing out traps. Those who demanded the final submission of Germany warned against the revival of peace hopes. Undue optimism about Allied success at the front was described as 'a danger to sustained war effort'.[6] The Austro–Hungarian proposals in September were greeted as 'An Impudent Sham' by the *Daily Mail* and Northcliffe's *Evening News* claimed 'Austrian Peace Trap a Dismal Failure'.[7] In the correspondence columns of *The Times*, they were described as: '. . . insidious German attempts to hearten the so-called "moderate" people who seem to think it would be safer to finish the war without winning it'.

The German peace note in October, which heralded a genuine suing for peace, was designated by *The Times*'s editorial as 'intended to avert . . . what [the Allies] are determined to secure', namely, a crushing victory. Lord Westbury declared in *The Times*: 'The Allies will not negotiate the peace terms. They will dictate them', and Professor Spencer Wilkinson, in another letter, added his name to those who thought that 'We have not sent our sons to die for the sake of a peace acceptable to Germany. Their blood calls for complete victory and an unconditional surrender.'[8]

Northcliffe vehemently attacked waverers, especially in the government: those of Lloyd George's 'satellites who have frigid feet'.[9] For instance Milner, who believed 'the demands of the English press (led by Northcliffe) for a humiliating peace with Germany were against the best interests of the British Empire',[10] was accused by Northcliffe in a note to the *Daily Mail* of 'losing his grip'.[11] Northcliffe's propaganda therefore concentrated on denigrating peace negotiations and reviving the crimes of Germany. He congratulated the *Daily Mail* for reprinting the *Lusitania* picture: 'I am glad to see it,' he wrote. 'It is a sufficient answer to Lord Milner, Lord Lansdowne and company and their "be kind to Germany".'[12] *The Times* declared its intention to remind people of the crimes of Germany 'lest there should be any weakening of moral fibre under the influence of good news from the front'.

The message of the Tory press and of Northcliffe's newspapers was that nothing less than the unconditional surrender of Germany was a suitable finish to the war. Negotiations were out of the question. Thus the *Evening Standard* warned in its editorial:

We are dealing with an enemy to whom generosity in adversity signifies a foolish weakness . . . We are fighting a foul and worse than bestial thing on which kindness and chivalry are worse than thrown away. However long Germany is able to hold out, we must fight on until she is beaten to the knees and the world is made a safe place for free men.[13]

The scurrilous *John Bull* expressed it more graphically. Its call for revenge reached the expected crescendo in Bottomley's declared cam-

7

paign to wipe Germany off the map of Europe. 'Destroy the Blond Beast' was his chosen slogan. 'Beware of the men in black coats who will let the blond brute of Middle Europe loose upon the world once more, to procreate their lustful and bloody greed and pollute the human race with their lewd, coarse and savage strain. The people's mandate is – Destroy the Blond Beast.' By way of punishment they demanded that the Kaiser be handed over, that the German people should be 'sentenced to redeem by the sweat of their toil . . . the precious treasure we poured out in this struggle for Freedom and Right', and that 'their War Lords must pay with their heads for the blood we have lost'. He listed twenty 'Huns to be Hanged', starting with Hindenburg.[14]

The demand for unconditional surrender in the press found its echo in an undercurrent of public opinion which was already in favour of vengeance. The *Nation* noted 'unshaken hatred, anger, just and unjust, the promptings of mean spirits and impulses of generous ones, all will [Germany's] destruction and would drive us to accomplish it'. The writer feared that at this critical time desire for revenge would 'corrode the peace and prolong the war'.[15] A letter published in the *Morning Post* indicates the mood at the time:

If the criminal people of Germany, after having in wanton aggression bathed mankind in blood and broken all laws human and divine, were permitted to escape penalty, then the nations leagued in defence of right would be betrayers of that right and they would brand themselves in ineffaceable shame . . . Clear and short is the answer to be given. 'Your crimes stink before Heaven. Man's justice demands your punishment . . . to negotiate with you would be pollution. Our only terms are your unconditional surrender. Until then, we fight on.'[16]

In *The Times* a correspondent wrote: 'Why all this slop about the German people? They should be arraigned as they have "bled us white".'

On 2 November a large meeting at the Albert Hall passed a resolution 'that there shall be no peace negotiations with either the Kaiser or his present government, and that the unconditional surrender of the enemy should be the first condition of any peace discussion'. All the prominent right-wing agitators were there, including Horatio Bottomley, Lord Charles Beresford, the 'bent and crippled' Havelock Wilson, Mrs Dacre Fox, Arnold White of the *Daily Express*, Ben Tillett and Marshall Hall. It was an early indication that such seasoned campaigners were unlikely to keep silence on the matter of peace.

Such demonstrations led 'Wayfarer' (H. W. Massingham) in the *Nation* to plead:

Would that this tragedy of a people and a civilization had found magnanimity in its avengers! The peace spells at least temporary ruin for Germany. If its terms are not abated the disaster may extend from this generation to the next and the impoverishment of the most industrious of the European people pass, like blight in an orchard, from one industrial group to another till it involves them all.[17]

Liberal supporters of both Asquith and Lloyd George favoured some sort of retribution from Germany, and most favoured justice against war criminals. No Liberal paper indulged in the excesses of the Tory and Northcliffe press, but expressed more concern for securing peace and finding means of preventing future wars.

Whether it was to be a peace of justice or a peace of vengeance wrought by a nation which had been fed on a diet of hysterical anti-Germanism was to be the key issue of the 1918 election.

The election platform of the Coalition was for a stern and just peace. But before the ink had dried on the Armistice, the cry went up for revenge. It was sections of the press which led the call. When it appeared that the public was responding to this call, they were followed rapidly by a number of candidates who came out with statements described later by Arnold Bennett as 'appealing chiefly to . . . the baseness and fury which lies always with us waiting to be stirred . . . They are competing with each other in a deliberate attempt to arouse in the average man the emotions of a frenzied brute.'[18] Though the brutalizing effects of war itself may well have already aroused these emotions, the election propaganda carried out in, initially, the press, deliberately heightened and exploited them. The press provided the spark which ignited a volatile mood, and transformed the possibility of justice into the certainty of crippling revenge.

As the election campaign progressed, it deliberately focused the attention of electorate and candidates on to two main issues: the treatment of the Kaiser, who had been made the scapegoat of the war, and the treatment of Germany, the guilty nation. In the general atmosphere of renewed Hun-hating, 'our Huns' – enemy aliens – also attracted the attention of those campaigners who bracketed them with the evil German race.

The call for the extradition and trial of the Kaiser appeared first in the pages of the Tory press and in Northcliffe's papers. The demand to 'mete

out heavy punishment against the Kaiser' was expressed first in Conservative circles, notably by Lord Curzon. Two days after the Armistice,
in a letter to Lloyd George, he justified stern punishment with the
argument:

Public opinion will not willingly consent to let this arch criminal
escape by a final act of cowardice. The supreme and colossal nature of the
crime seems to call for some supreme and unprecedented condemnation.
Execution, imprisonment, these are not, or may not be, necessary. But
continued life, an inglorious and ignoble exile under the weight of such a
sentence as has never before been given in the history of mankind, would
be a penance worse than death.[19]

Very soon this was translated into the demand to 'Hang the Kaiser'.
The *Daily Express*, in typically alarmist language, demanded tough terms
for the Kaiser. 'Hand Him Over!' was the headline on the day after the
Armistice, 'The Kaiser and his tribe must be brought to judgement and
at least held in safe keeping lest the world perish.' It substantiated this
spurious claim with ominous predictions of events in Germany: 'Abdica-
tion that Might be a Threatened Sham' and 'Possibility of Great German
Plans to Trick the Allies. Seize the Kaiser' were the headlines within a
week.[20] Under the headline 'Menace of Europe', they argued that 'while
the ex-Kaiser is free to come and go, [peace] is impossible. He cannot
be permitted any further political activity. His very existence is a
menace.'[21]

John Bull was equally vociferous in demanding that Germany pay for
the war. It deplored the Allies' failure to claim the prize of unconditional
surrender, by calling the settlement 'A Sham Armistice'. 'The government,' railed Horatio Bottomley, 'is preparing us for a weak Peace Treaty
in which, for example, neither indemnity nor the surrender of the Kaiser
will be found . . . The main thing to insist upon is that Germany must not
only restore the damage done – she must foot the whole bill of the war.'
He based his campaign around the demand that 'in the re-making of
Britain, and the strengthening of the Empire, Germany is made to pay;
that none of her bestial blood shall be given place or privilege among us;
that such weapons of trade and commerce as we can forge shall be used
against her.'[22]

The Northcliffe press became more vehement. Throughout the
election campaign Northcliffe used his newspapers in a concerted
attempt to steer the election towards what he thought were the main
issues, particularly by chivvying candidates and leaders, and encouraging

Figure 25 *Passing the Doctor*

Election slogans, *Evening News*, 1918

the electorate to demand of them more definite answers on the issues of the Kaiser, reparations and enemy aliens.

Northcliffe believed that the only way to prevent the rise of Germany was for the Allies to impose tough terms at the Peace Conference. He was also suspicious of Lloyd George, with whom his relationship was rapidly deteriorating, and equally suspicious of Conservative intentions, particularly those of Sir George Younger, Chairman of the party, whom he called 'the great wire-puller'. He feared that 'Liberal sentimentality' would lose the peace, but he was equally concerned that the machinations of Younger, who 'makes no pretence of dealing with any other task than that of running a party of wealth' would impose on Lloyd George reactionary ministers who would block reconstruction – which Northcliffe supported – and prevent him carrying out 'such reforms as will prevent revolution'. 'The dead weight of the preponderance of reactionary Coalitionists', he wrote to Dawson, editor of *The Times*, 'will impose on the Prime Minister Old Gangers who have shown themselves in the last few years to be without prevision.'[23] He deplored the Coalition's failure to placate the Labour Party, and devoted a daily column in the *Daily Mail* to their election campaign.

His main concern boiled down to the nature of the peace, however. His own attitude to Lloyd George chimed with that of Marlowe, his *Daily Mail* editor, who wrote, 'Lloyd George is acting on the belief that Englishmen like to shake hands after a fight. So they do – but not this time.'[24] Northcliffe's mistrust of Lloyd George increased as the campaign progressed; he accused him persistently of 'evading main issues'.[25]

Northcliffe's attitude to what he saw as the 'main issue' of the Kaiser was made plain in the *Daily Mail* of 13 November. To the question 'What to do with him?' the answer rang loud and clear – 'HANG HIM!' Three days later, the leader asked: 'Is the Kaiser to escape?', and continued, 'Is the Kaiser to be handed over now, later – or never? His internment is an utter farce . . . Plain justice demands that the man who is accused as the arch criminal of the War shall be surrendered and put on his trial – a full and fair trial – without further ado.'[26] The *Daily Mail*'s line on reparation was made clear on 13 November: 'THE HUNS MUST PAY'. Later it developed into the demand that Germany pay for the whole cost of the war.

The *Daily Mail* was prominent also in using the election to further a renewed campaign against enemy aliens. Lord Charles Beresford, in the House of Lords, revived the subject by deploring the government's silence on the issue. He said:

The nation is clearly determined to have done with the Hun and his descendants for many a generation, and it is not disposed to regard the matter as one which a glorious victory in the field renders unimportant. No victory won by blood and bravery abroad will be complete until it has been confirmed by drastic alien legislation at home.

The *Daily Mail* capped the report of his speech 'WHAT ABOUT OUR

HUNS? ARE THEY TO RUN LOOSE AGAIN?' These were trailers to a campaign which hotted up in the last two weeks of November, and which included the continuing denigration of the German race. For instance, a daily column written by Henry de Halsalle (author of *Degenerate Germany* etc.) expounded on 'Criminal Germany' with such titbits of Victorian melodrama as 'lust murder – a Teutonic species of crime' and 'girl-stabbing', an example of Teutonic blood-lust, as elaborate illustrations of the essentially criminal nature of the German race.

On 21 November, the *Daily Mail* started the first of its 'Tests for Candidates'. These not only gave great prominence to those questions which the *Daily Mail* – and Northcliffe – thought were the main issues, but also encouraged the electorate, a considerable proportion of whom were voting for the first time, to act on their guidelines. The first took the form of a letter from Viscount Templeton, who commented on the hundreds of letters received by the *Daily Mail*, asking: What can be done about our Huns? 'The *Daily Mail* gives the answer,' he said. 'Refuse to vote for any Member of Parliament who will not give a definite pledge that he will stand for the total eradication of German influence from our country.' He called for meetings up and down the country to pass resolutions 'that England shall be freed once and for all from all Germans and German influence', and advised that voters should send postcards to their prospective candidates asking 'Will you pledge yourself to work for the radical cleansing of the United Kingdom from Germans and German influence?' and then vote according to the reply.

When Lloyd George, in answer to an interruption, designated the problem as a 'side issue' (Wolverhampton, 23 November) it prompted almost a week of letters in the *Daily Mail* published under the heading 'Mr Lloyd George and Our Huns'. 'It is a matter more discussed than any other at the present moment,' protested the author of the interruption. 'Is [the Prime Minister] prepared to support a measure that will clear out and keep out the damnable, dirty, contemptible and despicable Hun?' Another correspondent wrote 'If every Hun is not bundled out and kept out, we have lost the war' (26 November), and Mr R. R. Neeld contributed the observation that 'No Hun ought to be allowed to trade or work in Britain, taking the bread out of the mouths of our countrymen ... Let Britain be in the future for Britons and not the dumping ground for traitors and spies.'[27]

The press campaign was backed up by the British Empire Union. A demonstration in Hyde Park on 24 November attracted reported crowds of 10,000. Resolutions from three platforms were passed stating that 'so loathed are the Germans for their foul acts that all present would boycott them socially and economically as long as they live'. Messages of support were sent from Arnold White, Ben Tillett of the British Workers' League, Will Crooks, M.P., and Captain Charles Craig.[28] Prebendary Gough, a man of God, hoped 'the Kaiser would be hanged – as he ought to be'. Mr Perkins Bull, K.C. expressed his demented hope that 'at Christmas nobody would allow children to touch toys that could be suspected of having been tainted by German hands', an observation matched only by *John Bull*'s apoplectic rage at a local education authority's decision to teach German in its schools. 'The vilest of all tongues for a girl to understand is assuredly that of the Hun – a tongue so vile, indeed so infamous, in its degradation of heart and mind that it is amazing to us any mother should wish her daughter to learn it . . .'[29]

The British Empire Union put a number of candidates into the field to propagate their views, though none were elected. Mrs Dacre Fox, the leading light in anti-alien agitation, contested Richmond on the sole issue of whether the country was to be rid of Germans. Mrs Hope of Luffness received favourable mention in the Tory Press for standing against 'Wait and See' Asquith in East Fife on the platform 'Britain for the British'. Her programme called for 'the body of the Kaiser to be tried by a just jury over here; the repatriation of all Germans, naturalized or not; jobs for all our British disabled soldiers and sailors before a single job is given to a foreigner'.[30]

Those interested in propagating anti-Germanism were helped by the publication of a government report on the treatment of British prisoners, which confirmed rumours that had been circulating in the press for some time. It was compiled under the chairmanship of Robert Younger, brother of Sir George Younger, chairman of the Conservative Party, who was at the time carrying most of the credit for the astute organization of the election in favour of his party. It was published at exactly the right time to have maximum impact on public opinion. The details of prisoners left without food, being released to walk to the border, and sickness and death in prison camps, were sufficiently appalling to prompt an official government protest to the German government. A flood of anger and indignation against German barbarism swelled in the columns of the press, providing further argument for tough terms against Germany.

Up till the last week of November ministers had been hesitant to declare themselves outright on either the treatment of the Kaiser or the

German indemnity. As Churchill noted, recognition that such a burden as the whole cost of the war would not only cripple Germany but would prevent payment, and might also damage the recipients, had governed comment on the indemnity issue; considerations of whether an indictment against the Kaiser could be upheld had determined circumspection in comments on his treatment.

But there was increasing evidence that the press campaign was finding a responsive echo in the electorate. Candidates began to trim their statements to chime with what appeared to be emerging as the dominant public mood.

Winston Churchill, in retrospect, described how he himself gave in to this apparent pressure. In his own constituency, Dundee, he was, he maintained, faced with 'an earnest and deep seated demand from all classes and parties . . . that the Kaiser should be hanged'. Under this pressure, he confesses: 'I was constrained to support his being brought to trial.'[31] On reparations, 'the crux of the election', he recorded similar pressure. The evidence of police reports indicated that 'even those who, a few weeks ago, were agitating for peace now say "the Germans should pay every penny of the damage, even if it takes them a thousand years"'. The practical argument that it would cripple Germany and ultimately the recipients was, he said, in the atmosphere of the time, 'unseasonal' and 'their mere statement would expose the speaker to accusations of being pro-German'. Everyone was 'unconsciously or wilfully blind to the stubborn facts'.[32]

In his Dundee speech of 26 November, he stated:

Practically the whole nation was guilty of the crime of aggressive war conducted by brutal and bestial means. It is no use pretending the late government is solely to blame. They were all in it, and they must all suffer for it. Reparations must be made for the damage she has done. I cordially sympathize with those who say 'Make them pay the expense of the war'. If the Allies have not claimed this it is for one reason only. It is not physically possible to do so.

Later he succumbed to what he called 'the blatancies of electioneering': 'We will make them pay an indemnity (cheers). We will make them pay a large indemnity (cheers). They extracted from France a large indemnity in 1871. We will make them pay ten times as much (prolonged cheers).'[33] It was an astute example of manipulation. He had made a calculation that the sum mentioned approximated to what Germany could be expected to

7*

pay, but the impression he gave satisfied the audience of the enormity of the cost, and of the resoluteness of the speaker.[34]

Other accounts pointed to a changing popular mood. *The Times* election reports noted that new issues were

gradually emerging from the apparent confusion of the moment and by no means all are concerned with the problem of reconstruction. The nature of the peace which is about to be made is a very burning question to the great mass of men and women in this country and candidates are finding it necessary to give more and more attention to it. The test for the simple elector is simply the position of the Kaiser.[35]

The *Glasgow Herald*, a Rothermere paper, reported that the clearest feature of the election was the 'almost universal support for . . . "relentlessly just" peace terms'.

Some candidates concluded that no candidate had the least chance of being elected if he showed any weakness on the main issues of the election, and those who failed to clarify their attitude were heckled. J. W. Grieg, Coalition Liberal candidate, commented after campaigning in working class districts that 'The meeting would hardly listen to me because I was not strong enough at the early meetings on the question of indemnity and reparation.' He, Addison, former Minister of Reconstruc- tion, and Fisher, all reported after meetings in major industrial centres that interest was almost exclusively on 'the expulsion of all the Germans in the district' and 'the trial and execution of the Kaiser'.[36]

The anti-Germanism which was sweeping the election campaign as effectively as the influenza rapidly infected ministers. Candidates' statements became wilder and more irresponsible. With all the authority of the Attorney General, F. E. Smith stated on 29 November that 'The German criminals will be punished . . . So far as our power enables us we will insist on the personal accountability of the Kaiser (cheers) for the crimes for which he is personally and chiefly responsible.'[37] Who could doubt his word? Next day, G. N. Barnes, whose connection with the Labour Party was now severed, stated: 'The Kaiser has been mentioned . . . I am for hanging the Kaiser . . . I say it would be a monstrous thing if the greatest culprit of murder in history escaped the great penalty of his crimes.'[38]

Lloyd George's position appeared, by contrast, equivocal. He had, up till then, retained his qualifying statements on what had become the two great issues of the election, and had attempted to keep reconstruction in the foreground. However, he was leading a Coalition composed of Conservatives, some of whose die-hard attitudes were increasingly being expressed publicly, and Liberals, whose plan for reconstruction and social reform had formed the basis of the initial election manifesto, agreed in Downing Street on 12 November. The Liberal Party itself was divided between the Lloyd George coalitionists on the one hand, and the Asquith supporters on the other, who now firmly believed that Lloyd George was officiating at the grave of Liberalism, and could see no hope for Liberal principles in a coalition with what seemed to be the overwhelming weight of reactionary conservatism. They were constantly sniping at Lloyd George for his conduct of the campaign.

The most crucial political factor was that, under the Coalition arrangement, the Conservatives had the overwhelming advantage. They had more official candidates in the field. They also found that, for the first time since 1905, public opinion was moving quite definitely in their favour. Part of the reason for this was that their commitment to a just and very stern peace was popular. Lloyd George was in the position of having to retain as many of his Liberal supporters as possible – which led him to make open accusations of treachery against the Asquith sections of the party during the election campaign – as well as keeping up with his Tory coalitionists.

Meanwhile, he was accused in the press persistently of lagging behind public opinion and was twice shouted down at public meetings for not giving definite answers about the treatment of Germany and the Kaiser. On 29 November he succumbed to the pressure from his Tory colleagues and from the press, though he still managed to retain some of his qualifying statements. At Newcastle, he succeeded in reversing his previous statement on reparations. The peace of 1871 was taken, not, as previously, as an example to avoid, but as one to follow. 'When Germany defeated France,' he said, 'she made France pay. That is the principle which she herself established. There is absolutely no doubt about the principle, and that is the principle we should proceed upon – that Germany must pay the cost of the war up to the limit of her capacity to do so.' His comments on the Kaiser were equally inflammatory. 'Someone has been responsible for this war that has taken the lives of millions of the best men in Europe. Is no one to be made responsible for that?' He reported that the Attorney General and some of the best jurists in the country had concluded after careful investigation that the Kaiser was guilty of an indictable offence and ought to be held responsible. On aliens, he used language

which the British Empire Union could have applauded. 'These people . . .
abused hospitality to betray the land that received them; . . . to plot
against its security, to spy on it, and to supply information and weapons
to enable the Prussian War Lords to inflict . . . damage and injury on the
land which had received them. Never again!'[39]

Even this volte-face did not satisfy the patriots thirsting for the head of the
Kaiser and the life blood of Germany. The *Daily Mail* kept up the pressure.
It received the speech with a leader headed 'Wobbling', and accused:

On the only questions the electors were asking, he is still vague . . .
Is Germany to pay up?
Are all the Huns to be sent out and kept out?
Is the Kaiser to be surrendered?
On all these points there must be no shadow of an excuse for the suspicion
that the government has cause for tenderness to the Hun.[40]

It published a running list of candidates who had given definite replies.

What was being demanded was the simplifications which are the stock-
in-trade of propaganda. When the world was on the brink of one of the
most complicated reorganizations in history, the election was reducing
politics to a series of simple slogans. Arnold Bennett, writing in the *Daily
News*, paused for thought on the tide of hysterical anti-Germanism which
was about to be enshrined in the terms of peace. He questioned whether
it was a passion for 'justice and retribution' or 'very different passions for
revenge and vindictiveness' which now inspired the election. The Kaiser,
he believed, must be brought to trial, but the statesmen 'must act like
great men and not like hounds after quarry'.[41]

Northcliffe, the leading hound, kept up the pressure on the candidates,
the leaders, and the electorate. In reply to those who claimed that
Germany could not pay the whole cost of the war, the *Daily Mail* raised
the spectre of discredited 'international financiers', who, friends of
Lloyd George according to its editor, Marlowe, were exploiting 'British
sportsmanship', that is, British sense of fair play and justice. Marlowe
wrote to Northcliffe: 'I hope you will ram this "stunt" down [Lloyd
George's] throat.'[42] Northcliffe firmly believed that the British people
would be 'cheated'.[43] Thus the *Daily Mail*'s reply to the argument that
Germany could not pay was that

the theory emanates from a small financial group in the City of London
with tentacles in Manchester, Glasgow and other centres, with one
tentacle reaching to Berlin via Holland.

The people should realize that if the Germans are not made to pay, then the employers and workers of this country will be put under bondage for a century in order that we may become debt free.[44]

Next day, the government, on the basis of the Law Officers' reports, endorsed the extradition and trial of the Kaiser. Meanwhile in France Madame Prieur, the widow of a Paris tradesman, started proceedings in the name of herself and her four children against the Kaiser, on the charge of murder.

Investigations were started into the indemnity question. A Cabinet Committee, chaired by the Hun-hating Prime Minister of Australia, Billy Hughes, the Treasury, and the Board of Trade each set about separately calculating the sum to be paid by Germany. Figures ranged from £24,000 million from Hughes (Lloyd George called this 'a wild and fantastic chimera'[45]) to £2,000 million from the Treasury, backed by J. M. Keynes. On 30 November Lloyd George told Lord Riddell privately 'of course the Germans must pay to the uttermost farthing . . . the question is how they can be made to pay beyond a certain point'. Publicly, businessman Sir Eric Geddes made the graphic and memorable declaration: 'We must squeeze the German lemon till the pips squeak.'

Even these government concessions did not deter Northcliffe. When Lloyd George was about to speak at Leeds, Northcliffe sent a personal telegram warning him that the public (for whom Northcliffe now felt qualified to speak) were dissatisfied with the phrase 'limit of her capacity', which they said could mean anything or nothing, and were expecting him to give a definite account of cash reparations to Germany. Northcliffe feared serious trouble in the country on that score. Lloyd George scolded him: 'Don't be always making mischief.'[46]

Northcliffe's 'mischief' was, however, bearing fruit. By 11 December the caution and qualifications which had restrained principal speakers was thrown to the wind. Germany, said Lloyd George, at Bristol, must pay to the last penny 'and we shall search their pockets for it'. The Allies had 'an absolute right to demand the whole cost of the war from Germany, and we propose to demand it'.[47] 'Hang the Kaiser' and 'Make Germany Pay' had become the official slogans of the Coalition campaign. It was the final triumph of the propaganda of hate.

Sections of the press had been viewing the election with increasing alarm, particularly the Liberal press which watched Liberalism and justice drown in the sink of reaction and prejudice. The *Manchester Guardian* summed it up in an editorial headed 'Vulgarizing the Issue'

three days before polling. 'Thus are the nations to be regenerated . . .
thus are the spirits to be uplifted to a high destiny . . . we venture to say
that in no election within living memory have the issues . . . been so
paltry or the mode of their presentation been so reckless and vulgar.'
C. P. Scott, the editor, had written to J. L. Hammond: 'George, who at
the start meant very well, (he spoke to me of his determination to stand
for a just peace with obvious sincerity) has gone downhill under stress of
the election.'[48] John Dillon, the Irish Nationalist leader, wrote to Scott in
blunter terms: 'Do you remember anything more contemptible in your
life experience of public affairs than George's recent election speeches?
He has got pretty near the level of [Horatio] Bottomley . . .'[49]

The result of the election was an overwhelming mandate for the
Coalition government and 'the Man who had won the War'. 339 Coalition
Unionists and 136 Coalition Liberals were returned, giving the Conservatives the first majority since 1905 – a majority which would probably
have been greater had it not been for the coupon arrangement. The
Labour Party increased its representation to 59 seats, almost all of whom
were trades union candidates. The triumph of nationalism in the election
campaign resulted in the complete elimination of all candidates branded
as pacifists. Henderson, MacDonald, Snowden, and Jowett all failed to
be returned. More astounding, though the coupon arrangement helped to
ensure the result, was the shattering defeat of the Asquith Liberals.
Their party was reduced to a representation of thirty-three members.
Almost every office holder in the last Liberal administration was defeated,
including Asquith, McKenna, Runciman, Simon, Samuel, McKinnon
Wood and J. J. Tennant. Some of them actually lost their deposits.
McKenna wrote to Gardiner of the *Daily News*: 'Anti-Germanism and
the desire for revenge were strong amongst large masses of people . . . the
Liberals are not thought as a party to be sufficiently venomous.'[50] The
split in the Liberal ranks later broke the Liberal Party. The Labour
Party benefited from the steady defection of Liberals, including wartime
radicals, nonconformists and leading politicians like Haldane, who found
their sympathies lay with the maligned wartime pacifists and pro-peace
groups who now led the new Labour Party.

With the election won, the new government, tied by its pledges, had to
turn to the wider sphere of peace-making. The mandate was for a peace of
vengeance. Churchill commented of Lloyd George's position: 'He
reached the Conference somewhat dishevelled by the vulgarities and
blatancies of the recent General Election. Pinned to his coat tails were the

posters "Hang the Kaiser", "Search Their Pockets" and "Make Them Pay"; and this detracted from the dignity of his entrance upon the scene.'[51]

The complex issues of the Peace Conference did not deter Northcliffe's press from harping continually on the pledges made at the election. He was convinced that the British delegation was becoming 'soft on Germany', particularly in modifying its claims against her. He subscribed to the belief that indemnities were the only way of preventing a resurgence of a powerful Germany – and of securing the peace for the Allies. It was a mistake of historic magnitude which left its legacy on the next generation. Between 7 April and 30 June 1919, on his instructions, the slogan 'Those Junkers will Cheat You Yet' appeared regularly in the *Daily Mail*. In another black box was printed 'Lest We Forget – Killed 670,986. Wounded 1,041,000. Missing 350,243.' He was constantly nudging the editor of *The Times*: 'Anxious about reparations', he telegraphed to Dawson, 'Unless strongest pressure be placed upon George burden of war expenses will be transferred from German to backs of British workers and businessmen . . . Insist that he carries out his promises.'[52] To his brother, Rothermere, he wrote, 'The Germans are cheating' and, later, 'I personally have no intention of spending the rest of my life swotting to pay excess profits tax and supertax for the benefit of Germany, if I can help it. I do not believe the tales of German hardupness. I know that if we let her, she will dodge and cheat.'[53] His views were expressed by his newspapers. In April he warned against surrender, declaiming: 'It is not our business to ask what Germany will think of the terms. Our duty is to dictate such terms as shall give a material guarantee for security, and let the Hun think what he likes about them.' Kennedy Jones, prompted by Northcliffe, his former employer, was the author of a telegram from 370 mainly Tory MPs on 8 April to Lloyd George in Paris demanding reassurance that he stick to his election pledges. Lloyd George reaffirmed this intention. When he returned to the House of Commons he mounted a full-scale attack on Northcliffe's 'diseased vanity' and his 'ridiculous expectations' and accused him of 'the crime of sowing dissension between great lands'. He revived his pledge of the earlier part of the election, to work for a peace 'not to gratify Vengeance but to vindicate Justice',[54] and evoked the supreme duty of statesmen, parliaments, and those who guide public opinions 'not to soil this triumph of right by indulging in the angry passions of the moment, but to consecrate the sacrifice of millions to the permanent redemption of the human race from the scourge and agony of war'.[55]

Northcliffe had achieved his object, however. The natural outcome of the excesses propagated during the war was a blighted peace.

Postscript

During the First World War, Britain, along with the other belligerents, discovered that total war necessitated propaganda on a greater scale than ever before. Never before had the temper of the civilian population had such crucial bearing on the outcome of the war. The development of propaganda as an instrument for waging war was the product. Propaganda was, in the words of J. F. C. Fuller, 'a democratic instrument' only in the sense that the opinions and emotions of the large mass of people became an essential reckoning in the actual conduct of the war. It was in fact an instrument for the control of democratic opinion. The mass had to be manipulated in definite directions: diverted away from criticism and towards action which promoted national unity.

Afterwards, however, a period of disenchantment set in when the belligerents sat down to survey the effects of the war and the achievements of the peace. The causes of disenchantment were complex. Suffice it to say, in the brief space available, that part of that disenchantment stemmed from a recognition that the expectations of a brighter future – a new world for which the war had supposedly been fought – had not been realized in the fraught aftermath of the peace, and that the nation had been deceived by propaganda.

This mood of disenchantment was expressed in a wealth of published material, which detailed the falsehoods and the consequences of propaganda. There were the writings of men like Arthur Ponsonby, a dissenter during the war but who now had considerable influence, and who expressed the view in *Falsehood in Wartime* that propaganda had lied to the Allies, especially about atrocities. And there were the books written by returned soldiers, many of whom, like C. E. Montague in *Disenchantment*, emphasized the contrast between the propaganda image of war and their own experiences.

J. M. Keynes formulated a powerful critique of the peace settlement in his book, *The Economic Consequences of the Peace*, which had considerable influence at the time. In it, he pointed to the folly of the British mandate on the question of the German indemnity, and criticized the subsequent campaign 'for securing out of Germany the general cost of the war' as 'one of the most serious acts of political unwisdom for which statesmen have ever been responsible', since, not only did it lead to 'an unjust and unworkable basis to the Treaty with Germany',[1] it also threatened the future financial prospects for Europe. That mandate was the product of the 1918 election, an election in which anti-German propaganda, focusing on the demand to 'Make Germany Pay', had a dominating influence in making the participants wilfully blind to the future implications of their pledges.

It is arguable that in Germany, also, reaction to Allied propaganda may have had some influence in defining certain post-war attitudes, though only in conjunction with more complex factors. Ludendorff, for one, was impressed by Allied propaganda. He wrote: 'We were hypnotized by Allied propaganda as a rabbit is by a snake. It was exceptionally clever and conceived on a grand scale. It worked by strong mass suggestion kept in the closest touch with the military situation, and was unscrupulous as to the means it used.'[2] His comments, however, must be taken in the context of a Germany which was not only experiencing the aftermath of a Peace Settlement which repudiated all the promises made in Allied propaganda about a peace based on justice not revenge, but which was also searching for an explanation of how the greatest army in Europe could possibly have been defeated. The legend was growing that the German army had been 'stabbed in the back' by socialists and civilians on the home front who had subverted the war effort. In so far as it was expedient to the argument, Allied propaganda and Soviet revolutionary propaganda were accorded the blame for having supposedly helped in that subversion.

Germany, like all belligerents, came to recognize the value of propaganda in total war, but in Germany the realization dawned later. German propaganda was undoubtedly less effective than Allied propaganda. Hitler, who accorded propaganda a central role in the building of the National Socialist movement, castigated the former German leaders for having made propaganda 'the last way for officeless politicians to make a living . . .', whereas for the Allies, he wrote in *Mein Kampf*, propaganda counted 'as a weapon of the first class'.[3] Hitler's elaboration of the theory that it was the feebleness of Germany's leaders which had made Germany vulnerable to external propaganda gained currency after 1933. The argument that there should be no repetition of history, that Germany should not fall prey to such techniques again, provided justification for some of the excesses of Nazi propaganda. Germany, argued Goebbels in 1941, 'now knew how to handle the weapon of Truth with sovereign certainty. Her news policy was now quick, experienced, clear and effective. She has formed a very detailed system of the highest perfection in the treatment of the opinion of the people and of the public opinion of the world.'[4]

The experience of the first total war brought with it a redefinition of the value and necessity of propaganda carried out on an unprecedented scale. Organized propaganda, using increasingly sophisticated and efficient communications techniques deliberately to manipulate the opinion of the mass of the people, became an indispensable adjunct to twentieth-century politics.

Notes to the Text

Chapter 1

1. Quoted in Bramsted, *Goebbels and National Socialist Propaganda, 1925–1945*, p. 29.
2. Goebbels to Werner Stephen, 1943, quoted in Bramsted, p. 269.

Chapter 2

1. Quoted in I. S. Clarke, *Voices Prophesying War*, p. 118.
2. Norman Angell, *The Great Illusion*.
3. T. C. Horsfall, *National Service and the Welfare of the Community*, 1906, quoted in A. Marwick, *The Deluge*, p. 26.
4. *Daily Mail*, 24 September 1897.
5. Quoted in Pound and Harmsworth, *Northcliffe*, p. 252.
6. Quoted in D. Boulton, *Objection Overruled*, p. 66.
7. Quoted in I. S. Clarke, *Voices Prophesying War*, p. 149.
8. ibid, p. 145, quoted from Bernard Falk, *Bouquets for Fleet Street*, p. 65.
9. Quoted in Clarke, op. cit., p. 145.
10. 16 December 1911, Blumenfield Papers, quoted in S. Koss, *Scapegoat for Liberalism*, p. 105.
11. 22 September 1912, Blumenfield Papers, quoted ibid, p. 106.
12. *Daily Mail*, 24 April 1907.
13. Quoted in L. W. Martin, 'The Navy Race Begins', Purnell *History of the Twentieth Century*, no. 7, p. 172.
14. From *Nauticus* 1900, quoted in Berghahn, *Germany and the Approach of War in 1914*, p. 29.
15. Quoted in Berghahn, op. cit., p. 31.
16. Quoted ibid, p. 44.
17. Quoted in A. M. Gollin, *The Observer and J. L. Garvin*, p. 19.
18. Parliamentary Debates, vol. 185, cols 366–9, 2 March 1908, quoted in Gollin, op. cit., p. 55.
19. Northcliffe Papers, Garvin to Northcliffe, 14 July 1909, quoted in Gollin, op. cit., p. 147.
20. *Daily Mail*, 16 March 1909.
21. *Daily News*, 22 March 1909.
22. *Daily Mail*, 31 March 1909.
23. Winston S. Churchill, *The World Crisis*, p. 39.

24. A. M. Gollin, op. cit., p. 129.
25. ibid, p. 130.
26. Fisher to Garvin, 22 January 1910, Garvin Papers, quoted in Gollin, op. cit., p. 131.
27. Quoted in Pound and Harmsworth, op. cit., p. 389 (4 January 1910).
28. Winston S. Churchill, *The World Crisis*, p. 42.
29. Quoted in Pound and Harmsworth, op. cit., p. 464.

Chapter 3

1. Asquith in the House of Commons, 27 August 1914.
2. Asquith in Cardiff, 2 October 1914.
3. IWM pamphlet, *The Fight for Right Movement*, p. 5.
4. *Daily News*, 14 August 1914.
5. *Annual Report*, CCNPO, 1916.
6. *Report*, National Relief Committee in Belgium, May 1916.
7. *The Times*, 20 September 1914.
8. House of Commons, 6 August 1914.
9. Edward Cook, *The Press in Wartime*, p. 42.
10. PRO. INF. 4/1B Secret Report, Military Press Control. *A History of the Work of M.I.7 1914–1919*, p. 9.
11. Quoted in R. D. Blumenfield, *All in a Lifetime*, p. 130.
12. Lt Col. Sir E. Swinton, *Eye Witness*, p. 53.
13. Basil Clarke, *How the Progress of the War was Chronicled by Pen and Camera*, quoted in J. Terraine, *Impacts of War*, p. 95.
14. Asquith to Venetia Stanley, 5 September 1914, quoted in Martin Gilbert, *Winston S. Churchill*, vol. III, p. 71.
15. ibid, p. 70.
16. Asquith to Venetia Stanley, 5 September 1914, quoted in Gilbert, op. cit., p. 71.
17. Douglas Brownrigg, *Indiscretions of a Naval Censor*, p. 13.
18. ibid., p. 33.
19. 68 House of Commons, 11 November 1914, col. 19.
20. L. Masterman, *C. F. G. Masterman*, p. 275.
21. PRO. INF. 4/5, Second Report of the Work Conducted for the Government at Wellington House, C. F. G. Masterman, February 1916.
22. Resolution passed at the Inaugural meeting of the NWAC, 4 August 1914, Queen's Hall.
23. PRO. INF. 4/4A. All quotes from Report (Secret) NWAC, *Home Publicity during the Great War*, National War Aims Committee, p. 2.
24. ibid.
25. ibid., pp. 5, 6.

26. Pound and Harmsworth, *Northcliffe*, p. 648.
27. Caroline Playne, *Britain Holds On*, p. 171.
28. ibid., p. 173.
29. Hartley Withers in the *Economist*, 10 January 1917.
30. Kennedy Jones in Edinburgh, 19 May 1917, quoted in Playne, op. cit., p. 66.
31. ibid., p. 65.
32. M. MacDonagh, *In London During the Great War*, 26 December 1916, p. 164.
33. Beaverbrook, *Men and Power*, p. 266.
34. PRO. INF. 4/6, *Report: War Cabinet Committee on Overlapping and Production and Distribution of Propaganda*, Minute on the Cinema Industry and its Relation to the Government, John Boon, 8 June 1918.
35. ibid.
36. *The Bioscope*, 12 October 1916.
37. *The Bioscope*, 10 September 1914.
38. Charles Edmonds, *A Subaltern's War*, p. 188.

Chapter 4
1. Eric Field, *Advertising: The Forgotten Years*, pp. 28–9.
2. ibid., p. 29.
3. Basil Williams, *Raising and Recruiting the New Armies*, p. 17.
4. ibid., p. 18.
5. Minutes of the Parliamentary Recruiting Committee, 27, 31 August 1914, add. MSS. 4192, quoted C. Hazelhurst, *Politicians at War*, p. 141.
6. W. H. Oakley, *Guildford in the Great War*, pp. 32–8.
7. M. MacDonagh, *In London During the Great War*, p. 51, 3 January 1915.
8. Quoted in M. Rickards, *Posters of the First World War*, p. 14.
9. MacDonagh, op. cit., p. 79, 6 October 1915.
10. *Daily Telegraph*, 4 September 1914, quoted in M. MacKenzie, *Shoulder to Shoulder*, p. 286.
11. Quoted in David Mitchell, *Women on the Warpath*, p. 40.
12. ibid., p. 40.
13. MacDonagh, op. cit., p. 44, 16 December 1914.
14. Quoted in James Walvin, *The People's Game*, pp. 88–9.
15. E. Arnold Bennett, *Journal 1896–1926*, p. 98, 10 August 1914.
16. C. E. Montague, *Disenchantment*, p. 10.
17. J. B. Priestley, *Margin Released*, p. 82.
18. *Letters of Charles Sorley*, p. 263.
19. Private interview with the author.
20. ibid.

21. S. Sassoon, *Memoirs of an Infantry Officer*, pp. 16–17.
22. E. Wrench, *Struggle 1914–1920*, pp. 112–13, quoted in A. Marwick, *The Deluge*, p. 41.
23. *The Times*, 5 September 1914.
24. Quoted in L. Masterman, *C. F. G. Masterman*, p. 296.
25. Phillip Gibbs, *The Battles of the Somme*, pp. 16–17.
26. L. Houseman, *Letters of Fallen Englishmen*, p. 30, 6 November 1916.
27. S. T. Kemp, unpublished manuscript, written in 1920.
28. Montague, op. cit., pp. 76–7.
29. S. Sassoon, *Memoirs of an Infantry Officer*, p. 155.
30. Kemp, op. cit.
31. *The Times*, 26 April 1915.
32. L. Houseman, op. cit., p. 117.
33. D. Lloyd George, *Memoirs*, vol. IV, p. 2036.
34. Kemp, op. cit.
35. ibid.
36. Montague, op. cit., pp. 108–9.
37. C. Edmonds, *A Subaltern's War*, p. 203.
38. ibid.
39. ibid.
40. Kemp, op. cit.
41. ibid.
42. ibid.
43. Phillip Gibbs, *Realities of War*, p. 110.
44. Martin Gilbert, *Winston S. Churchill*, vol. III, pp. 556–7.
45. Quoted in D. Owen, *Tempestuous Journey*, p. 458.
46. David Mitchell, *Women on the Warpath*, p. 59.
47. *The Times*, 15 January 1918.
48. Lloyd George, op. cit., vol. 5, p. 2605.

Chapter 5

1. H. D. Lasswell, *Propaganda Techniques in World War I*, p. 9.
2. M. MacDonagh *In London During the Great War*, p. 6, 3 August 1914.
3. Wickham Steed, *Through Thirty Years*, p. 37.
4. *Morning Post*, 22 June 1915.
5. *The Times*, 16 January 1918.
6. Ian Hay, *The First Hundred Thousand*, p. 224.
7. Quoted in Hamilton Fyffe, *Northcliffe, An Intimate Biography*, p. 175.
8. Lasswell, op. cit., p. 82.
9. Norman Angell, *The Public Mind*, p. 58.
10. Robert Graves, *Goodbye to All That*, pp. 99–100.

11. C. Dowling, 'The Campaign of Hate', *History of the First World War*, Purnell, no. 29, p. 792.
12. *Daily Chronicle*, 'Where the German Army Has Passed', 1915.
13. General Ludendorff, *My War Memoirs*, p. 31.
14. German War Book Memorandum, 1915.
15. *Kölnische Volkzeitung*, 15 September 1914.
16. *The Times*, 1, 2 and 24 June 1915.
17. Quoted in A. Marwick, *The Deluge*, pp. 212–13, from official figures published by the *Observer*, 12 January 1919.
18. Lasswell, op. cit., p. 84.
19. Siegfried Sassoon, *Memoirs of an Infantry Officer*, p. 273.
20. *Land and Water*, May 1915, quoted in A. Ponsonby, *Falsehood in Wartime*, p. 146.
21. Article by Ed Berwick, *Foreign Affairs*, July 1922, quoted in Ponsonby, op. cit., p. 146.
22. 27 February 1915, Richmond Diaries, quoted in Colin Simpson, *Lusitania*, p. 40.
23. PRO. ADM. 116/1359, 23 December 1914, quoted in Simpson, op. cit., p. 40.
24. ibid.
25. D. F. Fleming, *Origins and Legacies of the First World War*, p. 200.
26. D. Lloyd George, *Memoirs*, vol. II, p. 661.
27. Churchill to Runciman, 12 February 1915, Runciman MSS., quoted in Cameron Hazelhurst, *Politicians At War*, p. 189.
28. B. H. Liddell Hart, *History of the First World War*, p. 72.
29. D. F. Fleming, op. cit., p. 206.
30. Simpson, op. cit., pp. 91–8.
31. ibid., p. 16.
32. ibid.
33. T. Werner Laurie, *Thou Art The Man, Daily Express* War Book, p. 90.
34. W. N. Willis, *The Kaiser and His Barbarians*, p. 8.
35. Austin Harrison, *The Kaiser's War*, p. 99, November 1914, (extracts from the *English Review*).
36. Sir Theodore Cook, *The Mark of the Beast*, pp. 206–7.
37. 'On Forgiving our Enemies', pamphlet for SPCK series *Wartime Tracts for the Workers*, no. 15, 1915.
38. July 1916, quoted in C. Playne *Society at War*, p. 212.

Chapter 6

1. *Daily Mail*, 26 October 1914.
2. M. MacDonagh, *In London During the Great War*, p. 15, 11 August 1914.

3. ibid., p. 32, 28 October 1914.
4. *Daily Mirror*, 25 August 1914.
5. *Daily Mail*, 17 October 1914.
6. *Daily Mail*, 16 October 1914.
7. House of Commons, 17 December 1917, quoted in *The Times*, 18 December 1917.
8. PRO. INF. 4/9, report on *The Organisation of the Services of Military Secrecy, Security and Publicity*, section III: 'Military Security', prepared by the General Staff, War Office, October 1917.
9. *Daily News*, 16 October 1914.
10. *Daily News*, 19 October 1914; *Daily Mail*, 19 October 1914.
11. *Daily Mail*, 19 October 1914.
12. *Daily News*, 19 October 1914.
13. *Globe*, 5 October 1914.
14. PRO. HO. 45/267450, correspondence between DPP and Lord Charles Beresford, October 1914.
15. Letter to *Daily Mail*, 13 October 1914.
16. *Daily Mail*, 16 October 1914.
17. *Daily Mail*, 14 October 1914.
18. *John Bull*, 29 October 1914.
19. *John Bull*, 14 November 1914.
20. *Daily Mail*, 3 October 1914.
21. Hansard, vol. 18, no. 5, House of Lords, 25 November 1915.
22. MacDonagh, op. cit., pp. 32–3, 28 October 1914.
23. C. Playne, *Society At War*, p. 267.
24. Major General Sir Charles Callwell, *Experiences of a Dug-Out*, pp. 33–4.
25. L. T. Hobhouse to Simon, 22 October 1914; Simon to Hobhouse, 26 October 1914 (copy), Simon MSS., quoted in Cameron Hazelhurst, *Politicians At War*, pp. 145–6.
26. D. Lloyd George, *Memoirs*, vol. I, p. 221.
27. Quoted in David Mitchell, *Women on the Warpath*, p. 326.
28. Northcliffe to Bonar Law, 6 November 1914, Northcliffe MSS, quoted in Hazelhurst, op. cit., p. 145.
29. S. Koss, *Lord Haldane, Scapegoat for Liberalism*, p. 126.
30. ibid., p. 130.
31. Richard Aldington, *Portrait of a Genius, But . . .* , pp. 184–91.
32. Martin Gilbert, *Winston S. Churchill*, vol. III, pp. 144–8.
33. Quoted ibid., p. 152.
34. *The Times*, 30 October 1914.
35. *The Times*, 4 August 1914.
36. Letter to Haldane, 26 May 1915, quoted in J. Terraine, *Impacts of War*, p. 88.
37. Quoted ibid., p. 83.

38. Leo Maxse to R. D. Blumenfield, 3 March 1915, Blumenfield Papers, quoted in Koss, op. cit., p. 176.
39. Quoted in Koss, op. cit., p. 164.
40. Haldane, *Autobiography*, pp. 282-3, quoted in Terraine, op. cit., p. 85.
41. *Daily Express*, 8 May 1915.
42. ibid.
43. *Weekly Dispatch*, 9 May 1915.
44. *John Bull*, 15 May 1915.
45. C. S. Peel, *How We Lived Then*.
46. Sylvia Pankhurst, *The Home Front*, p. 171.
47. Simon to C. P. Scott, 14 May 1915, Scott Papers, quoted in Koss, op. cit., p. 155.
48. MacDonagh, op. cit., p. 61, 11 May 1915.
49. *Weekly Dispatch*, 16 May 1915.
50. *John Bull*, quoted in Julian Symons, *Horatio Bottomley*, p. 166.
51. MacDonagh, op. cit., p. 63, 13 May 1915.
52. BEU Leaflet No. 9.
53. BEU Leaflet No. 3.
54. BEU Leaflet No. 9.
55. MacDonagh, op. cit., p. 152, 1 December 1916.
56. Gilbert, op. cit., p. 749.
57. F. Owen, *Tempestuous Journey*, p. 485; *The Times*, 27 June 1918.
58. *Daily Mail*, 8 June 1918.
59. R. Pound and G. Harmsworth, *Northcliffe*, p. 644.
60. Northcliffe to H. G. Wells, 29 June 1918, quoted ibid., p. 649.
61. ibid., pp. 645-6.
62. *The Times*, 31 July 1918.
63. Quoted in Pound and Harmsworth, op. cit., p. 653.
64. Lloyd George, op. cit., vol. I, p. 221.
65. *The Times*, 18 December 1917.
66. M. Hankey, *The Supreme Command, 1914-1916*, pp. 220-21.
67. *Daily Mail*, 12 July 1918.
68. BEU monthly record, February 1918.
69. Quoted in Pound and Harmsworth, op. cit., p. 653.
70. *Daily Mail*, 12 July 1918.
71. *The Times*, 15 July 1918.
72. MacDonagh, op. cit., p. 308, 24 August 1918.

Chapter 7

1. Phillip Snowden, *Autobiography*, p. 366.
2. Ramsay MacDonald to C. R. Buxton, 8 October 1915, Buxton Papers,

quoted in M. Schwarz, *The Union of Democratic Control in British Politics During the First World War*, p. 70.

3. Ponsonby to Morel (Private), 19 July 1917, Morel Papers, quoted in Schwarz, op. cit., p. 213.
4. Quoted in A. J. P. Taylor, *The Trouble Makers*, p. 123.
5. UDC, June 1918, quoted in Schwarz, op. cit., p. 206.
6. ILP manifesto, *Labour Leader*, 13 August 1914.
7. Labour Year Book, 1916, p. 15, quoted in A. Marwick, *The Deluge*, p. 28.
8. *Labour Leader*, 6 August 1914.
9. *Labour Leader*, 25 March 1915.
10. ILP manifesto, *Labour Leader*, 13 August 1914.
11. Quoted in E. Hughes, *Keir Hardie*, p. 236.
12. NAC statement to members, *Labour Leader*, 13 August 1914.
13. Quoted in David Mitchell, *Women on the Warpath*, pp. 275–8.
14. ibid., p. 318.
15. ibid., p. 323.
16. Quoted in T. Wilson, *The Downfall of the Liberal Party*, p. 34.
17. *Labour Leader*, 6 January 1916.
18. Quoted in A. Marwick, *Clifford Allen: The Open Conspirator*, pp. 21–2.
19. Quoted in Martin Gilbert, *Plough My Own Furrow*, pp. 43–4.
20. Letter to Barrett Brown, 19 December 1916, quoted in Gilbert, op. cit., p. 65.
21. *Daily Express*, 11 September 1914.
22. MacDonald to Trevelyan, 5 August 1915, Trevelyan Papers, quoted in Schwarz, op. cit., p. 106.
23. PRO. HO. 45/10741/263275/43, 19 June 1915.
24. *Morning Post*, 10 September 1915.
25. *Daily Express*, 25, 29 November 1915.
26. Quoted in M. MacDonagh, *In London During the Great War*, p. 90.
27. *Daily Sketch*, 30 November, 1 December 1915.
28. Quoted in Schwarz, op. cit., p. 105.
29. ibid., p. 105.
30. Quoted in Francis Williams, *A Pattern of Rulers*, p. 68.
31. PRO. HO. 10801/307402/75.
32. ibid., NCAC Pamphlet No. 3.
33. *Labour Leader*, 6 January 1916.
34. ibid.
35. *Daily Express*, 29 January 1916.
36. *Daily Express*, 10 April 1916.
37. Quoted in Robert Graves, *Goodbye to All That*, pp. 283–6.
38. ibid., pp. 284, 287.

39. ibid., p. 283.
40. House of Commons, 26 July 1916.
41. Labour Year Book, 1916.
42. Ministry of Munitions 5. 73: 'Memorandum on Clyde and Tyne', Macassey, 10 December 1915, quoted in James Hinton, *The First Shop Stewards' Movement*, p. 127.
43. CWC leaflet c. 1915 in *Beveridge Collection on Munitions*, iii, p. 95, quoted in Hinton, op. cit., p. 128.
44. From D. Mackenzie, *Labour Conditions and Industrial Relations*, p. 601, quoted in Keith Middlemas, *The Clydesiders*, p. 61.
45. Sir Hubert Llewellyn Smith, Permanent Secretary at the Ministry of Munitions, in *Beveridge Collection on Munitions*, iii, p. 218, quoted in Hinton, op. cit., p. 143.
46. D. Lloyd George, *Memoirs*, vol. I, p. 325.
47. ibid., p. 334.
48. *Daily Express*, 31 March 1916.
49. Snowden, op. cit., p. 430.
50. House of Commons, 23 February 1916.
51. *UDC*, February 1916.
52. *UDC*, October 1916, 'The Great Push'.
53. Morel speech, 22 October 1916.
54. Lloyd George, op. cit., vol. II, pp. 853-4.
55. UDC General Council 7, Second Annual General Meeting, 10 October 1916, quoted in Schwarz, op. cit., p. 81.
56. Lloyd George, op. cit., vol. III, p. 1110.
57. ibid., p. 1114.
58. *UDC*, February 1917.
59. Trevelyan to Norman Angell, 22 December 1916, Angell Papers, quoted in Schwarz, op. cit., p. 136.
60. ibid., p. 137.
61. *Herald*, 4 August 1917, 'Who Aims at Conquests?'.
62. C. Playne, *Britain Holds On*, p. 109.
63. House of Commons, 16 May 1917, quoted in Snowden, op. cit., p. 449.
64. ibid.
65. *Labour Leader*, 9 August 1917.
66. S. Pankhurst, *The Home Front*, p. 328.
67. *Common Sense*, 25 August 1917, quoted in Playne, op. cit., p. 134.
68. *Morning Post*, 10 May 1917.
69. B. Pribićević, *The Shop Stewards' Movement and Workers Control*, p. 95.
70. *Morning Post*, 19 May 1917.
71. G. D. H. Cole, *Trade Unionism and Munitions*, p. 145.
72. *Morning Post*, 14 May 1917.

73. Milner to Lady Roberts (copy), 25 February 1916, Milner Papers, quoted in A. M. Gollin, *Pro-Consul in Politics*, p. 539.
74. *Daily Express*, 29 April 1915.
75. Milner to Lloyd George, 26 May 1917, quoted in Gollin, op. cit., p. 544.
76. Milner to Lloyd George, 1 June 1917, confidential memorandum, 'Mission of the ILP and SLP to Russia', Lloyd George Papers, quoted in Schwarz, op. cit., p. 174.
77. ibid., quoted in Schwarz, op. cit., p. 175.
78. ibid., quoted in Schwarz, op. cit., p. 174.
79. Quoted in Schwarz, op. cit., p. 161.
80. PRO. CAB. 23/3, WC Minutes 154(22), (Secret), 5 June 1917.
81. HC Deb (99), 13 November 1917, col. 286.
82. HC Deb (99), 13 November 1917, col. 311.
83. Quoted in Schwarz, op. cit., p. 191.
84. PRO. HO. 45/10743/263275/265, Thomas Cox to Secretary, Home Office, 15 November 1917, quoted in Schwarz, op. cit., p. 190.
85. Minute by Thomson, 26 November 1917, ibid.
86. PRO. CAB. 23/4. WC Minutes 245(20), (Secret), 4 October 1917.
87. PRO. CAB. 24/28. GT 2274, Memorandum by Roberts, 10 October 1917.
88. *Lord Riddell's War Diary*, p. 293, 24 November 1917.
89. *Daily News*, 14 August 1917.
90. *Economist*, 3 June 1917.
91. *Nation*, 4 August 1917.
92. Lloyd George, op. cit., vol. V, p. 2483.
93. ibid., p. 2483.
94. *Lord Riddell's War Diary*, p. 303.
95. Quoted in F. Owen, op. cit., p. 441.
96. J. R. Clynes, *Memoirs*, vol. I, p. 235.
97. *The Times*, 7 January 1918.
98. Lloyd George, op. cit., vol. V, pp. 2660–61.
99. Quoted in Hinton, op. cit., p. 256.
100. ibid., p. 257.
101. February 1918, quoted in Hinton, op. cit., pp. 260–61.
102. PRO. MUN. 2. 14, 26 January, 2, 9, 16 February 1918; PRO. CAB. 23/5, 5 February 1918, quoted in Hinton, op. cit., p. 264.
103. *Daily Herald*, 9 February 1918.
104. F. E. Smith to the New York Bar Association, quoted in Playne, op. cit., pp. 280–81.
105. Quoted in R. Pound and G. Harmsworth, *Northcliffe*, p. 646.
106. *Morning Post*, 13 September 1918.

Chapter 8

1. *The Times*, 18 November 1918.
2. *The Times*, 13 November 1918.
3. Letter to *The Times*, 31 July 1918.
4. ibid.
5. *The Times*, 26 August 1918.
6. *Weekly Dispatch*, 15 September 1918.
7. *Evening News*, 17 September 1918.
8. *The Times*, 9 October 1918.
9. Northcliffe to T. P. O'Connor, 18 October 1918, quoted in R. Pound and G. Harmsworth, *Northcliffe*, p. 668.
10. Haig Diary, quoted Pound and Harmsworth, op. cit., p. 668.
11. Office message to *Daily Mail*, 21 October 1918, quoted Pound and Harmsworth, op. cit., p. 669.
12. Office message to *Daily Mail*, 22 October 1918, quoted ibid., p. 669.
13. *Evening Standard*, 1 November 1918.
14. *John Bull*, 26 October 1918.
15. *The Nation*, 26 October 1918.
16. Quoted in C. Playne, *Britain Holds On*, p. 364.
17. Quoted ibid., p. 387.
18. *Daily News*, 5 December 1918.
19. Lord Beaverbrook, *Men and Power*, p. 305.
20. *Daily Express*, 14, 19 November 1918.
21. *Daily Express*, 19 November 1918.
22. *John Bull*, 16 November 1918.
23. Quoted in Pound and Harmsworth, op. cit., p. 680.
24. Marlowe to Northcliffe, quoted in Pound and Harmsworth, op. cit., p. 679.
25. Northcliffe to Dawson, 30 November 1918, quoted ibid.
26. *Daily Mail*, 16 November 1918.
27. *Daily Mail*, 27 November 1918.
28. *Daily Express*, 25 November 1918.
29. *John Bull*, 16 November 1918.
30. *Daily Express*, 27 November 1918.
31. Winston Churchill, *Aftermath*, p. 44.
32. ibid., p. 46.
33. ibid., pp. 46–7.
34. ibid.
35. *The Times*, 29 November 1918.
36. Quoted in Trevor Wilson, *The Downfall of the Liberal Party*, p. 192.
37. *Daily Mail*, 30 November 1918.
38. *Daily Mail*, 2 December 1918.
39. *The Times*, 30 November 1918.

40. *Daily Mail*, 30 November 1918.
41. *Daily News*, 5 December 1918.
42. Quoted in Pound and Harmsworth, op. cit., p. 679.
43. ibid.
44. *Daily Mail*, 2 December 1918.
45. F. Owen, *Tempestuous Journey*, p. 543.
46. ibid., p. 503.
47. *The Times*, 12 December 1918.
48. Scott to Hammond, 4 December 1918, quoted in Wilson, op. cit., p. 362.
49. December 1918, Scott Papers, quoted in Trevor Wilson, *The Political Diaries of C. P. Scott*, p. 362.
50. Quoted in Wilson, *The Downfall of the Liberal Party*, p. 189.
51. Winston Churchill, op. cit., p. 135.
52. Quoted in Pound and Harmsworth, op. cit., p. 711.
53. Northcliffe to Rothermere, 10 April 1919, quoted in Pound and Harmsworth, op. cit., p. 712.
54. 16 April 1919, quoted in Owen, op. cit., p. 540.
55. ibid., p. 542.

Postscript

1. J. M. Keynes, *The Economic Consequences of the Peace*, p. 134.
2. General Ludendorff, *My War Memoirs*, p. 360.
3. A. Hitler, *Mein Kampf*, p. 84.
4. J. Goebbels, *Die Zeit Ohne Beispiel* (Munich, 1941), p. 292, quoted in Bramsted, *Goebbels and National Socialist Propaganda, 1925–1945*, p. 443.

Bibliography

Books, Biographies, Contemporary Material, Secondary Material

ALDINGTON, Richard, *Portrait of a Genius, But . . .* , Four Square, 1963.

AMERY, Julian, *The Life of Joseph Chamberlain*, vol. VI: 'Joseph Chamberlain and the Tariff Reform Campaign', Macmillan, 1969.

ANGELL, Norman, *The Public Mind*, Noel Douglas, 1926;
The Great Illusion, Heinemann, 1910.

ANONYMOUS, *Frightfulness in Retreat*, Hodder & Stoughton, 1917.

ASTON, Major General Sir George, *The Triangle of Terror in Belgium*, John Murray, 1918.

BAIRNSFATHER, Bruce, *Bullets and Billets*, Grant Richards, 1916.

BEAVERBROOK, Lord, *Politicians and the War, 1914–1916*, Collins, 1960;
Men and Power, 1917–1918, Oldbourne (London), 1959.

BENNETT, E. Arnold, *Journals, 1896–1928*, vol. II: 1911–1921, edited by Newman Fowler, Cassell, 1932.

BERGHAHN, V. R., *Germany and the Approach of War in 1914*, Macmillan Papermac, 1973.

BERGONZI, Bernard, *Heroes' Twilight*, Constable, 1965.

BETTEY, J. H. (editor), *English Historical Documents, 1906 to 1939*, Routledge, & Kegan Paul, 1967.

BLUMENFIELD, R. D., *All in a Lifetime*, Ernest Benn, 1931;
The Press in My Time, Rich & Cowan, 1933.

BLUNDEN, Edmund, *Undertones of War*, Richard Cobden Anderson, 1928.

BOOTH, J. B., *The Gentle Cultured German – The Road Hog of Europe*, Grant Richards, 1915.

BOULTON, David, *Objection Overruled*, MacGibbon & Kee, 1967.

BRAND, Carl F., *The British Labour Party*, Stanford University Press, 1965.

BRAMSTED, Ernest K., *Goebbels and National Socialist Propaganda, 1925–1945*, Cresset Press, 1965.

BRERETON, Cloudesley, *Who is Responsible? Armageddon and After*, George Harrap, 1914.

BRIGGS, Asa, *They Saw It Happen, 1897–1940*, Blackwell, 1962.

BROWNRIGG, Rear Admiral Sir Douglas, *Indiscretions of the Naval Censor*, Cassell, 1920.

BRUNTZ, George B., *Allied Propaganda and the Collapse of the German Empire in 1918*, Stanford University Press, 1938.

Report of the Committee on Alleged German Atrocities (Bryce Report), Cmnd 7894, 1915.

Appendix to Report on Alleged German Atrocities (Bryce Report), Cmnd 7895, 1915.

BUCHAN, John, *Memory Hold the Door*, Hodder & Stoughton, 1940.

CALLWELL, Major General Sir Charles, *Experiences of a Dugout, 1914–1918*, Constable, 1920.

CARTON DE WIART, H., *The Way of Honour*, George Allen & Unwin, 1918.

CHURCHILL, W. S., *The World Crisis*, Macmillan, 1943; *The World Crisis – The Aftermath*, Thornton Butterworth, 1929.

CLARKE, I. F., *Voices Prophesying War*, Oxford University Press, 1966.

CLARKE, Tom, *My Northcliffe Diary*, Gollancz, 1931.

COLE, G. D. H., *A Short History of the British Working Class Movement*, George Allen & Unwin, 1948; *Trade Unionism and Munitions*, Clarendon Press, 1923.

Commissions of Inquiry Into Industrial Unrest, Cmnd 8662 to 8669, 1917.

COOK, Sir Edward, *The Press in Wartime*, Macmillan, 1920.

COOK, Sir Theodore A., *Kaiser, Krupp and Kultur*, John Murray, 1915; *The Mark of the Beast*, John Murray, 1917.

CREEL, George, *How We Advertised America*, New York, 1920.

Daily Chronicle *Black Book of the War*, 1914.

Daily Chronicle: *Where the German Army Has Passed*, 1915.

DANGERFIELD, George, *The Strange Death of Liberal England*, Constable, 1936.

DAVIGNON, Henry, *Belgium and Germany*, Thomas Nelson, 1915.

DAWSON, William Harbutt, *What Is Wrong With Germany?* Longman Green & Co., 1915.

DAY LEWIS, C. (editor), *Collected Poems of Wilfred Owen*, Chatto & Windus, 1971.

DONINGTON, Robert and Barbara, *The Citizen Faces War*, Gollancz, 1936.

DOWSE, Robert E., *Left in the Centre*, Longmans, 1966.

DRIBERG, Tom, *Beaverbrook*, Weidenfeld & Nicolson, 1956.

EDMONDS, Charles, *A Subaltern's War*, Peter Davies Ltd, 1929.

ENSOR, R. C. K., *England, 1870–1914*, Oxford, 1966.

Daily Express War Book, *Thou Art The Man*, T. Werner Laurie, no date.

FERRIS, Paul, *The House of Northcliffe*, Weidenfeld & Nicolson, 1972.

FERRO, Marc, *The Great War, 1914–1918*, Routledge & Kegan Paul, 1973.

FIELD, Eric, *Advertising: The Forgotten Years*, Ernest Benn, 1959.

The Field Supplement, *German Atrocities on Record*, 13 February 1915.

FISCHER, Fritz, *Germany's Aims in the First World War*, Chatto & Windus, 1967.

FLEMING, D. F., *The Origins and Legacies of the First World War*, George Allen & Unwin, 1969.

FRANKAU, Gilbert, *The City of Fear*, Chatto & Windus, 1917.

FULLER, Major General J. F. C., *The Conduct of War, 1789–1961*, Eyre & Spottiswoode, 1961.

FYFFE, Hamilton, *Northcliffe, An Intimate Biography*, George Allen & Unwin, 1930.

GALLACHER, W., *Revolt on the Clyde*, Lawrence & Wishart, 1949.

GIBBS, Phillip, *The Realities of War*, Heinemann, 1920.

GILBERT, Bentley, *British Social Policy, 1914–1939*, Batsford, 1970.

GILBERT, Martin, *Winston S. Churchill*, vol. III: 1914–1916, Heinemann, 1971; *Plough My Own Furrow. The Story of Lord Allen of Hurtwood as Told Through His Writings and Correspondence*, Longmans, 1965.

GOLLIN, A. M., *Pro-Consul in Politics*, Anthony Blond, 1964; *The Observer and J. L. Garvin*, Oxford University Press, 1960.

GRAVES, Robert, *Goodbye To All That*, Jonathan Cape, 1929.

GREY OF FALLODEN, Viscount, *Twenty Five Years*, Hodder & Stoughton, 1925.

HANKEY, Lord, *The Supreme Command, 1914–1916*, George Allen & Unwin, 1961.

HARRISON, Austin, *The Kaiser's War*, George Allen & Unwin, 1914.

HAY, Ian, *The First Hundred Thousand*, William Blackwood & Sons, 1916.

HAZELHURST, Cameron, *Politicians At War, July 1914 to May 1915*, Jonathan Cape, 1971.

HINTON, James, *The First Shop Stewards' Movement*, George Allen & Unwin, 1973.

HITLER, A., *Mein Kampf (My Struggle)*, Hurst & Blackett, 1933.

HOBSON, J. A., *The Psychology of Jingoism*, Grant Richards, 1901.

HOUSEMAN, L. (editor), *War Letters of Fallen Englishmen*, Gollancz, 1930.

HUGHES, Emrys, *Keir Hardie*, George Allen & Unwin, 1956.

HYMAN, Alan, *The Rise and Fall of Horatio Bottomley*, Cassell, 1972.

JONES, David, *In Parenthesis*, Faber, 1937.

JONES, Kennedy, *Fleet Street and Downing Street*, Hutchinson, 1920.

JONES, C. Sheridan, *The Unspeakable Prussian*, Cassell, 1914.

KEMP, S. T., *Unpublished Manuscript on First World War*, 1920.

KEYNES, J. M., *The Economic Consequences of the Peace*, Macmillan, 1919.

KOSS, Stephen E., *Lord Haldane: Scapegoat For Liberalism*, Columbia University Press, 1969.

LAMBERT, Richard S., *Propaganda*, Thomas Nelson, 1938.

LASSWELL, Harold D., *Propaganda Techniques in World War I*, Knopf, 1927.

LIDDELL HART, B. H., *History of the First World War*, Pan, 1972.

LIPPMANN, Walter, *Public Opinion*, George Allen & Unwin, 1922.

LLOYD GEORGE, D., *War Memoirs*, 6 vols., Ivor Nicholson & Watson, 1933–6. *The Truth About the Peace Treaties*, Gollancz, 1938.

LOW, Rachel, *The History of the British Film, 1914–1918*, George Allen & Unwin, 1950.

LUDENDORFF, General, *My War Memoirs*, Hutchinson, 1919.

LUMLEY, Frederick E., *The Propaganda Menace*, The Century Company, 1933.

LYTTON, Neville, *The Press and the General Staff*, Collins, 1920.

MACDONAGH, Michael, *In London During the Great War*, Eyre & Spottiswoode, 1935.

MACKENZIE, Midge, *Shoulder to Shoulder*, Knopf, 1975.

MALINS, Geoffrey, *How I Filmed the War*, Herbert Jenkins, 1920.

MARJORIBANKS and COLVIN, Ian, *The Life of Lord Carson*, vol. III, Gollancz, 1936.

MARWICK, Arthur, *The Deluge*, Penguin, 1967;
Clifford Allen: The Open Conspirator, Oliver & Boyd, 1964.

MASSART, Jean, *Belgians Under the German Eagle*, T. Fisher Unwin, 1916.

MASTERMAN, L., *C. F. G. Masterman*, Nicholson & Watson, 1939.

MAYES, W. L., unpublished manuscripts, *The Origins of an Art Collection*, I.W.M.

MIDDLEMASS, Keith, *The Clydesiders*, Hutchinson, 1965.

MITCHELL, David, *Women on the Warpath*, Jonathan Cape, 1966.

MONTAGUE, C. E., *Disenchantment*, MacGibbon & Kee, 1968;
The Front Line, Hodder & Stoughton, 1917.

MURPHY, J. T., *Preparing for Power*, Jonathan Cape, 1934.

NICOLSON, Harold, *Peacemaking*, Constable, 1933.

OAKLEY, W. H., *Guildford in the Great War*, Billing & Sons, Guildford, 1934.

OWEN, Frank, *Tempestuous Journey: Lloyd George, His Life and Times*, Hutchinson, 1954.

OWEN, Harold, *Disloyalty, The Blight of Pacifism*, Hurst & Blackett, 1918.

PANKHURST, E. Sylvia, *The Home Front*, Hutchinson, 1932.

PARSONS, I. M. (editor), *Men Who March Away*, Chatto & Windus, 1965.

PEEL, C. S., *How We Lived Then*, John Lane The Bodley Head, 1929.

PELLING, Henry, *History of British Trade Unionism*, Penguin, 1963.

PLAYNE, Caroline, *Society at War*, George Allen & Unwin, 1931;
Britain Holds On, 1917–1918, George Allen & Unwin, 1933.

PRIBIĆEVIĆ, Branko, *The Shop Stewards' Movement and Workers' Control, 1910–1922*, Blackwell, 1959.

PRIESTLEY, J. B., *Margin Released*, Windmill Press, 1962.

PONSONBY, Arthur, *Falsehood in Wartime*, George Allen & Unwin, 1928.

POUND, Reginald, and HARMSWORTH, Geoffrey, *Northcliffe*, Cassell, 1959.

RAE, John, *Conscience and Politics: The British Government and the Conscientious Objector to Military Service, 1916–1919*, Oxford University Press, 1970.

Lord Riddell's War Diary, Ivor Nicholson and Watson, 1933.

ROBBS, P. H., 'The Great War – Leaflet Evaluation', in *Psywar Society Bulletin*, no. 8, 1959.

ROETTER, Charles, *Psychological Warfare*, Batsford, 1974.

ROTHWELL, V. H., *British War Aims and Peace Diplomacy*, Clarendon Press, 1971.

ROBERTS, B. C., *The Trades Union Congress, 1868–1921*, George Allen & Unwin, 1958.

SASSOON, Siegfried, *Memoirs of a Fox Hunting Man*, Faber & Gwyer, 1928; *Memoirs of an Infantry Officer*, Faber & Faber, 1966; *The Complete Memoirs of George Sherston*, Faber & Faber, 1972.

SCHWARZ, Marvin, *The Union of Democratic Control in British Politics During the First World War*, Clarendon Press, 1971.

SILKIN, Jon, *Out of Battle*, Oxford University Press, 1972.

SIMPSON, Colin, *Lusitania*, Longman, 1972.

SNOWDEN, Phillip, Viscount, *Autobiography*, Ivor Nicholson & Watson, 1934. *The Letters of Charles Sorley*, Cambridge University Press, 1919.

SQUIRES, J. D., *British Propaganda At Home and in the United States from 1914 to 1917*, Cambridge, Massachusetts, 1935.

STEED, Henry Wickham, *Through Thirty Years*, Heinemann, 1924.

SWINTON, Major General Sir Ernest D., *Eye Witness*, Hodder & Stoughton, 1932.

SYMONS, Julian, *Horatio Bottomley – A Biography*, Cresset Press, 1955.

STALWORTHY, Jon, *Wilfred Owen, A Biography*, Oxford University Press and Chatto & Windus, 1974.

TAYLOR, A. J. P., *English History, 1914–1945*, Clarendon, 1965; *The Trouble Makers. Dissent Over Foreign Policy, 1792–1939*, Panther, 1969; *Beaverbrook*, Penguin, 1974; (editor) *Lloyd George. Twelve Essays*, Hamish Hamilton, 1971; *The First World War*, Penguin, 1963.

TERRAINE, John, *Impacts of War*, Hutchinson, 1970; *The Western Front, 1914–1918*, Hutchinson, 1964.

THOMSON, Sir Basil, *Scene Changes*, Collins, 1939; *The History of the Times*, vol. IV, 1952.

THORNTON, A. P., *The Imperial Idea and Its Enemies*, Papermac, 1966.

TUCHMAN, Barbara W., *August 1914*, Constable, 1962.

WELLS, H. G., *Mr Britling Sees It Through*, Cassell & Co., 1917.

WILLIAMS, Basil, *Raising and Recruiting the New Armies*, Constable, 1918.

WILLIAMS, Francis, *A Pattern of Rulers*, Longmans, 1965.

WILLIS, W. N., *The Kaiser and His Barbarians*, Anglo-Eastern Publishing Co., no date.

WILLMORE, J. Seldon, *The Great Crime and Its Moral*, Hodder & Stoughton, 1917.

WOOLFF, Leon, *In Flanders Fields*, Longmans, 1959.

WRENCH, John Evelyn, *Geoffrey Dawson and Our Times*, Hutchinson, 1955.

WILSON, Trevor (editor), *The Political Diaries of C. P. Scott, 1911–1928*, Collins, 1970;
The Downfall of the Liberal Party, 1914–1935, Fontana, 1968.
ZEMAN, Z. A. B., *Nazi Propaganda*, Oxford University Press, 1964.

Government Publications and Other Sources

Public Records Office:
Home Office files.
Ministry of Information files, including files of the Press Bureau, 1914–1918.
Official History of the Ministry of Munitions, 8 vols., 1918–1922.
Cabinet records.

House of Commons debates, Hansard.
House of Lords debates, Hansard.
Trades Union Congress library – Peace Movement, 1914–1918;
Shop Stewards, 1914–1918;
I.L.P. N.A.C. Reports.

Imperial War Museum Reference Library and Art Department

For pamphlets and leaflets of:
British Empire Union
National War Aims Committee
Parliamentary Recruiting Committee
Fight for Right Movement
Central Committee for National Patriotic Organizations.

Newspapers and Periodicals

The *Call*
Daily Chronicle
Daily Express
Daily Graphic
Daily Mail
Daily Mirror
Daily News
Daily Telegraph
Evening News
Evening Standard
Forward

The *Herald*
John Bull
Labour Leader
Manchester Guardian
Morning Post
Nation
National Review
New Statesman
Observer
Punch
Solidarity
The *Suffragette* – later *Britannia*
Sunday Pictorial
The Times
The *Tribunal*
Weekly Dispatch
Woman's Dreadnought – later *Workers' Dreadnought.*

Index

Aberystwyth demonstration, 114
Addison, Christopher, 192
Agadir crisis (1911), 19
Alexandra, Queen of England, 28
Alien Committee, 135
Alien Watch Committee, 137
Aliens Investigation Committee, 135
Aliens Restriction Act (5 August 1914), 111
Allen, Clifford, 147–8, 150, 152
Allen, Maud, 130
Allendale, Viscount, 117
America Latina, 38
American Chemical Warfare Service, 98
Angell, Norman, 6, 85–7, 143, 150
anti-alien campaign, in Britain, 110, 120, 128, 130–31, 133–5, 137–9
Anti-German League, *see* British Empire Union (BEU)
Antwerp, 87, 96
Arras, battle of (9–14 April 1917), 78
ASE, *see* Engineers, Amalgamated Society of
Asquith, Miss Elizabeth, 55
Asquith, Herbert Henry, 75, 120, 130; attitude to press, 34, 37; coalition government, 75; and conscription, 76–7; defeat in election after Armistice, 196; enforcement of dilution, 158, 165; on peace groups, 160; as president of CCNPO, 27; as president of NWAC, 40, 170; as president of PRC, 53; publication of Bryce Report, 93; speech on 6 August 1914, 22–4
atrocity stories, 38, 84–9; and Bryce Report, 93–4; photographs as evidence of, 87–8
Audacious (battleship), 35, 122
Austro–Hungarian peace proposals, 183

Bairnsfather, Bruce, 74
Balfour, Arthur James, 18, 19, 27
Barnes, G. N., 40, 165, 170, 192
Battenburg, Prince Louis of, 121–2, 123
Battle of the Somme, The (propaganda film), 45
Beaverbrook, Lord, 26, 40, 44, 46, 131
Belgian Committee of Inquiry, 93, 94
Belgian Relief Fund, 28
Belgique, La, 90

Belgium: British moral obligation towards, 22, 24, 25; *francs tireurs* in, 88–9, 95; German terrorization in, 88, 89, 94, 103, 109, 125; National Relief Committee in, 28
Bell, Tom, 158, 159; *see also* CWC
Bennett, Arnold, 25, 26, 63, 185, 194
Beresford, Lord Charles, 16; anti-alien campaign, 109, 122, 126, 128, 129; on peace negotiations, 184, 188; speech at Aberdeen (2 October 1914), 114–15
Berliner Lokalanzeiger, 88, 90, 91
Bernhardt, Sarah, 46
Bertie, Lord, 95
Billing, Pemberton, 130, 131, 135, 139
Blackwoods Magazine, 7
Blatchford, Robert, 18, 108, 109, 125
Blumenfield, R. D., 8, 11, 124
Bone, Muirhead, 45
Bottomley, Horatio, 61–3, 106, 122, 183–4, 186; call for reprisals on Germans in Britain, 126–7
boycott, of German goods, 115–17, 128–9, 130, 131
Bradford Pioneer, 142
Brailsford, H. N., 163; 'A Peace by Satisfaction', 160
Brangwyn, Frank, 28, 55–6
Brassey, Lord, 173
Bridges, Robert, 27
Britain Prepared (propaganda film), 45
Britannia (magazine), 57
British Empire Union (BEU): anti-alien campaign, 109, 117, 128, 129, 131, 135, 139, 189–90, 194; meetings in Hyde Park, 137
British National Workers' League, 153
British Naval Intelligence, 102
British War Mission, 40
British Workers' League, 167-8
Brockway, Fenner, 147, 150
Brooke, Rupert, 6, 65, 70
Brownrigg, Douglas, 35
Brunner, Sir John, 16, 17, 120
Bryce, Lord, 93
Bryce Report, *see* Secret War Propaganda Bureau, Bryce Report
Buchan, John, 25, 40
Bull, Perkins, K. C., 190
Bülow, Bernard von, 13, 14

Burn, Reverend P., 106-7
Burns, John, 22
Buxton, C. R., 143; 'The Terms of Peace', 160

Callwell, Sir Charles, 188
Carson, Sir Edward, 40, 44, 137, 149, 170
Cassell, Colonel E., 178
Cave, Sir George, 113, 134, 135
Cavell, Edith, 89-90, 129
Caxton Advertising Agency, 51-2
CCNPO, see Central Committee for National Patriotic Organizations
Cecil, Lord Hugh, 28, 182
Cecil, Lord Robert, 91, 165
censorship, see press; propaganda
Central Committee for National Patriotic Organizations, 27, 41, 95, 102, 170
Central Withdrawal of Labour Committee, 157-8, 159
Centre d'Action de Propagande Contre l'Ennemie, 47
Chamberlain, Austen, 44
Chamberlain, Joseph, Tariff Reform campaign, 15
Chaplin, Charlie, 45
Charteris, Brigadier-General, 91
Chesney, Lt Col. Sir Tomkyns, serial: 'The Battle of Dorking', 6-7
Childers, E., The Riddle of the Sands, 7
Churchill, Clementine, 130
Churchill, Winston, 17, 18, 19; Aftermath, 179; attitude towards information, 30, 33, 34, 35; comment on Lloyd George's position in Peace Conference, 196-7; comment on Prince Louis' position, 122-3; on conscription, 75, 76; as Minister of Munitions, 177; obituary for Rupert Brooke, 70; policy as First Lord of Admiralty, 98-9, 100; speech in Dundee (26 November 1918), 191
Clarion, 18
Clarke, Basil, 33
Clowes, W. L., The Great Naval War of 1887, 7; and The Siege of Portsmouth series, 7
Clyde District Committee of the Federation of Engineering and Shipbuilding Trades, 177
Clyde Workers Committee, 157
Clynes, J. R., 175
Coalition: campaign, 180, 185, 188, 193, 195; government, 196
Coats, Sir Stuart, 134
Commissions of Inquiry into Industrial Unrest, 165
Committee on Public Information (American), 47, 48

conscientious objectors, 148, 156
conscription: campaign against, 151, 152, 158; campaign for, 75, 76, 77, 141; industrial, 158; introduction of (1916), 49
Conservative Party, 19, 75, 76, 77, 193; in Coalition government, 196
Cook, Sir Edward, 27, 30
Cook, Sir Theodore, 105
Coolidge, President Calvin, 1
Cooper, Sir Richard, 134, 135-7
Corriere della Sera, 87
COs, see conscientious objectors
Cox, Thomas, 170-71
Craig, Captain Charles, 190
Criminal Investigation Department (CID), 171
Crooks, Will, 190
Culling Carr, F. E., 128
Curzon, Lord, 75, 186
Cust, H. C., 27
CWC, see Central Withdrawal of Labour Committee

Dacre Fox, Mrs, 137, 184, 190
Daily Chronicle, 131, 135
Daily Express, 8, 11; anti-alien propaganda, 116, 124, 125; call for tough terms for Kaiser, 186; on pro-peace activities, 149, 150, 153, 160, 167-8
Daily Herald, 142, 146, 172
Daily Mail, 8, 13, 16-18, 29, 62; anti-alien campaign, 131, 133, 135; and anti-conscriptionist campaign, 153; call for boycotting German goods, 115, 131; demonstrations against, 75-6; on German peace proposals, 183; on German spies, 111, 113-14, 117, 119, 120; on Lloyd George's position on German reparation, 194, 197; Lord Northcliffe's campaign of conscription in, 10; on Lusitania sinking, 102, 183; on pro-peace activities, 174; revives hate propaganda, 178-9, 188; Sir W. B. Richmond's letter to, 105
Daily Mirror, 29, 59, 88, 111, 125
Daily News, 5, 12, 17, 18, 26, 82, 85; on pro-peace activities, 174; on riots in Deptford, 114
Daily Sketch, 34, 150
Daily Telegraph, 15, 34, 174
Dalziel, Sir Henry, 126, 129, 135
Dane, Phyllis, 62
Dardanelles campaign, 35, 75
Darling, Justice, 130
Dawson, Geoffrey, 167, 197
Defence of the Realm Acts (DORA), 30, 96, 111, 158, 159, 164, 173
Denaturalization Bill, 137

Department of Information, *see* Information
Department of Public Prosecutions (DPP), 149
Deptford riots (18 October 1917), 114
Derby, Lord, 52; Scheme, 76
Despard, Mrs Charlotte, 146, 164
Dickinson, C. Lowes, 143
Dillon, John, 196
dilution, 158, 165
Donald, Robert, 40
DORA, *see* Defence of the Realm Acts
Doyle, Arthur Conan, 25, 81
DPP, *see* Department of Public Prosecutions
Dreadnought programme, 12–13, 16, 17
Dublin Rebellion, 77
Dumfries Standard (16 September 1914), 84
Duncan, Charles, 168

East London Suffrage Federation, 119
Economist, 183
Edmonds, Charles, 73
Edward VII, Prince of Wales, 28
Engineers, Amalgamated Society of, 157, 176
England's Call (recruiting film), 45
Entente Cordiale, *see* France, British Entente Cordiale with
Esher, Lord, 19, 123
Espelho, El, 38
Evening News, 103, 119–20, 171
Evening Standard, 84, 183

Falaba (British liner), 101
Fawcett, Mrs, M., National Union of Suffrage Societies, 20, 22, 57, 77
Fell, Sir Arthur, 134
Field, 105
Field, Eric, 52
Film propaganda, *see* propaganda
Financial Times, 128
Fisher, Admiral Sir John ('Jacky'), 12, 16, 19, 75, 123
Fisher, Victor, 167, 168, 192
Fitzgerald, Admiral Penrose, 56
food rationing, 39, 43–4, 103
Football Association, 59
Ford, Ford Maddox, 121
Forward, 142, 158
Foy, H. S. A., 128
France: British Entente Cordiale with (1904), 22, 50, 174; propaganda in neutral countries, 47
French, Sir John, 146
Fuller, General J. F. C., 199

Gallacher, Willie, 157, 158, 159
Gardiner, A. G., 5, 196
Garvin, J. L., 15–16, 17, 19, 68
Geddes, Sir Auckland, 77–8, 176
Geddes, Sir Eric, 195
Germany: British blockade of, 99, 101; call for peace, 161, 162, 163, 177; internal and external propaganda, 200; naval expansion, 12, 13, 17; peace proposals, 102, 183; propaganda in America, 39; strike action in, 177; unrestricted submarine warfare, 98, 102, 103; White Book on Belgian civilians' atrocities, 95; *and see* Navy Laws, German
Gibbs, Phillip, 68, 74
Gladstone, William E., 7
Glasgow Herald, 192
Globe, 122
Goebbels, Joseph, 3, 200–201
Gollin, A. M., 19
Gore Booth, Eva, 146
Gosse, Edmund, 25
Gough, Prebendary, 190
Graves, Robert, 87, 156
Great War, The, 88
Greene, Sir Graham, 46
Gregory XV, Pope, 1
Grenfell, Julian, 70–71, 72
Grey, Sir Edward, 20, 49, 77, 151, 161
Grieg, J. W., 192
Griffith, D. W., 45; *Hearts of the World*, 46
Guest, F. E., 40, 170

Hague Convention, 94
Haldane, Lord, 11, 12, 120, 130, 178, 196; campaign against, 120, 121–2, 123–5
Hall, Captain Reginald, 102
Hall, Marshall, 184
Halsalle, Henry de, 189
Hammond, J. L., 196
Hankey, Lord, 134
Harcourt, Lewis, 22, 120
Hardie, Keir, 20, 144, 150
Hardy, Thomas, 25
Harmsworth, Alfred, *see* Northcliffe, Lord
Harrison, Austin, 105
Hassall, John, 28
Henderson, Arthur, 53, 158, 196; resignation from Cabinet, 165; visit to Petrograd, 165
Henley, W. E., 6
Herald League, 163
Hesperia, 38
Hicks, Joynson W., 128, 129, 134, 135
Hicks, Seymour, *England Expects*, 62
Hindenberg, Field-Marshal, 184

Hitler, Adolf, *Mein Kampf*, 200
Hobhouse, L. T., 118
Hobhouse, Rosa, 146
Hobson, J. A., 143; *The Psychology of Jingoism*, 79
Hodge, Herman, 18
Hodge, John, 168
Hughes, Billy (Prime Minister of Australia), 108–9, 195
Hughes, Spencer, 44
Hume, Grace, 84

Illustrated War News, 38
ILP, *see* Independent Labour Party
Imperial Maritime League, 17, 18
Imperialist, see *Vigilante*
Indépendance Belge, L', 38, 90
Independent Labour Party (ILP), 22, 156, 168, 175–6; anti-war stand, 141, 142, 143–4, 149, 167; manifesto (August 1914), 140; meetings, 155, 167; Peace Negotiations Committee (Autumn 1916), 164
Information: Department of (1917), 39, 40, 149; 'film tag', 46; Ministry of (1918), 40, 44, 45, 182; propaganda films, 46

Jellicoe, Lord, 35
Joffre, General, 33
John Bull (magazine), 61, 62, 115, 116, 120, 122, 183, 186, 190
Johnson, Dr Samuel, 44
Jones, Kennedy, 7, 43, 135, 197
Jury, William, 46

Kadaver, use of word, 91–3
Kaiser, *see* William II
Karlsruhe raid, 96
Keeling, F. H., 90
Kemp, Private S. T., 69, 72–3, 74
Keynes, J. M., 195; *Economic Consequences of the Peace, The*, 199–200
Kipling, Rudyard, 25, 27, 46, 81
Kirkwood, David, 159
Kitchener, Lord, 32, 33, 50; *Daily Mail*'s attack on, 75–6; recruiting poster, 53–5, 158
Kölnische Zeitung, 87

Labour Leader, 142, 148, 149, 152, 153, 167, 174
Labour Party, 19, 20, 22; in coalition government, 196; Conference (August 1917), 164; Memorandum on War Aims (28 December 1917), 41, 164, 165, 175; pacifists, 141; and Soviet call for Conference in Stockholm, 165

Langdon Davies, W., 150
Lansbury, George, 145, 152, 153, 163
Lansdowne, Lord, 161, 174, 183
Lasswell, H. D., 1
Law, Bonar, 37, 40, 53, 120, 125, 170, 180
Lawrence, D. H., 121
League of Nations, 180
Le Bas, Hedley, 51
Leete, Alfred, 53
Leith of Fyvie, Lord, 116–17, 128, 129
Le Queux, William: *England's Peril*, 7; *The Invasion of 1910*, 10–11
Liberal Party, 19, 20, 21, 22, 141, 148, 193; in coalition government, 196; returned to power at 1906 election, 13
Lindsay, A. D., 27
Liverpool, 52–3, 126
Lloyd George, David, 17, 19, 22, 24, 28, 133; anti-alien campaign, 134–5, 138; attacks on working class, 159; budget of 1909, 19; on censoring publications advocating peace, 171; and conscription, 75; criticism of McKenna's actions, 118, 133–4; election campaign after Armistice, 180–81, 189, 192–3; interview to President of United Press of America (26 September 1916), 161; Lord Northcliffe's attitude to, 187–8; rejection of German call for peace, 163, 178; speech on 19 September 1914, 83; speech to trades union audience (January 1918), 41; view on conscientious objectors, 156; visit to Glasgow (December 1915), 158; war aims speech (5 January 1918), 175, 176; War Memoirs, 49, 71, 76, 78; Wolverhampton speech (23 November 1918), 181, 189
London, bombed, 96, 97
London Opinion, 53
Loos (offensive of September 1915), 71, 72, 74
looting, 126
Louvain, German bombing of (25 August 1914), 88
Ludendorff, General, 47, 89, 200
Lugard, Lady, 28
Lusitania, sinking of (7 May 1916), 90, 93, 95, 101–2, 103, 108, 109, 125, 183; medal for, 102
Lyttleton, Hon. Mrs Alfred, 28

MacDonagh, Michael, 55, 56, 59, 79; anti-alien campaign, 110–11, 117, 129, 138
MacDonald, Ramsay, 22, 61, 196; anti-war campaign, 142, 143, 144, 148, 150, 151; prevented from sailing to Petro-

grad, 165, 168; resignation from Labour Party leadership (7 August 1914), 151
MacLean, John, 156, 158, 159
Maison de la Presse, 47
Mallins, Geoffrey, 46
Manchester Geographical Society, 85
Manchester Guardian, 12, 18, 40, 143, 163, 174, 195–6
Manningham Buller, Lt Col., 128
Manpower Bill, 176, 177–8
Manpower Conference (18 January 1918), 176
Marshall, Catherine, 146, 152
Masefield, John, 25, 27
Massingham, H. W., 152, 185
Masterman, Charles, 37–8, 91, 93, 95; use of film for propaganda, 45
Matin, Le, 87
Maubeuge, German bombardment of, 116
Maude, Colonel, 97–8
Maurier, Guy du, *An Englishman's Home*, 11
Maxse, Leo, *National Review*, 11, 120, 121, 124
McDowell, Lt J. B., 46
McKenna, Reginald, 17, 19, 77, 161, 196; actions against enemy aliens, 111, 113, 118, 124, 133
McNeil, Ronald, 128, 134
Merchant Seaman's League, 137
Mesopotamia, surrender of British troops in (29 April 1916), 77
Messer, James, 157
Meyer, Reverend F. B., 107
Michaelis, Chancellor, 163
Military Service Acts, 77, 149, 151–2, 175
Mond, Sir Alfred, 120
Mons, British retreat from, 33, 51
Montagu, Lord, 97
Montague, C. E., 63–5, 69, 73; *Disenchantment*, 199
Montague, Edwin, 159
Moore, Arthur, 33
Morel, E. D., 142, 143, 150, 168; *How the War Began*, 143; *Truth and the War*, 143, 173
Morgan, H. E., 28
Morley, Lord, 22
Morning Post, 11, 33–4; on anti-war activities, 149, 155–6, 167, 174; campaign against Lord Haldane, 124; on peace terms, 184
Morrell, Philip, 143, 147
Morrison, Herbert, 147
Mothers of France (French film), 46
Muir, John, 158, 159
Munitions, Ministry of (1915), 63
Munitions of War Acts, 157, 159, 165

Murphy, J. T., 159
Murray, Gilbert, 25, 26

Nash, Paul, 45
Nation, 5, 152, 163, 173, 184, 185
National Committee, 176
No Conscription Fellowship (NCF), 146; manifesto (September 1915), 147; *Tribunal*, 148
National Council Against Conscription (NCAC), 153
National Daily News, 163
National Labour Press, 149
National Liberation Federation, 53
National Party, 109, 129, 137, 139; mass meeting in Manchester (24 July 1918), 137; mass rally at Albert Hall (30 July 1918), 137
National Registration Bill (15 July 1915), 76–7
National Relief Fund, 27, 28
National Review, see Maxse, Leo, *National Review*
National Sailor's and Fireman's Union, 165, 168
National Service Journal, 10
National Service League, 8, 10, 12, 50, 75, 167
National Shop Stewards' Agreement, 176
National Union of Suffrage Societies, *see* Fawcett, Mrs, National Union of Suffrage Societies
National War Aims Committee (NWAC), 40–41, 42, 170, 177, 182
Navy Laws, German (1898, 1900 and 1908), 12, 13
Navy League, 14, 17
NCAC, *see* National Council Against Conscription
NCF, *see* National Conscription Fellowship
Neutrality Committee, 20, 26
Neutrality League, 20, 143
Nevinson, C. R., 45
Newbolt, Henry, 25, 27
Newman, Major, 134
News Chronicle, 40
News of the World, 40
Newspaper Proprietors' Association, 32
New York Times, 91
Nield, Herbert, 133
No Conscription Fellowship, 22, 141, 147
Norman, C. H., 147
Northcliffe, Lord, 5, 8, 11, 13, 15, 16, 20; anti-alien campaign, 131–3, 135, 139; attacks on Kitchener, 75; attitude to Lloyd George, 187, 188, 197–8; campaign for conscription (1907), 10; com-

Northcliffe, Lord, *continued*
    missions Robert Blatchford to write
    for *Daily Mail*, 18; at Department of
    Information, 25, 40; as Director of
    Propaganda to enemy countries, 25, 44,
    46, 131; and dispatch from Amiens in
    The Times, 33; on films used for propa-
    ganda, 45; on German reparations,
    197–8; as pacifist, 149; Portsmouth
    election (1895), 7; on recruitment
    campaign, 67–8, 83; revives hate propa-
    ganda, 178, 183, 187–8
Noyes, Alfred, 27
NWAC, *see* National War Aims
    Committee

Observer, 6, 15, 16, 18, 19
O'Grady, James, 168
Once a Hun, Always a Hun, 129
One Flag League, 178
Optimist, 107
Orczy, Baroness, 57
Owen, Wilfred, 72
'Oxford Pamphlets', 26–7

Page, Croft, Brig-Gen. H., 129, 135, 137,
    138
Pall Mall Gazette, 84
Pan German League, 14
Pankhurst, Emmeline and Christabel,
    146; Women's Social and Political
    Union, 22, 57
Pankhurst, Sylvia, 77, 119, 126, 146, 153;
    Federation of Suffragettes, 145;
    Workers' Dreadnought, 146
Parker, Gilbert, 25, 38
Parliamentary Recruiting Committee
    (PRC), 49, 51, 95, 96; posters, 53–5, 57
Passchendaele, battle of, 78, 174
Peace Conference, 180, 187, 196, 197
Peace Treaty, 186
Pease, Jack, 22
Peet, Hubert, 148; *see also* NCF
Pemberton, Max, *Pro Patria*, 7
Pethwick Lawrence, F. W., 147, 152
Pethwick Lawrence, Mrs, 146, 164
Pick, Frank, 56
Ponsonby, Arthur, 142, 143, 150, 174
    Falsehood in Wartime, 199
Portsmouth Daily Mail, 7
Powell, Dr T. Ellis, 128
press: attitude to government, 37; censor-
    ship in, 35, 37; propaganda through, 2,
    29, 37, 67
Press Bureau: and atrocity stories, 85;
    censorship through, 30–32, 34, 67,
    171; on Zeppelin raids, 96
Priestley, J. B., 65

propaganda: in America, 25, 38–9; censor-
    ship and, 3; and disenchantment, 199;
    in enemy countries, 46–7; films used as
    medium for, 45; French, 47; German,
    39, 47, 200; against Germany, 5–6,
    7–8 10–11, 19, 109–10, 179, 182, 190;
    official government, 4; for peace, 173;
    through posters, 53; and the press, 2, 29,
    67, 110–11; for recruitment, 63–5, 67,
    75
Prothero, G. W., 27
Prothero, Rowland, 44

Quakers, 119, 141, 147
Queen Mary's Needlework Guild, 28
Quiller Couch, Arthur, 25

Raemaekers, Louis, 28
Rawlinson, Sir Henry, 53
recruitment campaign, 49–52, 53–5, 59,
    61–3, 67
Reform Act (1918), 180
Resolution of the Socialist International
    Conference (1907), 143
Rheims Cathedral, bombarded (22 Sep-
    tember 1914), 82, 105, 106
Rhondda, Lord, 44
Richmond, Sir W. B., 105
Riddell, Lord, 32, 37, 40, 173, 195
Roberts, Lady, 167
Roberts, Lord, 8, 10, 17, 124; National
    Service League, 11, 50; speech in
    Manchester (1912), 11–12
Rolland, Romain, 173
Rosebery, Earl of, 27
Rosner, Herr Karl, 90, 91
Rothermere, Lord, 46, 68, 197
Routledge, Edwin, 65–6
Rowntree, Arnold, 143
Runciman, Lord, 77, 100, 146, 161, 196
Russell, Bertrand, 143, 147, 150, 152, 173
Russia: withdrawal from war, 163;
    Revolution of 1917, 161, 163

'Saki', *When William Came*, 7
Sanders, Lt. Col. R. A., 40
Sankey, Mr Justice, 135
Sassoon, Siegfried, 66, 69, 71–2, 96–7, 146
Scott, C. P., 40, 143, 196
Schedule of Protected Occupations, 165
Secret War Propaganda Bureau, 37, 39,
    40, 44, 45, 91, 101; Bryce Report (May
    1915), 38, 93–5, 102, 109, 125
Selborne, Lord, 85
Selfridge, Mr Gordon, 102
Seymour Cocks, Sir, 150
Shaw, George Bernard, 25
Shee, George, 'The Briton's First Duty –
    The Case for Conscription', 8–10

Sheffield Trades Council, 177
Shop Stewards and Workers Committee Movement, 157, 176; National Administrative Council of, 176
Simon, Sir John, 22, 76, 77, 118, 128, 149, 196
Simpson, Colin, *Lusitania*, 100
Sinn Fein, 148
Smillie, Robert, 152, 163
Smith, F. E., 33, 192
Smith, Lydia, 148
Snowden, Mrs Ethel, 146, 164
Snowden, Philip, 22, 142, 160, 163, 196
Social Democratic Federation, 167
Socialist Labour Party, 141, 156
Socialist National Defence League, 167
Socialist Party, British, 141, 156
Somme battle (July to November 1916), 74, 160
Sorley, Charles, 65, 72
Spencer Pryce, Gerald, 55, 56
Speyer, Sir Edgar, 120
Stanley, Sir Albert, 131
Stanton. C. B., 168
Star, 84
Steed, Lancelot, 46
Steed, Wickham, 20, 79–81
Stockholm, 164–5, 168, 176–7
strikes, 165–7, 170, 176
submarine warfare, 98–100, 101, 102
Suffragist, 57
Sunday Chronicle, 85
Sunday Pictorial, 62
Swanwick, Helena, 146, 164
Swinton, Lt Col. Sir Ernest, 32

Tariff Reform League, 129
Templeton, Viscount, 189
Tennant, Sir Edward, 17
Terry, Ellen, 46
Thomson, A. M., 168
Thomson, Sir Basil, 133, 171
Thorne, Will, 150, 168
Tillett, Ben, 184, 190
Times, The, 5, 17, 28, 29, 61; anti-alien campaign, 133, 137; on atrocity stories, 84, 87; and British Workers' League, 167; campaign against Lord Haldane, 123; communiqué from Sir Basil Thomson to, 133; dispatch from Amiens (31 August 1914), 33; on German peace proposals, 183; on German spies in Britain, 116; on issues of election, 192; on the Kaiser, 106; leader of 31 July 1914, 20; on Lord Lansdowne's letter in the *Daily Telegraph*, 174; on Louvain bombing, 88; on Prince Louis' resignation, 123;

protestations to, 84–5; publication of Rupert Brooke's poem, 70; report on German corpse factory, 90–91; revives hate propaganda, 178, 184; and sinking of *Audacious*, 35
Tirpitz, Admiral von, 13, 100–101
Trade Committee, 46; *see also* film propaganda
Trades Union Council, 152
Treasury Agreements, 157
Trevelyan, C. P., 143, 150, 162
Tribunal, 142, 148, 173
Troup, Sir Edward, 149

U-boats, 98–9, 100, 101
UDC, *see* Union of Democratic Control
UDC, the, 142
Unfit (Hepworth film fantasy), 45
Union des Grandes Associations Contre la Propagande Ennemie, 47
Union of Democratic Control (UDC), 168, 175–6; anti-war campaign, 141, 142, 143, 149, 150, 160, 161, 162, 178; meetings, 167
Unionist Enemy Influence Committee, 134–5
Unionist Party, 15, 19, 128; in Coalition government, 196
Unionist War Committee, 44
United States of America: agreements with Germany on ships (6 June and 17 August 1915), 102; Atlantic trade routes, 99; and British interference with freedom of seas, 99; British propaganda in, 38–9; Committee on Public Information, 47; declare war on 6 April 1917, 102, 162; German propaganda in, 39; official propaganda in, 47; Secret War Propaganda Bureau in, 25

Vickers Maxim, 45
Vigilante, 130
voluntaryism, 50, 75, 76, 77, 103
Vote, 146

Walpole, Hugh, 25–6
Walsh, Stephen, 168
War Loan Schemes, 43, 62–3, 77
War Office, 30, 32, 46, 49; Cinematograph Committee, 46; embargo on war correspondents, 67; and German 'corpse factory', 91–2; recruitment methods, 51–2
War Propaganda Bureau, 100
Warrington Steevens, George, 8
War Savings Committee, 43
War Savings Schemes, 77

Watson, William, 27
Webb, Henry, 120
Webb, Sidney, 178
Wedgewood, Josiah, 173
Weekly Dispatch, 108, 125
Wellington House, *see* Secret War Propaganda Bureau
Wells, H. G., 5, 25, 26, 42, 133, 173
Westbury, Lord, 183
Westminster Gazette, 84
White, Arnold, 124, 184, 190
Wilde, Oscar, 130
William II, Emperor of Germany, 14, 15, 82, 91, 103, 105-7, 179, 184; call for extradition and trial of, 185-7, 190-91, 193-5
Wilkinson, Professor Spencer, 183
Willies, A., 168
Willson, Beckles, 7
Wilson, Havelock, 128, 137, 165, 168, 184
Wilson, H. W., 10
Wilson, President, 38, 47, 100; peace note (29 December 1916), 161, 162, 174;

peace speech (January 1918), 162, 174, 176, 178
Women of England's Active Service League, 57
Women's International League, 146, 164
Women's Peace Crusade, (July 1916), 164
Women's Social and Political Union, 146
Wood, McKinnon, 196
Worker, 142, 158
Workers' Committees, 159, 176
Workers' Dreadnought, 145, 154; *see also* Pankhurst, Sylvia
World Crisis, 100, 122
Worthington Evans, Sir L., 91

Younger, Sir George, 187, 188
Younger, Robert, 190
Younghusband, Sir Francis, 'Fight for Right Movement', 25

Zeppelin raids, 31, 96-7, 126
Zimmern, Herr, 91
Zimmerman telegram, 102